Australia 63

AUSTRALIA 63

ALAN ROSS

With a New Introduction by the Author

THE PAVILION LIBRARY

First published in Great Britain in 1963

First published in the Pavilion Library in 1991 by
PAVILION BOOKS LIMITED
196 Shaftesbury Avenue
London WC2H 8JL

Series Editor: Steve Dobell

A CIP catalogue record for this book
is available from the British Library

ISBN 185145 6686

Printed and bound in Great Britain
by Biddles Limited, Guildford

INTRODUCTION

Re-reading this account of Test matches played nearly thirty years ago is to recognise the disappointment of the series as a spectacle. There were three drawn games, and the two matches that achieved a result did so rather one-sidedly. In the Postscript I tried to analyse why the matches were not more absorbing or entertaining, so there is no point in going into it again. What I had forgotten over the years was how much good cricket was played, especially by England, who, given little chance before the tour began, came nearer of the two sides to winning. What worked against real tension was the reluctance of either captain to set challenges that might result in defeat. There is nothing new or shaming in a Test context about that. Unfortunately the pitches were generally slow, the stroke-making batsmen tended to get out early, and the heat of the day was borne by batsmen of lesser gifts struggling to hang on.

A drawn series rarely catches the imagination, but I can remember a great deal about this one with pleasure. Nothing perhaps was more exciting or relevant than the batting of Dexter in both innings in the First Test at Brisbane, and the bowling of Benaud in the same match, each captain striving to impose himself on the other at the outset. With Dexter making 70 and 99, and Benaud taking 6 for 115 and 1 for 71, it was never less than compulsive watching.

At Melbourne England won decisively, largely due to magnificent bowling by Trueman. The batting, in contrast to some fairly stodgy performances by the Australians, was splendidly fluent and uninhibited, Sheppard, Dexter and Cowdrey all playing at or near their best.

The Third Test, at Sydney, was fairly even over the first

innings, Titmus taking 7 for 79 in 37 overs to keep Australia to a lead of 40. Davidson, in a superb opening spell, removed the top three English batsmen for 25, and by the end of the third day England were reduced to 86 for 6. England's last four opening partnerships between Pullar and Sheppard had produced 0, 5, 4, 0. The match was quickly over next day.

The Adelaide Test, very uncharacteristically, was spoilt by rain. Davidson, hit for 30 in three overs by Barrington, limped off, never to reappear. Harvey made 154, Barrington 195 in the match for once out, and Dexter an imperious 61. In the end, with England needing 356 to win and only four hours left, the match petered out, England comfortably placed at 223 for 4.

The weather in Sydney for the final Test was wretched, bad light interrupting play on each of the first three days. Barrington made 101 out of 321, and Burge 103 out of the Australians' 349. Dexter, after England had made 268 for 8, declared, leaving Australia to make 241 in four hours. Trueman bowled Simpson for 0, and then Allen took 3 for 26 in 19 overs. Burge and Lawry dug in and that was that.

No one was really to blame that, finally, the series ended in anti-climax. Each side had its moments, but there were not quite enough of them for either to gain a decisive advantage. Warily, in the manner of Sumo wrestlers, the two sides circled each other, never quite getting to grips.

There were incidental curiosities. For Australia, Harvey and Davidson had come to the end, and Benaud almost. For England, two who played little part in the series, and could have been considered to have had their better days behind them, Tom Graveney and Raymond Illingworth, in fact had their greatest triumphs ahead. Graveney in his maturity was to display, especially against West Indies, the full glory of his stroke play, and Illingworth, at the age of 37, was to become not only a successful England captain, recovering the Ashes on England's next tour of Australia, but a Test all-rounder of considerable quality.

A.R., 1990

AUSTRALIA 63

BY

ALAN ROSS

WITH DRAWINGS BY
RUSSELL DRYSDALE

1963
Eyre & Spottiswoode
LONDON

Acknowledgments

Acknowledgment is due to the following:

The *Sydney Morning Herald* for photographs Nos. 2, 3, 5–14, 16–21, and 24, and for the cartoons by George Molnar.

Sport and General Press Agency Ltd. for photographs Nos. 4, 22, 28, 29, and 30.

Central Press Photos Ltd. for photographs Nos. 1, 23, and 25.

The *Adelaide Advertiser* for photographs Nos. 26 and 27.

The *Observer* for photograph No. 15.

The *Daily Mail* for the cartoon by Jon.

Contents

Introduction – Before the First Test

The seven weeks of M.C.C.'s first circuit of Australia, between October 16, when they played their opening match against a West Australian Country XI at the gold mining city of Kalgoorlie, and November 30, the date of the First Test at Brisbane, is always crucial. It has never been more so than this year when Dexter arrived with a party far from experienced in Australian conditions, which depended ultimately on how the several newcomers developed, and on how the players settled down together as a team. The fact that the M.C.C. arrived at Brisbane seemingly less co-ordinated than they looked to be at Perth and with no very clear tactical propositions in mind, is an indication of how difficult the various adjustments were. But that is anticipating rather.

The choosing of the team in the first place threw up a lot of problems. With Peter May's reluctance to commit himself to another overseas tour, the choice of his successor lay between Cowdrey, Dexter, and Sheppard, the latter having announced his availability for Australia early in the 1962 season. Of these the conventional selection would have been Cowdrey, who had captained England a number of times during May's different absences, usually in a brisk and efficient manner. His only notable failure had been against Australia at Lord's in 1961, when England were soundly defeated, though that was scarcely Cowdrey's fault in particular. He was the most experienced cricketer of the three, the most accessible and warm as a character. Against him were perhaps a certain fatalism of outlook, an absence of obvious drive, and the fact that around the time of the team's selection he was in and out of hospital with a series of minor ailments.

In Dexter's favour was his growing magnetism as a cricketer, the often thrilling and always dashing quality of his own all-round cricket, and the fact that he alone of the major contenders had been willing to take the side to Pakistan the previous winter. On the surface, there was little against him; what remained to be seen was whether he could thaw out sufficiently as a human being and make taking an interest in other people seem less of an obvious effort. Those who are neither good conversationalists nor natural mixers have obstacles to surmount in their dealings with others that are not achieved overnight. As a captain, Dexter had proved, mainly at county level, enterprising, wayward, but under pressure or when bored by adversity or lack of success, inclined to dissociate himself from the whole proceedings. He is a temperamental cricketer, and temperamental cricketers depend on the stars being right for them. Whoever captained England in Australia would need a cool head as well as an acute cricketing brain if they were to be any kind of match for Benaud's audacity and cunning. In this respect, Dexter was bound to be something of a gamble.

The latest contender of all, Sheppard, had played scarcely any first-class cricket for several seasons, was uncertain up to a point of finding a place as a batsman, and could, in any case, be available only for this one tour. His credentials were his remarkably successful captaincy of Sussex, his superbly opportunist and immediate recapturing of Test form in his two subsequent returns to Test cricket – especially against Australia in 1956 – and his generally authoritative personality. Inspired rumours began to circulate in the early summer that it was he whom the selectors really wanted. All he had to do was to find his form in the eight weeks first-class cricket he was allowing himself before returning to parish activities. He took a long time to do this, much longer than ever before. He looked for over a month heavy-footed and laborious, playing only a few long innings interspersed with several failures, and appearing in the field altogether slower in reaction than of old. At the very crucial moment, however, he made a fine hundred for the Gentlemen against the Players – a match that had all the implications of a Test trial for him – and the job appeared to be his. The captaincy had been delayed, it seemed, exactly for this. However, it gradually became apparent that, during this protracted period of form-finding, selectorial opinion, for one reason or another, was hardening against Sheppard. Possibly it was felt short-sighted for the captaincy to be given to someone for one Test series only. The Chairman himself, initially an enthusiast for Sheppard, began increasingly to blow hot and cold, and when it came to the point, Dexter convincingly carried the day.

Of the rest of the party, about half picked themselves. On current form and general experience, Cowdrey, Barrington, Sheppard, Pullar, Graveney and Parfitt were certainties among the batsmen, though, at the time, I had my own reservations about the class of Parfitt and would have preferred Sharpe or M. J. K. Smith. Nevertheless, Parfitt had succeeded quantitatively in his two Test series against Pakistan, for what that was worth, and his fielding was something to set against the vintage locomotion of some of the others. Statham and Trueman remained, in their thirties, our only two fast bowlers of quality, though the thirties tend to be more advanced an age for English fast bowlers than for Australians. As far as they were concerned, one had to bargain on freedom from injury, no over-bowling between Tests, and their standing up to the hardships of slow pitches without too much loss of pace or hope.

Who were to support them remained another matter. Since the departure of Laker and Wardle no class spinner of any kind had emerged; since Bailey's descent into county cricket no all-rounder of comparable stature had taken his place. Dexter had appeared, it is true, but the virtues he possesses are different in kind from Bailey's.

What was required now were a reserve pair of fast bowlers, two if not three spinners, an all-rounder, and a wicket-keeper plus deputy.

By reasons of current form and future promise, there was little alternative to Coldwell and Larter to fulfil the first of these places. Coldwell, at something under Bedser's pace, had nearly bowled Worcestershire to the championship, and though his dependence on pronounced in-swing and some help from the wicket might make him seem a bowler unsuited for export, he had at least the necessary accuracy and stamina. Larter, a gangling six foot seven, had youth, height and physique to set against obvious lack of experience and control. He could be expected to get plenty of bounce on Australian pitches, and with Tyson in mind – though Larter had nothing of his dynamism or speed – was as justifiable a gamble as any. As further support for the pace attack Knight, of Essex, an in-swing bowler with an indifferent action and of modest pace, was chosen, presumably on grounds of his aggressive batting. This was in fact to show its value in the early weeks of the tour. Unfortunately, none of these three would be likely to do anything but decrease the already precarious style and efficiency of the fielding.

As far as spin went, Allen, despite his low trajectory and rhythmic torpor, had proved his worth in the West Indies; if he had not developed as much as one had hoped since then, he was still the first choice. Lock, despite his total ineffectiveness in South Africa and again in Australia in 1958–9, was expected to accompany him, on grounds of variety if on none other. However, much to everyone's surprise, he was left out, two further off-spinners, Titmus and Illingworth, being chosen instead. Lock was immediately taken on by Western Australia, allowed to bowl round the wicket as he likes, instead of over as May had demanded of him, and by the time M.C.C. had reached Brisbane for the First Test he had become the leading Australian wicket-taker.

It was not easy to account for this overloading with off-spin. There was no leg-break bowler of sufficient class, and Lock, the only left-arm bowler worth even considering, perhaps was felt to have been too consistently unsuccessful abroad.

Tayfield's success in adapting himself to Australian conditions, Laker's effectiveness, and the decided usefulness of the

West Indian off-spinner Gibbs in Australia, probably settled it. But it was trusting in a steep rise on the previous form of Titmus and Illingworth to expect them to challenge the figures of such classic prototypes.

No one could find this array of English bowlers other than thin and monotonous. All that could be hoped for was that Trueman and Statham might make an early break, that thereafter the spinners could bowl accurately enough to carefully thought-out fields, and that Barrington and Dexter might pick up the odd wicket. It was not likely to be a spectacular business and it became increasingly hard to see where the wickets might come from. Lock's wholehearted aggression under any circumstances, and the mere fact of his left-handedness seemed qualities put aside for too little.

However, there it was. Murray, despite an unimpressive tour of Pakistan, remained the wicket-keeper in residence, and Smith of Warwickshire was somewhat unexpectedly picked as his stand-in. Myself, I should have preferred Parks to either, and it seemed to me, on the basis of his batting in the West Indies – when his scores of 43 and 101 not out saved the Fifth Test for England – to say nothing of his subsequent improved wicket-keeping, incomprehensible how he had been allowed to drift out of the Test running. On good wickets there are few better players of spin bowling in England and only the presence of a top-class leg-spinner would have made one think twice about his technical expertness as a wicket-keeper.

This then was the team:

E. R. Dexter
M. C. Cowdrey
D. A. Allen
K. F. Barrington
L. J. Coldwell
T. W. Graveney
R. Illingworth
B. R. Knight
J. D. F. Larter

J. T. Murray
P. H. Parfitt
G. A. Pullar
D. S. Sheppard
A. C. Smith
J. B. Statham
F. J. Titmus
F. S. Trueman

One's imagination played with the vast increase in potential which May, Parks, Wardle (now lurking in the Lancashire League) might have produced had they been chosen or available. But they were not, so that was that.

Alec Bedser was wisely chosen as Assistant Manager, the Duke of Norfolk, Earl Marshal of England, as Manager. The latter appointment was as surprising at the outset as if Mr Macmillan had suddenly volunteered for the job to escape the Opposition battering over the Common Market and to avoid an English winter. But once the initial stir had died down, it was seen to be an opportunist move, calculated to create publicity, to remove the main social burden from Dexter, and to demonstrate aristocratic adaptability to a notoriously egalitarian country. Whether the Duke himself in the long run, despite his organizational flair at high levels and a passionate, but unassuming, love of cricket, would find the brute necessities of the post more irksome than he might have appreciated, was a matter for conjecture. What seemed initially to be a stunt, with faint diplomatic overtones, could conceivably work miracles in terms of both public interest, and public relations. His Grace, from the outset, seemed determined that it would.

Finally, the party was made up by Sam Cowan, the Sussex masseur and former Manchester City footballer, giving Sussex a triple holding in administrative posts. One would miss George Duckworth, whom I remembered singing in a feathered hat at Brisbane at 2 a.m. in 1954, but if anyone could be expected to combine his worldly wisdom, apparent cynicism and professional shrewdness, then Alec Bedser was he.

The arrangements were that the players would fly to Aden, there pick up the *Canberra*, and complete the journey to Fremantle by sea. This meant that their six month absence from home would be significantly shortened, in itself a good thing. It allowed ten days for necessary acclimatization and discussion, without the tedium of a long sea voyage.

The two Perth matches, with pitches of a lush greenness found nowhere in the eastern states, bear little relation to the Tests. They allow the visiting side to sort themselves out, and they give Australians the chance to size them up. Richie Benaud flew over for this very purpose. The results, a ten wicket victory over Western Australia and a ten wicket defeat by the Combined XI, were symptomatic of the violent instability that was to last until Brisbane. More importantly, they seemed to indicate the levels at which M.C.C. looked either a good or indifferent team.

The opening day, against Western Australia, was warm, but overcast, and not without its shocks, for M.C.C. lost seven wickets for 161, four of them to the fast bowling of Hoare. Not one of Pullar, Cowdrey, Graveney, Barrington and Parfitt reached 25, and only 76 by Dexter – the first of a thrilling sequence of innings that continued unbroken on the initial circuit of Australia – redeemed the early batting from the kind of paralysis M.C.C. are prone to abroad. Titmus, 88, and Smith, 42, added 119 for the eighth wicket, and M.C.C. scrambled to 303.

Just over two hours later, with Statham and Larter making impressive use of a lively pitch, Western Australia were out for 77. Of these, their left-handed captain, the burly Shepherd, who was to be Australia's twelfth man in Brisbane and to play at Sydney and Adelaide, contributed 41. He had, I recollected, made a great impression on me at Bunbury in 1954, when he can have been little more than a schoolboy. Western Australia managed 274 in their second innings; Statham again bowling well to take 4 for 49. Pullar and Cowdrey knocked off the 49 required to win without actually being separated. So far so good. Lock, as a member of the opposition, had scored 0 not out and 9 not out and taken 4 for 68 in M.C.C.'s first innings.

The Combined XI, reinforced by Lawry, Simpson, and O'Neill, sent M.C.C. in to bat, and at the end of the first day were 96 for 0, having shot M.C.C. out for 157. Hoare took 3 for 42, McKenzie 4 for 38, and only Sheppard, with 43, and Knight with 65 not out got beyond twenty. Cowdrey, going in first, made the first of three successive noughts. The Combined XI, after being 170 for 2, with Simpson making 109, were cut back by some steady bowling from Allen and reached only 317. Allen failed to get another wicket before the First Test and, disintegrating under some heavy punishment by O'Neill at Sydney, lost his place. In their second innings M.C.C., despite an impressive 92 by Sheppard, a flamboyant 60 by Dexter, and 44 from Barrington, were out for 270. Graveney failed for the second time, adding 2 to his 1 in the first innings, and Hoare took another five wickets for 60. The Combined XI knocked off the 115 needed to win with contemptuous ease, Simpson making 66 not out in only eighty minutes. Trueman and Coldwell had been the fast bowlers this time, making much less impression than Statham and Larter. O'Neill, in Combined XI's first innings, had struggled amnesiacally for over an hour for 15.

So to Adelaide, with proportion restored, and much thinking to be done. Here, on another cool cloudy day, Cowdrey lost the toss, and South Australia by the evening were 324 for 7. Sobers, temporarily disguised as an Australian, scored 42 of these, and there were useful innings from Lill, McLachlan, Chappell and Hawke. Statham, rolling up the innings quickly on the second morning, finished with 4 for 58, Larter with 2 for 76.

M.C.C., after losing Cowdrey for nought, batted agreeably all down the line. Barrington collected the first hundred of the tour, Graveney got 99, Titmus 137 not out, Knight and Smith

55 each. Cowdrey was able to declare at 508 for 9. Rain spoiled the last day when, after Favell had declared at 283 for 7, M.C.C. at 95 for 1 were only 15 short. Sobers was run out for 99, Statham took three more wickets, and Cowdrey, with 32 not out, at last got off the mark again.

For the Australian XI match at Melbourne, M.C.C.'s batsmen were offered only cut-price bowling, and they savaged it accordingly. Pullar and Sheppard went fairly cheaply, but Dexter annihilated Misson, Guest, Martin and Veivers in turn. His hundred, scored in only 110 minutes, contained thirteen fours and two sixes, and what sceptics still remained about Dexter's legendary advance on the scratchy performances of 1958–9 had to retire to comfort themselves according to taste. At the end of the first day M.C.C. were 458 for 5, and Dexter batted on until the 600 was passed for only seven wickets. Such profligacy, whatever the quality of the bowling, had not been seen from M.C.C. for many a moon. Barrington was undefeated for 219 – reaffirming his unique (among English batsmen anyway) appetite for runs – Cowdrey at number four achieved a rehabilitating 88, and Knight made 108, full of flourishes and aggressive driving.

The Australian XI, without great trouble, reached 451, both Simpson, seemingly impregnable already, and Shepherd making hundreds. Dexter strove to give some point to the last day by hustling to a declaration, but in the process M.C.C. lost five wickets in rather an undignified fashion for 68. The match was drawn nevertheless, the Australian XI settling for some batting practice and finishing with 201 for 4.

By now, M.C.C. had impressed many with their lavish stroke play, a scoring rate of at least sixty runs an hour having been maintained all the way through, but the spin bowling had achieved next to nothing, and the fielding, with catches going begging in every game, had deteriorated rather than improved. The initial success of the fast bowlers at Perth had, predictably enough, not been maintained. Trueman had bowled scarcely at all; Larter, on the flawless Adelaide pitch, had come to realize that all was not honey and roses, Coldwell had been unfit, and Knight looked short of pace and accuracy.

No one, however, was going to take M.C.C.'s batting at its face value until Davidson and Benaud had been encountered. The wicket for the New South Wales match at Sydney was on the slow side, and Dexter, winning the toss, batted. Davidson bowled five bewildering overs of late swing at the start which Sheppard and Pullar were fortunate to survive. After Sheppard had gone to Martin at 31, Dexter rattled up 42 in even time before hitting over a long hop. Cowdrey played smoothly for 50, but Graveney was out for nought and Parfitt, who had had little practice, managed only 17. That M.C.C. reached 348 all out by stumps was due largely to Pullar who battled on, in face of much discouragement from the Hill, for 132, an innings of patience and determination that lasted over four and a half hours. Benaud bowled twenty-five overs during the day, finishing up with the wickets of Parfitt, Illingworth and Smith for 61. It could hardly be said to have been decisive either way.

Trueman bowled magnificently on the second morning, but once he had retired with fibrositis, New South Wales had it all their own way. Simpson scored his third hundred against M.C.C. in a month, O'Neill hammered up 143, Booth, Harvey, Davidson, Flockton and Benaud each scored between 40 and 63, and the bowling began to look ragged and purposeless. Benaud declared at 532 for 6. Three gloomy and desperate hours later it was all over. M.C.C. through a succession of bad strokes (Dexter was caught off a full pitch, and Cowdrey off a long hop) were put out for 104, Benaud taking 7 for 18 in 18.1 overs. Parfitt got his head down for eighty-four minutes to make 22, but otherwise resistance was token. Five boundaries only were hit in the whole innings, one of them by Trueman. The peacock scores of 500 at Adelaide, of 600 at Melbourne, dwindled into sudden insignificance.

Since Old Trafford in 1961 – when Dexter was within minutes of destroying Benaud and winning England the series – this meeting with Benaud was always going to be the crucial moment of recognition. That it had gone so meltingly in Benaud's favour, with the First Test a bare fortnight off, could only be a matter for dismay. Technique where it has never properly existed cannot be developed against a bowler of Benaud's class in a matter of days. Batsmen accustomed to pushing stoically down the pitch are hard put to muster the necessary confidence for co-ordinated attack. Benaud, calculatingly slow of movement, his delivery a model of hallucinatory control, could afford now to stare down the wicket or gaze hypnotically back over his shoulder on the way to the next ball. He found himself suddenly holding all the cards, with the need to play very few of them.

Such confidence as had been developed among the English batsmen over the past few weeks was seen clearly to have been falsely based. Two delusive Test series against Pakistan bowlers were no kind of mental preparation to meet a bowler who required instinctive action based on correct premises. But what were these premises? No English batsmen, save Dexter, and he only for brief bouts of savagery, had found time to discover and relate them.

The Queensland match, however restorative in other ways, could offer no further practice against leg-spin. Queensland on the first day proceeded to 433 for 7 declared, Mackay entertaining himself with 105 not out. Coldwell, with 2 for 106, was the best of the M.C.C. bowlers. The fielding and catching were jeered by scoffers under the fig trees, as they had been at Adelaide. Dexter, as sometimes happens on these occasions, alienated himself from the action altogether, and the bowlers were left to their own, largely arbitrary, devices. The disintegration and disappointment had become dangerously near chronic.

On the Monday, things took a turn for the better. Wesley Hall, viewed with some apprehension, found the pitch too slow for him and looked anyhow to have shed the rough edge of his violence. He finished with 0 for 106, and the other Queensland bowlers did little better. Dexter declared at 581 for 6, everyone except Titmus making runs. Pullar had 'flu, and Parfitt, opening with Sheppard, helped to put on 101 for the first wicket. Sheppard got 94, Parfitt 47, Dexter 80 (in eighty-five minutes), Barrington 183 not out, Graveney 52, and Knight 81. Queensland, batting a second time, were all but bowled out by Dexter who took 4 for 8 in 8 overs. Queensland at the close were 94 for 7, Grout being unable to bat, Hall having removed him from the first Test by landing one on his jaw.

Certainly, the manner of England's batting showed a return of spirit and determination. But it was not at all the same thing as batting against Benaud and Davidson. For that we should have to wait another few days.

The England side, when it was announced late that night, was not without surprises. For a start, Smith was preferred to Murray. Dexter, having decided on only one off-spinner, settled on Titmus rather than Allen, which was in line with all-round form if not with intrinsic quality. Similarly Knight, on batting figures alone, had earned his place, especially since Larter, after being repeatedly no-balled at Adelaide for dragging, had since lost both rhythm and accuracy. The really contestable decision, though, was Parfitt to bat at number six, and not Graveney. Both averaged under 25, with only one decent innings – Graveney's 99 at Adelaide – between them. However apparently out of form, one would have expected Graveney, on the basis of experience and class, to have had the initial opportunity. But Parfitt's fielding could hardly be discounted in the circumstances, and that presumably was what ultimately counted. It must have been a sad setback for Graveney, after the long haul of the last two years, but in a sense he had only himself to blame.

The Australian team was as expected. The batsmen, save perhaps Lawry, were all in rampageous form, and the bowlers had all tasted blood. The length of the batting was such that Jarman, who came in for Grout and was no mean performer at all, found himself at number 11. It was scarcely possible to envisage England ever bowling them out. Trueman at this stage was an uncertain proposition, physically, and he had rarely been at full stretch. Dexter, save for that one purple patch against Queensland, had been bowling slower than his best speed. Knight, Barrington, and Titmus looked optimistic support for Statham, ever-reliable but no longer quite so whippy. And none of them seemed yet to have fixed on their most satisfactory method, with developed understanding of field placings, nor to have become a related part in a preconceived and thought-out strategy.

There is nothing quite like the assembling of teams, officials and Press on the eve of an England-Australian Test series. Everything lies ahead; the predictions of weeks can be made nonsense of in a few hours.

Each new flight from Sydney brought players from the other States. Lennons Hotel began to hum with excitement. The bar in the Rainbow Room swelled nightly and the barman who wore mauve eyeshadow was pirouetting from end to end of his command like a ballet dancer. A sexy-looking torch singer breathed huskily into her microphone while bronzed Brisbane couples smooched in the semi-darkness. A dozen oysters and a fillet steak took longer and longer to order, so in the end it was better and cheaper to settle for Chinese food round the corner. The coloured lights flickered along by the river where frangipani exhaled their musk alongside the poinsettias and the night air was exactly the right temperature.

1 Brisbane: The First Test

First Day: The toss, unanimously accepted as crucial to England's chances, was won by Australia, on a sunless, cloud-strewn morning. The scarlet poincianas shivered in a light breeze, the palm trees on the hill slung their branches over the red corrugated-iron roofs of the houses below them. On the grass banks in front of the stands it was for the most part bare legs and floppy white hats. A sweepstake in the Press Box for the day's total gave Australia scores varying from 270 for 7 to 350 for 2. Everyone was afraid that if any inroad was to be made into Australia's batting it had to be in the first hour. On the face of it, the pitch, a healthy camel-colour, looked good for thousands.

Statham, from the Pavilion end, bowled to Lawry, the latter, with a very short haircut, all baggy cap and nose, hunched over his bat like a kangaroo. Statham was immediately on a length, straight, with one that got up to hit Simpson on the gloves. Trueman, bowling down the slight slope, looked a shade quicker and twice Lawry all but played on. Now Trueman, bowling wide of the crease, concentrated on slanting the ball across Lawry's body towards the slips. Twice Lawry played and missed; one he watched go by, almost superciliously; then to the last ball of Trueman's second over, he pushed out along the line of the off stump, got an edge, and was caught at the wicket.

Simpson took two fours off Statham's next over, a handsome turn off his legs, and a slash that sent the ball scudding high over slips. Neither bowlers used third man or fine leg.

Trueman at once produced two leaping bouncers for O'Neill, one on a length that thudded up at O'Neill's heart, and one that he only came down on just in time. Off this latter, O'Neill hared off for an improbable single and, had Dexter at short leg picked the ball up cleanly, O'Neill would have been pushed to get home. As it was, he made his presence plain with a square cut off a short rising ball that sent it skidding between gully and cover. Trueman at this stage had two slips, two gullies and on the leg side a very close forward short leg, and two backward short legs.

He bowled again a shade short to O'Neill, O'Neill slashed and Sheppard, the finer of the gullies, knocked it up at full stretch. Parfitt threw himself from second slip, held it, only for the impact of his body on the ground to knock it out. A heroic effort, but he flung his cap on the ground in self-disgust. O'Neill was 6 at the time. It could have been the turning point.

Knight took over from Statham and the drop in pace was calculable in dozens of miles per hour. Trueman continued to harry both O'Neill and Simpson, and Simpson's bat on the forward stroke looked oddly irresolute – neither straight nor more than cardboard in substance. The ball had not swung all morning, but Trueman was digging it in to ferocious effect.

O'Neill, after a nervy, fidgety period, suddenly late cut Trueman with annihilating swiftness. Sheppard at gully was providently not in its way. In the same over, O'Neill glanced Trueman to the vacant long leg boundary. The opening hour of the series had produced 41 runs, with twelve overs being bowled.

Trueman now looked to be tiring. O'Neill swung at a no-ball and missed heavily. Next, however, Trueman managed to make one lift sharply, O'Neill took it on the glove, and Statham, running in from backward short leg, held a gentle catch.

Knight was varying his pace interestingly, and now and again his inward flight found the inside edge of the bat, sending the ball only feet wide of the two short legs. But once an over he overpitched or dropped short, and at his friendly pace, Simpson could pick his spot on the fence.

Harvey did well to survive two overs against Trueman. Twice Trueman beat him outside the off stump, twice he came down on straight ones at the last second, his bat at an angle. After seventy-five minutes, Trueman came off with 2 for 28 in 7 overs; there would be few better spells of fast bowling in the series. Not since Port-of-Spain, when he bowled out West Indies in the bottle-throwing Test, had he looked so hostile and accurate.

Knight changed ends, and Statham came back, the cross breeze helping his in-swinger to drift away from Harvey. Simpson, driving a half volley from Knight to the sightscreen, was looking ominously settled. Statham dropped one short to Harvey who hooked viciously, only to find Pullar at backward square leg all but cling on. It was a hit to waken the dead, and Pullar examined the ball as if it had materialized from the underworld. He looked astonished to find both ball and himself in the same place, intact.

At 77, a quarter of an hour before lunch, Titmus relieved Knight, Dexter took over from Statham. Harvey at once moved down the pitch to Titmus, and seemed to relish being able to do so. Simpson drove Dexter through the covers, reaching 50 in the process. He went to hook the next ball, a long hop of no great pace, mistimed it, and Trueman, looking suspicious at the laziness of it, caught him at mid-on. Australia, at lunch, were 97 for 3; altogether an absorbing morning.

Trueman now attacked Burge on the leg stump, digging the ball in, with Dexter close up on Burge's hip, and two other short legs squarer and deeper. Almost at once Trueman got one to lift, and Dexter, shooting up his right arm to its full extent, took a brilliant catch.

Trueman greeted Booth with a swift one to the jaw, embracing him with brotherly love at the end of the over. Booth got well over a short one on the off stump, steering it for four, then drove Trueman to the long-off boundary. At 128 for 4, Statham bowled for the first time from Trueman's end. He looked at first to be getting considerably less life from it, but after Harvey had driven past mid-off he twice had him feeling outside the off stump and getting perilously close. In his second over, he suddenly produced a beautiful ball that pitched on Harvey's off stump and came back between bat and pad to hit the middle. Harvey departed shaking his head as if satisfied nothing could have been done about it.

Dexter had bowled for half an hour fairly tidily from the pavilion end. Titmus, coming on under a now cloudless sky, immediately appealed loudly for l.b.w. against Davidson, but was refused. So Titmus changed ends and for some while he and Knight kept things surprisingly quiet. A stiffish breeze was helping Knight's in-swing, and Titmus used it to curve the ball away towards the slips. Davidson, after taking his ease for half an hour, crashed Knight through the covers, and Booth cut Titmus for four almost out of the wicket-keeper's gloves. Runs ticked up without either much distinction or difficulty, 50 coming in fifty-four minutes.

Dexter gave Barrington a go with the wind behind his leg-break. Davidson swung at a ball on the leg stump, and Trueman on the fence at long leg ran a few yards to take the ball before it crashed into the wood. In his fiftieth Test, he had had a hand in five of these first six wickets.

So Mackay loped in, chewing as demonstrably as for a TV commercial, with the new ball a couple of overs off. It was Booth, though, before and after tea, who took the brunt of the bowling, stroking Statham away to the long-off boundary and generally bestowing an air of uprightness and leisure. He stands straight, and, more than any of the others, gave the impression of having time and enough to get his body into the proper position. Anything remotely overpitched from Trueman or Statham he flashed to the boundary, the left arm beautifully in control. Once only was he made to look awkward, Trueman bringing one back sharply from outside the off stump to take the inside edge. Smith moved the wrong way and the ball shot to his left for four.

The fifty partnership went up in just under the hour, Mackay contributing seven of them. Self-effacement could go no further. The lack of a top class spinner began to show itself, for the fast bowlers were spent and the others looked increasingly amicable.

Mackay, after eighty minutes inharmonious stagnation, sliced Titmus past slip for four and, confidence achieved, twice carved Dexter through the covers. In the same over, Booth, just before five o'clock, stroked Dexter to the mid-wicket boundary to reach 100 in only his third test. He had scored his runs out of 165 made while he was at the wicket.

Barrington bowled again and Mackay began to acquire boundaries stealthily in all directions. Booth was resting up but the England attack seemed for the first time all day devoid of purpose. It is at such moments that Dexter's hold on the proceedings seems altogether too remote.

The hundred for the partnership went up, the fielders' shadows took on the elongated thin shapes of the sculptor Giacometti, and the play for the last forty-five minutes had a run-down automatic air. Booth eventually seemed to weary of it, and leaping down the pitch to Titmus he hit him hard and cross-batted to wide mid-on. Dexter, making ground, took a fine catch over his shoulder.

Without Booth it would plainly have been England's day. He and Mackay had added 103 and they had emphasized that, even after an early breakthrough, England just had not

AUSTRALIA – First Innings

W. Lawry, c. Smith, b. Trueman	5
R. B. Simpson, c. Trueman, b. Dexter	50
N. O'Neill, c. Statham, b. Trueman	19
R. N. Harvey, b. Statham	39
P. J. Burge, c. Dexter, b. Trueman	6
B. Booth, c. Dexter, b. Titmus	112
A. K. Davidson, c. Trueman, b. Barrington	23
K. Mackay, not out	51
R. Benaud, not out	13
Extras (b. 1, l.b. 1, n.b. 1)	3
Total (7 wkts.)	321

FALL OF WICKETS. 1—5, 2—46, 3—92, 4—101, 5—140, 6—194, 7—297.

the resources to press an advantage home on a good pitch and against such depth of batting.

Mackay reached 50 before the end, going about it with a mortician's lofty detachment from the irksome job in hand. He was chewing as frenziedly at the finish as at the beginning.

Second Day: Plainly if the striking achievements of Friday morning and afternoon were not to be wasted, England could afford little nonsense from Mackay and Benaud. The blue of the day before had given way to unbroken cloud and the leaves of the fig trees and poincianas still gleamed from a heavy breakfast time shower. Mackay, however, is not one to be distracted by aesthetic considerations, and while contriving to look as much on the run from trailing sheriffs as usual, he steered the fast bowlers at the most unlikely angles and with something approaching disdain. Benaud brings to batting a sense of pure pleasure, a feeling of adventure, and a correct technique. He hooked Trueman's bouncer, glanced Statham off his middle stump and evoked lively memories of his tremendous 97 in the Lord's Test of 1956. When he sees the ball as early as this he can be a formidable batsman. Trueman with little to encourage him grew nettled and fretful. Statham appeared slow enough for Mackay's hyperdermic stab to acquire overtones of acute voluptuousness. Titmus halted progress for a while by bowling four overs for one run, but he came comfortably on to the middle of the bat nevertheless. At the end of an hour, Australia were 50 runs on, and the attack seemed without further ideas. Knight bowled and, although he came within a whisker of getting Benaud l.b.w., one could only long for some of Bailey's intelligence and persistent accuracy. Once the fast bowlers were off the absence of penetration and control made batting seem an academic formality. Mackay once missed a sweep off Titmus and the bowler seemed justifiably aggrieved at the refusal of his appeal. Benaud reached 50 with a skimming off-drive but next ball, flicking Knight to leg, was neatly taken low down by Smith.

The last two wickets had added 194 runs. An over later Knight flung himself down the pitch to take a tumbling return catch from McKenzie. Mackay continued to scoop and swivel his way towards his first Test century, but the final non-consummation of it was largely his own fault. For if you waste as many runs as Mackay does there comes a limit to the time your partners may care to remain. Five minutes before lunch, Jarman drove a half-volley from Knight, who had collected all the three wickets to fall, and Barrington caught him at wide mid-on.

After being 190 for 6, with the new ball due, 404 was more than Benaud can have assumed. Yet he would always have the comforting knowledge that happen what may in the first hour or two, his own batting was as long as England's bowling was short.

The afternoon was no less cloudy, the cross-breeze a point or two brisker. Davidson, his breadth of shoulder seemingly vaster than in England, bowled to Pullar with an arc of four slips and two backward short legs. Pullar took six runs to leg off the first over, then Sheppard drove McKenzie through the covers. The innings was launched. For Sheppard, Davidson dispensed with cover and allowed Benaud to station himself off the batsman's hip. McKenzie's second over had Sheppard in real trouble. He shot one past the off stump, had him all but jab one off his ribs to backward short leg, and next saw Davidson at second slip fail to cling on to a low sharp chance to his right. Davidson's direction was more variable than usual and Pullar was soon able to put a full toss away to the fig-trees at square leg.

At 25, McKenzie changed ends, and Mackay bowled, or rather propelled the ball with convulsive jerk of the wrist. McKenzie's lift, accuracy and general aggression made him look every inch a bowler of the future. Benaud kept him going for eighty minutes, but at 40, came on himself. The whole match, it seemed, had been geared to this moment. From the beginning he turned the ball several inches and with the covers swoopingly patrolled by O'Neill, Harvey and others, was never easy to get away. Mackay came back and, pitching just short of a length, tied up the other end. Beer cans circulated under the eucalyptus and the packed shirt-sleeved gentlemen from the country grew vocal. Fifty was hoisted after an hour and a half: Benaud experimented with his flipper and bowled a wide: the picking up was precise, the throwing of a deadliness that never involved Jarman the wicket-keeper in more wrist movement than would flicking a cigarette lighter. Once Pullar hauled a full toss from Benaud for four, once Mackay got one to go the other way and Sheppard was perilously close to it. But for the most part there was little incident.

Then at 62 with sun shining and tea in sight, Pullar went to turn an off-break from Benaud to leg. The ball hung up somewhat in the air and Benaud received a dismally gentle return catch off the outside edge. In the last over before tea Benaud, throwing the ball up outside the leg stump with pronounced but laboured turn, and nobody deep, got Sheppard caught at backward short leg off an indeterminate prod. Benaud had taken two wickets for nought in eleven balls. No sooner had he come on than the batting degenerated into struggling diffidence.

After tea Davidson dug in a few at Dexter's ribs but a ferocious hook and two lovely straight drives returned authority to where Dexter clearly thought it belonged. And it stayed that way. McKenzie replaced Davidson while Benaud for over an hour spun away with fastidious nonchalance. Cowdrey was content to push amiably forward at the pitch of the ball while Dexter cut, pulled, and on the rare occasions Benaud overpitched, hit brutally hard. Together these two added 50 in forty-five minutes, Dexter's share being 40.

Benaud, having bowled eleven overs for 19, came off after his next two cost 22. Dexter had won his second victory of the evening. He reached 50 out of 66 and he had made them imperiously. Davidson returned and Dexter crashed his first ball to the screen. Mackay now bowled several searching overs at Dexter, keeping the ball up to him, bringing it in a bit and inviting him to hit over the top of mid-off and mid-on standing deep. Simpson bowled his leg-spinners at 141 and Cowdrey cut the first for four. The third was a long-hop and Cowdrey swung it hard and high to leg. He had the whole of that side to aim at and he compulsively picked the one spot where Lawry stood isolated on the fence. A quarter of an hour from stumps Benaud came back and now there were leg-spinners at both ends. With eight minutes to go Dexter, who had been taking it quietly for some time, lost sight of a high-flighted one from Benaud, hit over it and was bowled. His 70 had been finely etched and often thrillingly struck. Whether it would be enough remained to be seen.

AUSTRALIA – First Innings

W. Lawry, c. Smith, b. Trueman	5
R. B. Simpson, c. Trueman, b. Dexter	50
N. O'Neill, c. Statham, b. Trueman	19
R. N. Harvey, b. Statham	39
P. J. Burge, c. Dexter, b. Trueman	6
B. Booth, c. Dexter, b. Titmus	112
A. K. Davidson, c. Trueman, b. Barrington	23
K. Mackay, not out	86
R. Benaud, c. Smith, b. Knight	51
G. McKenzie, c. and b. Knight	4
B. Jarman, c. Barrington, b. Knight	2
Extras (b. 5, l.b. 1, n.b. 1)	7
Total	404

FALL OF WICKETS. 1—5, 2—46, 3—92, 4—101, 5—140, 6—194, 7—297, 8—388, 9—392, 10—404.

ENGLAND – First Innings

G. A. Pullar, c. and b. Benaud	33
D. S. Sheppard, c. McKenzie, b. Benaud	31
E. R. Dexter, b. Benaud	70
M. C. Cowdrey, c. Lawry, b. Simpson	21
K. F. Barrington, not out	13
A. C. Smith, not out	0
Extras (w. 1)	1
Total (4 wkts.)	169

P. Parfitt, B. Knight, F. J. Titmus, F. S. Trueman and J. B. Statham to go in.

FALL OF WICKETS. 1—62, 2—65, 3—145, 4—169.

Third Day: The leg-spinners began where they had left off, Simpson towards the pavilion, Benaud away from it – the end from which he had bowled Dexter, and from which he had seemed to get more turn. Simpson's third ball was a half-volley and Barrington drove it all along the ground to the long-off boundary. There were 26 runs to go to the new ball, if Benaud chose to take it. Benaud, using the full width of the crease, bowled a thoughtful maiden to Barrington. Off Simpson's next over both Smith and Barrington took fours, one on each side of the wicket. Then Smith swung Simpson off his leg stump past the square leg umpire's shins.

Barrington, taking note, did the same to Benaud, a stroke not without elements of risk. Benaud, seemingly unnerved, bowled two long hops and Barrington despatched both of them. The 200 went up, six boundaries coming in the first half-hour. O'Neill replaced Simpson, and Barrington swept him against the spin to long leg for four more.

So Davidson was summoned and at once took the new ball. He whipped one back to rap Smith on the pads, but was oddly wasteful outside the off stump. Smith steered McKenzie between the slips and 45 runs had come at one a minute. Davidson now softened up Smith by beating him continually outside the off stump, Smith's left foot getting further and further from the line of the ball. McKenzie got one to kick in the next over and Smith, who had taken a nasty blow from Hall in the Queensland match, turned his head at the last second and was caught off his glove.

Parfitt showed such immediate signs of life, scuttling between the wickets with Barrington like an old tug behind him, that Benaud returned earlier than he can have intended. McKenzie changed ends and Parfitt played him away off his legs and then hit him cross-batted through the covers. England at lunch were 264 for 5, Barrington, who had batted without suspicion of error or uncertainty, 63, Parfitt 22. Benaud after his opening overs, had looked tameable, Davidson, ageing.

Parfitt pulled a full toss from Benaud soon afterwards, which meant the second 50 partnership of the day. Barrington looked to be taking root again, as solidly as a gum-tree. But Benaud, bowling with dissembling ease, occasionally found him mistaking the googly for the leg-break, causing him hurriedly to change his mind about intended off-drives. Parfitt on-drove Benaud through two scarlet sunshades and only several brilliant one-handed stops by Lawry saved them being disturbed further. Mackay satisfactorily sealed up the other end, pitching on or about the off stump the whole time and every so often getting one to run away. He beat Barrington once like this, the only false stroke Barrington had played in two and a half hours. For twenty minutes Mackay tied up Barrington, and Benaud, Parfitt. The fielders swooped in like vultures and even for Parfitt, the short single, that might have broken up the pattern, dried up completely. There was accuracy to admire, and concentration, but no anecdote. The sun poured down. Three times Barrington drove hard and scattered the stumps at the bowler's end. He threw his cap down in frustration. It was difficult to discern whether Benaud or Barrington were running out of ideas quicker.

Parfitt now grew fidgety against Mackay, skying him suddenly just over the bowler's head. Both batsmen might have taken warning from this, but a drink, far from cooling Barrington down, launched him out against Benaud; he failed quite to get to the pitch, and Burge at extra cover took a spinning overhead catch. Barrington came in looking understandably fed up, for it was a wicket thrown away, when everything was in favour of grinding Benaud down until he was forced to come off. On such pitches the bowler can only hope for mistakes and the less hopeful he becomes, the more relaxing for the batsmen.

Titmus started perkily, taking four past slip off the bottom of the bat, and then carting Benaud over mid-wicket. So Benaud, after bowling twelve successive overs for 25 runs, gave Simpson a bowl, bringing Davidson on from the pavilion. Parfitt, glancing Davidson the thickness of glass from Jarman, reached 50, a consolidating innings of initiative and character. Scarcely a run had come off the front foot through the covers, but on the leg side he was neat and productive.

Titmus looked so costive against Simpson, that Benaud faced him with two silly mid-offs and two short mid-ons. He assumed the proportions of a small, docile animal in an ostentatiously barred cage. But he stuck it out till tea, or nuts, which seemed more apposite in his case. England then were 331 for 6, Parfitt 59, Titmus 12.

With Simpson and Mackay still bowling, the half-hour after tea produced 10 runs. Titmus was more bullyingly imprisoned than even before, and Parfitt used his pads to anything outside the off stump. The drive had grown obsolete. The 50 partnership, when it arrived at half-past four, had taken ninety minutes. Mackay bowled five overs for 8 runs, after which Benaud came on himself, with McKenzie relieving Simpson. The cricket had permanence, but no pride.

Benaud began throwing the ball up to Titmus who, deciding contrarily to fetch a leg-break from outside the off stump to mid-wicket, sliced it to slip. One run later McKenzie's first ball to Knight found the glove, and Davidson, moved across from slip to backward short leg by Benaud, received a comforting catch. With 0 for 77 at the time he was probably glad of it. He got further solace a moment later for Parfitt, putting scant faith in Trueman's scowling presence, lofted Benaud to him at deep mid-off. Three wickets had gone for one run.

Trueman succeeded, by some curious legerdemain, in hitting a full toss from Benaud over his own head, and then, after a variety of miscues, pulled him for four, four, six, one, off consecutive balls. McKenzie in the next over had him caught behind, a judgment Trueman accepted with some grudgingness. Benaud came out of the proceedings with 6 for 115, in 42 overs; something worth putting beside his 6 for 70 at Old Trafford, an honest reward for long accurate spells on a wicket that offered him little.

Australia therefore began their second innings 15 ahead,

with twenty-five minutes batting. Simpson faced Trueman, and the first ball he played down hard for it to roll back and nestle against the off stump without disturbing the bail. He snicked four runs between first and second slip, and played and missed at the next two. Trueman had reason now for grievance. Simpson, looking unhappy, appealed against the light, but was refused. Statham next beat him twice, and altogether he looked relieved to come in.

AUSTRALIA

First Innings		Second Innings	
W. Lawry, c. Smith, b. Trueman	5	not out	7
R. B. Simpson, c. Trueman, b. Dexter	50	not out	7
N. O'Neill, c. Statham, b. Trueman	19		
R. N. Harvey, b. Statham	39		
P. J. Burge, c. Dexter, b. Trueman	6		
B. Booth, c. Dexter, b. Titmus	112		
A. K. Davidson, c. Trueman, b. Barrington	23		
K. Mackay, not out	86		
R. Benaud, c. Smith, b. Knight	51		
G. McKenzie, c. and b. Knight	4		
B. Jarman, c. Barrington, b. Knight	2		
Extras (b. 5, l.b. 1, n.b. 1)	7	Extras	2
Total	404	Total (no wkt.)	16

FALL OF WICKETS. 1—5, 2—46, 3—92, 4—101, 5—140, 6—194, 7—297, 8—388, 9—392, 10—404.

ENGLAND – First Innings

G. A. Pullar, c. and b. Benaud	33
D. S. Sheppard, c. McKenzie, b. Benaud	31
E. R. Dexter, b. Benaud	70
M. C. Cowdrey, c. Lawry, b. Simpson	21
K. F. Barrington, c. Burge, b. Benaud	78
A. C. Smith, c. Jarman, b. McKenzie	21
P. H. Parfitt, c. Davidson, b. Benaud	80
F. J. Titmus, c. Simpson, b. Benaud	21
B. R. Knight, c. Davidson, b. McKenzie	0
F. S. Trueman, c. Jarman, b. McKenzie	19
J. B. Statham, not out	8
Extras (b. 4, l.b. 2, w. 1)	7
Total	389

FALL OF WICKETS. 1—62, 2—65, 3—145, 4—169, 5—220, 6—297, 7—361, 8—362, 9—362, 10—389.

Fourth Day: Dexter's policy could only be one of confinement. The chances of any serious inroad into Australia's batting on this pitch, without a back-of-the-hand spinner, were fairly remote. If he could prevent Benaud from declaring before the day's end, Dexter would have reason for satisfaction.

The first twenty minutes provided only three runs. Trueman again bothered Simpson, whose right foot tended to stray away from the line. Statham, bowling to Lawry, was unable to slant the ball across the left-hander's body, and Lawry tucked him away off his legs. Simpson began to play some pleasant strokes off the back foot, but when he was 21 he pushed forward too soon at Statham's slower ball, only for the incredulous bowler to put down a waist-high lob. Several fielding mistakes now, and an irrelevant overthrow to the boundary by Trueman, gave a sense of unearned ease to the batting.

Knight and Titmus bowled for forty minutes before lunch, without either incident or untidiness. Dexter set sensibly defensive fields and the bowlers bowled to them. It was much like the tactics of Benaud and Mackay the afternoon before, except that Benaud, even when his flights of fancy are curtailed by an unimaginative pitch, remains absorbing to watch. Five minutes before the interval Simpson's 50 and the 100 partnership had been recorded, and that was about all that could be said of them.

Dexter and Titmus bore the early heat of the afternoon, the batsmen rather more comatose than the fielders. After half an hour, Dexter decided to dispense with slip, Cowdrey moving into the covers. Simpson, a figure bereft of all company near the wicket, went to glance the next ball and Smith caught him on the leg side. Simpson walked without verdict. It had not been one of his more assured innings.

O'Neill took time to settle in, but a hook and a cut off Dexter recalled echoes of latent savagery. Knight offered him several succulent half-volleys, Titmus meanwhile feeding Lawry over-generously on the leg stump. The fielding alternated between brilliance and ineptness.

Statham returned, but he, too, seemed mesmerized by Lawry's leg stump, with the result that runs at last began to flow. O'Neill hooked Knight repeatedly, his field rapidly resembling a tiring off-spinner's. Trueman was reluctantly pressed back into service, his aspect suggesting that such unprofitable labour should be reserved for younger, fitter, and less precious men.

Lawry neared an unremarkable century, its assiduous inevitability being cut short two runs off when Sheppard fastened on to a hook off Titmus. Australia at tea, with the new ball just taken, were 223 for 2, O'Neill 41, Harvey 3.

Statham's opening over afterwards provided O'Neill with 11 runs, including a gorgeous hook, and Trueman's first ball, a half-volley, O'Neill hammered through the covers. Dexter's resources had begun already to look pitifully thin.

Fortunately, Statham now brought one back at O'Neill, who, pressing somewhat, was fulsomely l.b.w.

Harvey took over, placing Trueman through the covers and edging him wide of slip, while Trueman raised supplicating arms. Titmus bowled in place of Statham, and Smith failed to stump Harvey when, without announcement of intention, Harvey waltzed down the pitch. Dexter set no gully for Harvey, an unwise economy, for three times Harvey took fours for what would have been catches there.

Smith a second time failed to stump Harvey off Titmus, dropping the ball with Harvey well down the pitch. Evans at this stage of affairs was always able to keep the fielders from flagging, and the lack of someone with his ebullience and energy, to say nothing of his technical proficiency, was inevitably lowering.

Harvey continued to throw his bat fairly edgily but, when he did connect with Dexter, he sent a towering catch to Statham at deep mid-off. This followed some ragged fielding and throwing and Dexter, not daring to turn his head, waited interminably for applause or laughter. He was spared the latter.

Burge swept Titmus inconsequentially off his middle stump,

and several times drove Dexter past mid-off. Australia's lead passed 350 and, with half an hour left, it became plain that the threat of Dexter was deterring Benaud from an over-night declaration. In the circumstances, it appeared unduly deferential. For it was possible that Benaud, thanks largely to Lawry's reluctance to bestir himself, might now run out of time, but find himself with 70 or more useless runs in hand.

AUSTRALIA

First Innings		Second Innings	
W. Lawry, c. Smith, b. Trueman.......	5	c. Sheppard, b. Titmus...	98
R. B. Simpson, c. Trueman, b. Dexter ..	50	c. Smith b. Dexter.......	71
N. O'Neill, c. Statham, b. Trueman	19	l.b.w. b. Statham........	56
R. N. Harvey, b. Statham.............	39	c. Statham, b. Dexter....	57
P. J. Burge, c. Dexter, b. Trueman	6	not out	47
B. Booth, c. Dexter, b. Titmus	112	not out	19
A. K. Davidson, c. Trueman, b. Barrington	23		
K. Mackay, not out	86		
R. Benaud, c. Smith, b. Knight	51		
G. McKenzie, c. and b. Knight	4		
B. Jarman, c. Barrington, b. Knight.....	2		
Extras (b. 5, l.b. 1, n.b. 1)	7	Extras (b. 4, l.b. 10)	14
Total............................	404	Total (4 wkts.)..........	362

FALL OF WICKETS. *First innings*: 1—5, 2—46, 3—92, 4—101, 5—140, 6—194, 7—297, 8—388, 9—392, 10—404. *Second innings*: 1—136, 2—216, 3—241, 4—325.

ENGLAND – First Innings

G. A. Pullar, c. and b. Benaud..............	33
D. S. Sheppard, c. McKenzie, b. Benaud......	31
E. R. Dexter, b. Benaud....................	70
M. C. Cowdrey, c. Lawry, b. Simpson.........	21
K. F. Barrington, c. Burge, b. Benaud.........	78
A. C. Smith, c. Jarman, b. McKenzie..........	21
P. H. Parfitt, c. Davidson, b. Benaud..........	80
F. J. Titmus, c. Simpson, b. Benaud...........	21
B. R. Knight, c. Davidson, b. McKenzie........	0
F. S. Trueman, c. Jarman, b. McKenzie........	19
J. B. Statham, not out......................	8
Extras (b. 4, l.b. 2, w. 1)..................	7
Total	389

FALL OF WICKETS. 1—62, 2—65, 3—145, 4—169, 5—220, 6—297, 7—361, 8—362, 9—362, 10—389.

Fifth Day: This, patently, as far as England was concerned, would be the day of truth. Although Hutton had lost decisively at Brisbane, but recovered to win the series, no other English side had done so, and it needed no emphasizing that Dexter lacked the bowling guns to retrieve any violent upset.

Benaud delayed his declaration until after 11.30. Storms were forecast for later in the day and Pullar and Sheppard, with England wanting 378 to win or, more realistically, requiring to bat for six hours, began their innings under skies more grey than blue.

Davidson struck Pullar painfully on the knee in his first over, but Pullar took eight off McKenzie's next over, a streaky four through the slips and two nice strokes through the covers. Davidson shot several along the ground outside Sheppard's off stump, and Sheppard observed them quizzically. Then McKenzie, in his third over, got one to lift, it found the shoulder of Pullar's bat, and Pullar, about to depart, saw the ball comfortably into Jarman's gloves and incredibly plop out. Pullar was then 13.

Davidson this time was more variable in length than direction, three full tosses in one over to Pullar going unscathed. Benaud gave him five overs, then took over himself. The score was 31, fifty minutes had gone. Benaud's opening over was laconically to the point, each ball on a length, its rhythm balletic. Sheppard drove McKenzie to the sightscreen, having previously driven uppishly once or twice with the weight on the back foot. Benaud pitched into the rough outside Pullar's off stump, and Pullar thrust forward his right leg and took him on the pads. At noon Mackay replaced McKenzie, and stage two of Benaud's strategy was in operation. Benaud bowled more or less without regard to the batsmen's presence, so unobtrusive were they. After nearly four overs for one run, Pullar swept Benaud, not without a hint of desperation, to the mid-wicket boundary. Sheppard then drove a high-flighted one from Benaud off his legs past mid-on, sending up the 50 for the second time in the match, in eighty minutes. He tried next to cut a googly, smiling as he stabbed it gratefully towards gully. Pullar lifted Benaud over wide mid-on and Mackay, licking his fingers like a Post Office clerk, twice beat Sheppard outside the off stump.

Twenty minutes before lunch, Benaud had leg-spinners performing at both ends. Sheppard slashed Simpson through the packed covers and having sent them deeper took a quick single there. He hit Benaud to the fence off the back foot, a stroke that left O'Neill at cover stationary. Now Benaud flipped through several quicker and lower, drawing Sheppard forward and missing the edge by a hair's breadth. Pullar swung Simpson to the stand at long leg, and England were discernibly on the move. At lunch they were 83, Sheppard 41, Pullar 38. Benaud had bowled ten overs for 19 runs.

The clouds scattered under a brisk breeze, and the slopes below the poincianas and the figs began to thicken. Cattlemen under broad-brimmed hats and naked to the waist tossed beer cans around them as if they were peanut shells. Some preferred to doze on their backs well into the afternoon. Benaud changed ends, using McKenzie now as foil. Sheppard jumped out at Benaud, not quite getting to the pitch, and Lawry at silly mid-off failed to grasp a catch high to his right. Sheppard was 42. Pullar glanced McKenzie fine for four, then Sheppard, flicking him off his legs to the fence, sent up the 100. Both now stood on 49, Pullar steering McKenzie past gully to inch his way first to 50. Not since 1946–7, when Hutton and Washbrook made three successive such opening partnerships, had England passed a hundred for the first wicket in Australia. Sheppard quickly followed Pullar, and the running between the wickets became positively skittish.

So Davidson was restored, and Pullar, aiming to turn him to leg at once gave a trifling return catch off the outside edge. Dexter in the same over hit Davidson along the ground to the stand at long-on, but several shrewd overs from each end curbed his barely concealed aggressiveness. At length Dexter drove a widish leg-break through the covers and pulled the next ball for four. The slumberers on the slopes sat up and took notice. Sheppard in half-an-hour received two balls, such was Dexter's proprietary impatience. Dexter came down the track to Benaud, who gave himself a fifth fielder on the off side. The hour after lunch produced 52 runs, a prospect not altogether unpromising if Dexter could stay there.

But now he lost Sheppard, who, starved for so long of the strike, fended a lifting ball from Davidson off his gloves into Benaud's hands at gully. Dexter cut Benaud between cover and third man, and then with almost pagan follow-through smote Davidson to the cover boundary. Benaud came off, giving Cowdrey two fast bowlers to contend with. Dexter edged Davidson waist-high between slip and gully, reached across to slash him past cover, and in the same over drove him nearly to the extra-cover boundary. He jumped out to McKenzie, just clearing mid-on, and the handsome and the hazardous were jostling nerve-wrackingly together. Davidson, cutting the ball off the seam, continued to bowl calculatingly, but Dexter again crashed McKenzie through the covers, a stroke of devastating swiftness. A late cut took him to 50, scored out of 59, and Benaud, bowling to four men on the leg side, replaced Davidson.

Dexter immediately lay back to strike him savagely through the covers, all lying deep. With England 182 for 2, Dexter 56, Cowdrey 9, the two hours since lunch had brought 99 runs. The situation was that England, in the remaining two hours, needed 196, having taken four hours to make 182. Conversely, Australia, having taken two wickets in four hours, wanted eight in half that time.

The thunderstorm was rumoured still to be approaching, but the sky remained severely blue. Mackay was recalled and Dexter carted him high towards the fig-trees at mid-wicket. Benaud bowled a rank long-hop at Cowdrey and Cowdrey, out to a long-hop in the first innings, hit it straight back at the bowler. News came that the storm had 'levelled out'.

Barrington drove Mackay consolingly past mid-off to the scoreboard, and Dexter, hitting Mackay on the rise, found the mid-wicket fence second bounce. Harvey brought off a thrilling stop at square leg, and with one of three results conceivable, the cricket was vigorous and pointed. Barrington drove Benaud flaringly past extra, overhauling Cowdrey's monkish nine in a matter of minutes. Mackay, having conceded 18 in two overs, was withdrawn, Simpson providing leg-breaks of assorted length, but definite spin, in his place.

Dexter, chasing the unlikely but just possible, pulled Simpson over mid-wicket, then forced him airily just fine of cover. A googly from each end shot low past the stumps to give England seven in byes. Dexter, undeterred, lifted Simpson over mid-off, crashed him past cover, cut him late. Ten runs in three balls. Barrington, encouraged, swung a long-hop for four, drove the next to long-on. Nineteen off the over. The forty minutes since tea were worth 64 runs to England. Simpson, with 31 off three overs, retired in his turn, McKenzie taking over. Benaud was running out of partners. With seventy-five minutes left England needed 128.

Benaud gave Davidson the new ball. The hunt, from one point of view, had been called off. The next quarter of an hour resulted in two runs, Barrington being pinned down by McKenzie. Dexter lost the strike for close on twenty minutes, save for half-a-dozen balls from Davidson which demanded his full attention.

When he got it, his own score at 99, he drove slightly across one well up to him from McKenzie and was bowled. Barrington at the other end shut his eyes in dismay. It was cruelly unfortunate for Dexter that, once time had run out through no fault of his own, his innings necessarily lost momentum. But the spirit, the acceptance of challenge, and the sheer power in making strokes, remained indelible. He had turned a stubborn fight into a headlong chase, with, for about twenty minutes before the new ball, a dawning prospect of victory.

McKenzie gave Parfitt a testing start, and Benaud, with thirty-five minutes left, packed the close field. Barrington in Davidson's next over failed to get over a half-volley on the off stump and McKenzie took a sharp catch at gully. McKenzie now bowled to three slips, three short legs, with Benaud at silly mid-off. He got one to lift outside the off stump, Parfitt sparred at it, and the whole Australian side went up.

So Knight, facing a pair, came in with twenty-five minutes left. There were now eight men round the bat, Titmus again staring into four baggy caps, eight pairs of eyes at an accusatory proximity. Appeals of catlike ferocity accompanied nearly every ball.

For Knight, McKenzie had two forward short legs, two backward and fairly dug them in at him. The sun had gone, low cloud drew all the light out of the poincianas. Titmus appealed, but was turned down. The bars of the cage narrowed, a quarter of an hour to go.

Benaud called on O'Neill. O'Neill flighted one so generously it went over the wicket-keeper's head. A shaft of sun flooded the pitch. With seven minutes left, Benaud came on himself. Knight struck a long-hop for four. O'Neill bowled a maiden. On the stroke of six Benaud began the last over to Knight. Two minutes later the crowd swarmed like ants across the pitch. Benaud was four wickets short; Dexter, 100 runs. But for twenty minutes the wind had been put up the partisans of each side in turn, if not of the captains. Either way, it had been an absorbing day from which, considering the wicket, both teams emerged with credit. For England the figures of 1 for 71 against Benaud's name was the most pleasant sight of all. Australia had put down two catches, but in relation to Dexter's innings, crucial to the subsequently developing drama, they were probably irrelevant. For the first time since the war a Test Match at Brisbane had been drawn.

Retrospect: There was now three weeks breathing space for both sides. Australia could perhaps have done with Sincock, the South Australian leg-spinner, on this last day, but he could only come into the side at the expense of a batsman, Booth or Burge, and both of these had batted fluently. If anyone went at Melbourne or Sydney, it would probably be Burge. England conceivably might also keep this side for the next match, although its weaknesses were more apparent. Larter and Allen, on paper at least, would strengthen the bowling, but Larter, even supposing he could recover rhythm and control, remained a total liability as batsman and fielder, while Allen had been massacred at Melbourne and Sydney. Perhaps Dexter would soldier on with Titmus and Knight for the time being. The Australians appeared to have cottoned on to Knight's distaste for the short-pitched ball, which meant that his batting potential would be drastically reduced. Knight and Titmus as the second line of attack was painfully thin, but there seemed nothing to be done about it. Parfitt's batting, for all his limitations on the offside, was determined enough to make Graveney's imminent return unlikely. While neither Pullar nor Sheppard had ever got properly on top, two partnerships of 62 and 114 could scarcely be discounted. Pullar twice got himself out when going well, in identical fashion, playing across the line, and being caught by the bowler off the outside edge. Sheppard had grown visibly in confidence against Benaud, and when he was out in the second innings was stroking the ball in something like his old manner. There remained the problem of Cowdrey. Up to a point he had batted reasonably enough within himself, but it was so far within that the original was barely detectable. He gave the impression of being so absorbed in monk-like meditations of his own that when a really bad ball penetrated his consciousness he went haywire. Four times in a row, he had been out to rank long-hops and in eleven innings he had only twice exceeded 25. In a way, he seemed more out of humour than out of touch. Yet on his previous tours, he had made Test hundreds at Melbourne and Sydney, so one could only hope for the best.

Of the respective fast bowlers, Trueman and McKenzie had come out of the match the best. Trueman on the first day had bowled with real fire and aggression and he carried a threat which none of the others did. McKenzie was strong, straighter than usual, and got the occasional ball to hustle through or lift. Both Statham and Davidson showed signs of ageing, though being bowlers of classic quality had moments when the lineaments of passion showed through. The pitch was too sluggish for either of them, but at Sydney especially one could expect them to respond to conditions more wholeheartedly.

What this Test Match emphasized was that in all departments Australia were the stronger side. But it underlined also the fact that once Benaud was handled with anything approaching firmness, the Australian bowling revealed distinct limitations. England would have to rely on scoring heavily and fast, hoping for at least one break-through.

It was impossible to remember a series in which the personal encounter between the opposing captains was of such dramatic intensity: the greatest attacking batsman of the post-war period versus its most considerable leg-break bowler. It was a duel of heroic proportions, and it dominated the play to an extent that made the performances of the others seem insignificant in comparison. Dexter's batting, restless and impatient, scarcely induced a sense of comfort; for all the certainty of his stroke play, the serenity of his timing and technique,

AUSTRALIA

First Innings		Second Innings	
W. Lawry, c. Smith b. Trueman	5	c. Sheppard, b. Titmus	98
R. B. Simpson, c. Trueman, b. Dexter	50	c. Smith, b. Dexter	71
N. O'Neill, c. Statham, b. Trueman	19	l.b.w. b. Statham	56
R. N. Harvey, b. Statham	39	c. Statham, b. Dexter	57
P. J. Burge, c. Dexter, b. Trueman	6	not out	47
B. Booth, c. Dexter, b. Titmus	112	not out	19
A. K. Davidson, c. Trueman, b. Barrington	23		
K. Mackay, not out	86		
R. Benaud, c. Smith, b. Knight	51		
G. McKenzie, c. and b. Knight	4		
B. Jarman, c. Barrington, b. Knight	2		
Extras (b. 5, l.b. 1, n.b. 1)	7	Extras (b. 4, l.b. 10)	14
Total	404	Total (4 wkts. dec.)	362

FALL OF WICKETS. *First innings*: 1—5, 2—46, 3—92, 4—101, 5—140, 6—194, 7—297, 8—388, 9—392, 10—404. *Second innings*: 1—136, 2—216, 3—241, 4—325.

ENGLAND

First Innings		Second Innings	
G. A. Pullar, c. and b. Benaud	33	c. and b. Davidson	56
D. S. Sheppard, c. McKenzie, b. Benaud	31	c. Benaud, b. Davidson	53
E. R. Dexter, b. Benaud	70	b. McKenzie	99
M. C. Cowdrey, c. Lawry, b. Simpson	21	c. and b. Benaud	9
K. F. Barrington, c. Burge, b. Benaud	78	c. McKenzie, b. Davidson	23
A. C. Smith, c. Jarman, b. McKenzie	21		
P. H. Parfitt, c. Davidson, b. Benaud	80	c. Jarman, b. McKenzie	4
F. J. Titmus, c. Simpson, b, Benaud	21	not out	3
B. R. Knight, c. Davidson, b. McKenzie	0	not out	4
F. S. Trueman, c. Jarman, b. McKenzie	19		
J. B. Statham, not out	8		
Extras (b. 4, l.b. 2, w. 1)	7	Extras (b. 15, l.b. 10, n.b. 2)	27
Total	389	Total (6 wkts.)	278

FALL OF WICKETS *First innings*: 1—62, 2—65, 3—145, 4—169, 5—220, 6—297, 7—361, 8—362, 9—362, 10—389. *Second innings*: 1—114, 2—135, 3—191, 4—257, 5—257, 6—261.

Bowling Analysis

ENGLAND

	First Innings				Second Innings			
	O.	M.	R.	W.	O.	M.	R.	W.
Trueman	18	0	76	3	15	0	59	0
Statham	16	1	75	1	16	1	67	1
Knight	17.5	2	65	3	14	1	63	0
Titmus	33	8	91	1	26	3	81	1
Dexter	10	0	46	1	16	0	78	2
Barrington	12	3	44	1				

AUSTRALIA

	First Innings				Second Innings			
	O.	M.	R.	W.	O.	M.	R.	W.
Davidson	21	4	77	0	20	6	43	3
McKenzie	25.3	2	78	3	20	4	61	2
Mackay	28	7	55	0	7	0	28	0
Benaud	42	12	115	6	27	7	71	1
Simpson	18	6	52	1	7	0	48	0
O'Neill	1	0	5	0	2	2	0	0

UMPIRES: C. Egar and E. Wykes
Total Attendance: 63,416.
Total Receipts: £A17,861 13.

one was never sure from one ball to the next when his reluctance to accept imposed limitations might lead to disaster. The sight of mid-on and mid-off being waved deeper seemed merely to encourage him to want to hit over the top of them. In this he succeeded; and in general the savagery of his driving and hooking were in nice contrast to the delicacy of his cutting and placing to leg.

Benaud, laconic and thoughtfully hypnotic, bowled with a rhythmic control that was almost oriental in its consistency. His accuracy, whether with the leg-break, the googly or the flipper, was astonishing, and he varied them with a magician's sleight of hand. Only on the last afternoon, when the pitch should have suited him best, was he unable to make his spin bite in the way one expected. Possibly his shoulder held him back that final bit. However that might be, he bowled well enough for most purposes. The fact that he ended up with figures of 1 for 71 was rather an indication of the strides England's batsmen had made since Sydney.

If the match had a particular significance it was that the mere presence of Dexter deterred Benaud from an aggressive declaration. Had Dexter not been playing, Benaud would probably have given himself another hour to get England out. His calculation, in the circumstances, was shrewdly judged; but by reducing his chances of defeat he had to forfeit victory.

2 From a Journal I: Brisbane - Sydney - Melbourne - Adelaide

Australian cities – Brisbane, Sydney, Melbourne, Adelaide, Perth – are river-haunted, some more commercially than others. The river as recreation or as life-line. Coming in to land at Brisbane airport the wings of the Electra tilt over cranes, cargo vessels, derricks, wharves, launches, warehouses. Tall office blocks, hotel slabs rear over muddy water, the two banks of the city paper-clipped together by harp-like steel bridges. In Lennons Hotel you can hear the hoot of sirens above the low hum of the air-conditioning. The city itself, laid out on the American grid system, has a gimcrack, peeling forlornness, a scrawl of corrugated iron against squat irregular skyline. Palm trees and poincianas create an exotic context never convincingly fulfilled. It is almost the tropics, but not quite. Yet certain suburbs might be in Bridgetown, Barbados, or Georgetown, British Guiana; the same steeply-pitched red roofs, white wooden frames raised on stilts with a surrounding verandah. The stilts were, initially, to resist the white ant; now the space beneath has become a refuse dump for everything from old cans to rusting bedsteads.

Down river, the waterfronts are largely industrial; higher up, modern houses with private jetties bear sweeping lawns to the river's edge. At weekends motor boats churn up the water and skiers make U-turns past the Koala farm.

Each day the humidity rises, but the storms somehow evaporate outside Brisbane. They wait for our departure, the day after which roofs are ripped off suburban houses and the central streets turned into canals. Driving the 1,200 miles down the New England and Hume Highways towards Melbourne, the rain follows me as far as Sydney. The volcanic stumps of the Macpherson Range turn the colour of deep carbon, the lush Darling Downs disappear into mist. I lunch at Coochin, where for generations the best cattle has been raised by the Bells in an area largely colonized by Germans and Irish. The night before, three cows had been struck by lightning, an expensive accident of God. Now the great cattle and sheep boom is over; costs are trebled, but prices remain the same.

Getting back to the bitumen, I slither over red gravel roads, the intersecting creeks and gullies nearly all flooded. My new Arctic blue car is streaked like a Nolan painting. On either side of the bitumen dead ghost gums stalk and litter the plains that stretch away to the foothills of the Great Divide. Red, mauve and white against hard blue is what Australian landscape painters have conditioned us to. Under grey dripping skies, the country seems softer, more approachable.

Sometimes fifty miles pass at a stretch without noticeable habitation. Mostly the traffic consists of huge interstate trucks, lit up like fairgrounds, and carrying trailers laden with cars. Between the hiss of my windscreen wipers, I get sudden glimpses of alarmed cockatoos, rising in great flutters of grey and rose from isolated trees, and of the green-breasted galahs. Huge magpies flop on and off the road, seemingly top-heavy. At dusk I reach Glen Innes, showering and eating at the Astor Motel – unlicensed, a severe blow. Through bad weather I missed the Bell birds on Cunningham's Peck.

Between Glen Innes and Muswellbrook, nearly 250 miles, it rained steadily. One might have been driving up the A.1 except that scarcely a car passed all day. Australian country towns, sprawling and shack-like, make one realize how excess of space leads to architectural disaster. There is nothing to curtail or to give density to any of these monotonously similar places. They are shopping centres, nothing more. At night, the inhabitants retire to country properties, leaving the towns empty and devitalized, like abandoned ships on the ocean of the plains. The Hunter Motel at Muswellbrook reminds me of *Lolita*, only unlike Humbert Humbert I am unaccompanied, unpursued, and unobsessed. Rain beats down all night.

The morning is better, grey clouds lifting until by the time I reach the Pacific Highway for the long descent from Wyong into Sydney the light is as garishly bright as I remembered. Fruitstalls stacked with oranges line the roadside; oysters and fresh prawns are advertised on the hillsides above the silver waters of the Hawkesbury; the traffic thickens on the densely forested mountain switchback that winds into the north shore suburbs. The bridge soars into view, and soon I am curving left past Circular Quay, the Botanic Gardens, and into the newly-landscaped cuttings that swing you beneath King's Cross into Woolloomooloo. Tall slabs of glass on the skyline take the setting sun like stained-glass windows above the funnels of liners and streamlined dock terminals. From where I am staying in Potts Point, my window looking through palm trees across ships and warehouses at the glittering bridge, Sydney seems marvellously to have grown in promise and excitement.

Weekend in Sydney. Yachts like confetti litter the harbour, the beaches are packed though the water is still cold. Today the *Sydney Morning Herald* records deaths by redback spider, snake and shark – a reminder that nature in Australia, moving violently from drought to flood, is essentially hostile. People cavort in the shallows within the shark nets that encircle most inlets. On the surf beaches beyond Manly, the dumpers thunder in and rips whirling the unwary out, have life-savers in continual action. Half-a-dozen are drowned in New South Wales over the two days.

Breakfast of black coffee, paw-paws in brandy, orange juice. Then a tour of the city, the King's Cross galleries, the Opera House, the early wrought-iron balconies in Paddington and Argyle Street. The city soars above Macquarie Street, huge grey-green glass skyscrapers dwarfing the old mid-west brick buildings that carry the dying echoes of convict-built Sydney. Greenway's dream of a Georgian-colonial metropolis surrenders gallantly but not ungracefully to the American idiom of the 1960s. The art galleries sprout everywhere, for Australian painting has struck gold. Nolan and Drysdale fetch four figures, and their early work is unobtainable. Not far behind them, Blackman, Fairweather, Daws, Boyd, Olsen, Rapotec, Friend and Whitely fairly satisfy a gambler's market. The Opera House on Benelong Point will take another two years before its white sails unfurl against the blue water. Meanwhile the design continues to incur criticism on grounds of cost, technical inadequacy, insufficient seating, and general inaccessibility. But the daring and sheer lyrical power of the architects' model remains an encouragement to its backers.

Drive where you like in Paddington, and Darlinghurst, sloping street after street catches the eye, whether rusting or gleaming with new paint. Rather as happened to Chelsea fifteen years ago, tiny tenement-size houses change hands now at £10,000 to £20,000. The lacework balconies glisten in the sun, the weatherboarding, framed by palm-trees, looks as if it was hammered in yesterday. Further out towards the Heads at Point Piper, Double Bay and Vaucluse, the houses are enlarged copies with Vogue-style gardens. Flats a dozen stories high rear up off the water's edge, yachts and launches strewn at their base. At sunset the harbour is flooded with saffron and peach light, the North shore ferry boats puffing their way among warships and islands. With darkness, Sydney becomes magical, the headlands and bays flickering with reflection and the electric blue lights of the bridge arching over the estuary. Dining overlooking Double Bay, the only sound comes from the cicadae. The sky is like black velvet inlaid with diamond, the night an illuminated Cartier's window.

At King's Cross the espresso bars and night clubs give off an aroma of coffee, buried jazz and foreign accents far into the dawn.

A day with Arthur Mailey at Cronulla, a forty-minute drive through suburbs that stretch the built-up area of Sydney for thirty miles at its widest. Mailey's house, a fishing shack on a narrow promontory, dips down to the sea, the water in front scored with boats of all shapes and sizes. Each house has its lawn and its jacaranda and Mailey's, of course, its concrete cricket pitch and net. We ate mostly oysters picked that morning off the rocks and afterwards Mailey, with arm lower but eyes revived, fizzed leg-breaks and googlies of recognizable authority. I asked him about the alleged full toss with which he bowled Jack Hobbs, who was 100 not out overnight, first thing on the next morning of a Test Match. 'It was not a full toss, you know, it was a high one that dipped suddenly. A dangerous ball.' The eyes softened in fond recollection. We discussed Benaud's control, accuracy and string of maidens at Brisbane. 'I always used to regard maidens as a weakness, it meant a lack of imagination, I wasn't finding the edge. But then I am a smaller man than Richie, I had to throw the balls up more.' I questioned Arthur as to why he wasn't at Brisbane. 'I could never watch a Test,' he replied, 'in a State of which Mackay was a resident.' Round the walls of the shack are cricket books, photographs, a painting by Tom Roberts, and several by Mailey himself. On the verandah are painting materials, fishing equipment. A gramophone bears a pile of records and we have the first act of *Aida*. Arthur's fishing boats swing at anchor in light rain. Mr Menzies recently commissioned a cricket painting by Mailey, 'and he's paid for it, too'. A volume of Mailey's cartoons lies on a table. Above the corduroy trousers and loose blue shirt, a face of dignity, wit, integrity and devastating charm. 'I have to be prised out of this place,' he says, 'I've got everything I want – my boat, books, music and my painting. And I can sleep all day if I feel like it.'

Afterwards he drove with me past O'Neill's house, on the other side of the headland. When I put him down, he shambled into his shack, a Gauguin among leg-spinners, whose patient mastery of his own art had led him into an evening of articulate peacefulness. 'See you at Adelaide,' he called back, 'and Melbourne, too, when Mackay's out.'

A morning of awakening blue, that colour the eyes of certain blondes spasmodically acquire, all innocence and encouragement. Driving south along the Hume highway the gums rise above pale stubble, with mauve hills in the distance. Cattle and sheep roam the rolling plains; the blue almost hurts. This is Australia as the early Australian painters, Streeton and Roberts, painted it. In bare humps of earth and twisted tree trunks, the farms of Nolan and Drysdale emerge intact. I skirt Bowral, birthplace of Bradman, and the suburban names on the fronts of buses, sometimes unnervingly nostalgic – Brighton, Studley, Cambridge, Ipswich, Swansea, Picton – give way to the lilting aborigine Creek signs.

After three hours driving through country not noticeably changing – gums, grass, wheat, sheep, in recurrent patterns – I have covered 200 miles. The bitumen scalds. A café advertises a Hangover Breakfast – tomato juice, raw eggs, black coffee, aspirin, our sympathy – but is unable to offer a hangover-free driver lunch at 1.40. I drive on without, another 150 miles in softening heat, to Holbrook. At intervals, the road bears such signs as 'Is Fire Prevention Your Intention?', 'Alert Today, Alive Tomorrow', 'When you drive don't work'. The Cheryl Ann Motel stands off the highway facing into the bush, skeletal eucalyptus straggling the plain. No licence, and no dinner after 7.30. Just time for a quick couple of Scotches in the local hotel, the bar crowded with stockmen, graziers, construction workers, all broad-brimmed hat, dungarees and sweat. At 6.30 they are deposited outside, the bar closed for tea! Still, they have had a good two hours, and some of them look like it. The walls carry advertisements for rodeos. I return to Cheryl Ann clutching an undrinkable bottle of wine, ready for baked beans, ham and eggs, and compulsory commercial TV while I eat. During dinner I learn about Fruit Fly and how to deal with various pests. But not unfortunately with TV. Our spinners have been tonked about yet again by uncouth country batsmen, fresh from the milk round. Cowdrey has managed a century. I can sleep soundly.

Next day across the Victorian border and into the Ned Kelly country. The Riverina of the Wild Colonial Boys, of the ballads of Banjo Patterson. Rivers hung with willows and green swell of hills. Euroa where Kelly held up a bank, Glenrowan where he was finally tracked down, besieged and killed. Small country towns with nothing to reveal of their dramatic past. Corrugated iron roofs, a bank, a dozen stores, a post office, jacarandas thinning out into inevitable eucalyptus. Occasionally wattle in flower, a halo of bright yellow. The bitumen beckons, and by mid-afternoon I am enmeshed in suburban Melbourne traffic, clanging trams, and a cold grey wind.

Walking to Melbourne Cricket Ground from the Windsor Hotel in Spring Street across the Treasury Gardens is one of my remembered pleasures from 1955. It is as if Lord's was at the northern edge of Hyde Park and one was setting out from the Hyde Park Hotel in Knightsbridge. The grass under massed trees, few of them indigenous, is of a green seldom seen in Australia. Sprinklers play over vivid spring lawns where, on benches or in the shade, people lie on their backs, sleeping off something or perhaps simply opting out of commitments for a few hours. In the Fitzroy Gardens, an extension of them, the green conservatory, the pale colour of a water-ice, brings a Victorian elegance to a pastoral arcadia that is heavy with exotic aroma and steamy brilliance. Captain Cook's cottage, brought brick by brick from England by a euphoric business man, sheds a suitable nostalgic aura around it. The Treasury buildings themselves have the solid durability of Carlton House Terrace. In the morning, the gardens hum with expectancy and growing heat; on the way home mellow light floods them, the sultriness ebbs, the spires and skyscrapers of the city soften in saffron radiance. 'From five o'clock to eight is on certain occasions a little eternity,' Henry James wrote at the beginning of *Portrait of a Lady*, 'but on such an occasion as this the interval could be only an eternity of pleasure.' It is the more so when England have done well.

The great bowl of the stadium, able since the 1956 Olympics to take over 100,000, is not, for all its tree-clustered grass approaches, its accessibility and sheer capacity, everyone's idea of a perfect cricket ground. It is not mine. The vastness tends to remove and dwarf the spectacle, though when full it gives it an exciting gladiatorial quality. The pavilion, originally the Ladies' stand, and the one distinctive architectural feature in a waste of concrete, is shortly to come down. The dressing-rooms are below standard. Over and above this, the attendants have the ferocity and self-righteousness of guardians of the gates of heaven. Test-players arriving on the day of a match without their tickets have before now had to vault the barriers.

The absence of Dexter and the continued presence of Lawry over a day and a half put paid to the M.C.C.-Victoria match almost as soon as it had began. Dexter, I think, should have played both here and at Adelaide, but presumably he felt his 100 here against 'An Australian XI' in November would have to do for the local citizens and that his charms, not to be rashly dispensed, must be reserved for display at Adelaide, where he had not played on the first way round. The consequence was a significant drop in the gate, compared with the equivalent match on May's tour in 1958 – 14,000 on the Saturday as against 26,000 four years ago. Cowdrey put Victoria in and Lawry batted throughout the first day with excruciating unimaginativeness. Some years ago Lawry was dropped from the Victorian side for his gross immobility. He returned a season later with evident intentions to reform, made the side to England in 1960, and was sensationally successful, at least until August, when nearing his 2,000 runs, he relapsed into the old canniness. But against England at Lord's and against Surrey at the Oval, Lawry made hundreds that, as well as demonstrating sound technique against the moving ball and a fine temperament, were lavish in hooks and cover drives. Now, without reason, he looked back where he started. Levering himself forward on to the front foot almost before the ball had left the bowler's hand, he put himself into a position from which he could only prod woodenly, the bat well in the wake of the pad. Between lunch and tea, shrilly hooted by his own crowd, he gave an appalling exhibition of miserliness; he risked nothing, achieved nothing, merely existed and accumulated. Compared to his English form, he was as Grimmett was to Mailey. Statham, taking the second new ball after tea, was stung into something like full pace. But Lawry was there at the end, Victoria past the 250 with only three wickets down. Next morning, Statham got a few to whip back off the seam for almost the first time on the tour; Allen, in a long steady bowl, took 3 wickets for 57, his first since Perth, and Victoria lost their last 7 wickets for 81. Lawry finally departed for 177, the fact that he had acquired over half his side's total of 340 superficially seeming to have justified his methods. In truth, he caused several of his younger batsmen to throw away their wickets going for the runs he himself should have been making. Before the end, he showed for half an hour around noon that his cover drive had not ossified beyond recovery. Allen, for all his increased conviction, looked to have lost some of his flight and variety, and his rhythmic monotony, off a run too short to allow much change of pace, made him seem easy meat for any batsman willing to use his feet. Titmus, with his curving trajectory and ability to get the off-break to drift, still looked the best bet of the three off-spinners. Coldwell and Knight were predictably docile.

M.C.C.'s batting was, alas, no improvement. Parfitt and Sheppard went for 25, Pullar having strained his groin fielding and having been put down the order. Meckiff, bowling with an angle of delivery and occasional lift that only too plainly stemmed from a bent elbow, lacked pace and hostility. It was hard to credit that he had once shattered England in 1958 with 6 for 38 out of a total of 87.

Cowdrey and Graveney scratched about myopically against Kirby, a leg-spinner of variable length, but eventually Cowdrey, helping himself to an optimistic series of full tosses and long-hops, looked gradually to be finding his touch. Hitherto, he had been like a piano-tuner unaccountably gone hard of hearing; the notes seemed none of them to give off the right tone and in consequence he had tapped away speculatively without satisfaction or power. Now, just as confidence was emerging, he slipped on the turn when sent back by Graveney and was helplessly run out. Graveney, surviving an easy chance, never acquired any sort of fluency. His right hand repeatedly drew his bat across the line and in nearly two hours batting he failed to produce a commanding stroke. Five wickets went down for 116 but Pullar, limping in with a runner, saw out the day with Illingworth. Together, without discomfort, and at a sedate pace against modest bowling, they added 96, before, next morning, Meckiff bowled Illingworth round his legs with the new ball for 50. Pullar hung on to make 91, Smith made 41, and M.C.C. finished with 336, only four runs short. By the end of the day they had virtually bowled themselves into a winning position, Victoria being only 137 ahead with five wickets down. Lawry, who had been responsible for a run-out in the first innings, was now himself retributively sent back. Coldwell collected a wicket with his first ball, and then another, and Allen, again pretty much on the spot, took the other two. The last five wickets, after overnight rain, were shot out by Statham and Coldwell, Coldwell, doing just a little off the pitch, taking 6 for 49. The opposition, however, was negligible.

M.C.C. lost Pullar and Parfitt for 12, but Sheppard, 50, and Cowdrey, 63, saw the M.C.C. on the way to a comfortable five wickets win. Cowdrey that evening said he felt as excited as a schoolboy, having been able to play strokes for the first time since arriving in Australia.

Trees are the first thing one recalls about Melbourne – in the Fitzroy Gardens, down Collins Street, along the Yarra, off

St Kilda Road – and driving into the city, through the hideous jagged rectangle that forms the commercial centre, they are what alleviate the garish ugliness and at moments give it grace. Generally, the tree is a natural enemy to Australians; they dispose of them as greedily as of half-volleys, a tragic fact that robs them of much natural beauty and lately has resulted in a timber shortage. But the tree-lined swishing, switchback of Collins Street, a new mammoth glass slab drawing the eye skywards from churches, stores, scent shops, boutiques and doctor's consulting rooms, has a congenial quality unique in metropolitan Australia. Since 1955, espresso bars, exuding coffee smells among the trams, have become part of social life, with, at the high 'Paris' end of the street, coloured umbrellas actually inviting the puritan Victorian to take his ease outside. That scarcely any do is another matter; the invitation is there.

At the moment, gargantuan Father Christmases, looking down from emporium entrances, alternately shiver and sweat in weather that changes from the icy to the sultry in a matter of hours. It is nothing for temperatures to drop from over 100° to 60° in the same weekend.

At Aspendale, on Sunday, I walked on a grey morning by the beach, while parachutists made recreational jumps over the sea before floating like lotuses until they could be picked up. Aircraft patrolled on the watch for reported sharks, and the sea on inspection deterred immersion. By mid-afternoon the sky was blue, the sands golden, the water marvellous. Sunset was preceded by a metallic silver light, of a northern transparency, and gulls wheeled against the dipping sun. In the city one is conscious of the river, occasionally of the port, but never of the sea. Yet half an hour's drive through St Kilda miles of hard white sand curve round the shore of a generous bay. The beach houses all glass and wood, face due south and the waves beat at their feet.

The aspect of Melbourne has altered decisively, yet the atmosphere remains consistent – a mixture of Victorian pubs and music halls, bulbous many-domed railway stations, dilapidated suburban tenements with flaking cast-iron verandahs, a water front with landscaped contemporary villas looking over the river at the low commercial skyline of the city. Opposite Spring Street, the solid façades of the Parliament and Treasury buildings glisten grey and white among the vivid green of gardens raked by spires. Respectable conformity lingers on the brink of elegance; palm trees hint at the exotic. Down in Queen Street the tall offices soar shoulder to shoulder, an air of Wall Street pervading Manhattan. It is the best metropolitan area in Australia. But now, in St Kilda and South Yarra, luxury blocks form evening honeycombs of light above the poplars, glittering motels, all gold leaf and chromium, draw the traveller into oases of leafiness. Houses here vary from Mission-house Spanish and early colonial Georgian to sleek constructions of fibre and glass. You pay your money and you take your choice.

The 460 miles from Melbourne to Adelaide by the Western Highway route is for much of its length as straight as a ruler – not as unyieldingly direct as the 999 miles through the Karoo that links Johannesburg and Cape Town, but enough to remind me of it. In 1957, I drove that journey in a large American car at an overall average speed of seventy-five. In a Mini-Minor I found I could arrange sixty comfortably, except for the hour leaving Melbourne and entering Adelaide. The half-dozen agricultural towns *en route* bore names that were biblical, Australian or unashamedly English – Ballarat, Beaufort, Ararat, Horsham, Dimboola, Tailem Bend, Aldgate. They were more lavish and prosperous versions of those encountered on the Hume Highway between New South Wales and Victoria. At Ballarat a venerable, paunchy Father Christmas stumped off in the heat for his lunch. It seemed a disillusioning too-human thing for him to be doing. A Greek from Piraeus served me with sandwiches at Beaufort, an Estonian with fruit, a Sicilian with coffee. It was vaguely comforting. But always an

Australian drew the beer. All afternoon I drove through melting blue, wheatfields, half-harvested, dazzling blonde as far as the eye could see. The country is level, nothing above the height of the windscreen. Clumps of trees paddle the waving stubble, and occasionally on the skyline mauve hills surface and abruptly stop. There is an almost holy richness about it, with sheep cropping on intervening stations and the sun splintering off the corrugated iron of barns and homesteads. A yellow land bisected by bitumen and strung with Shell pumps and Caltex, gleaming white. I dined at Keith, catching the pubs with ten minutes to spare, and then, with the light fading, and the white bark of the eucalyptus dripping with apricot and violet, cruised in the darkness the last 150 miles into Adelaide. Stars flickered over the Mount Lofty hills, the air cooled until a jersey became scarcely enough, and suddenly over the summit, Adelaide was a blaze of squared light, gold and red and green, on its plain below. Just so does Port of Spain look, coming in over the mountains from Mayaro.

Adelaide, despite its Festival of the Arts, has habitually been the Australian city most resistant to change – politically, socially, architecturally, culturally. Perhaps its Englishness has something to do with it. Yet, added to its successful Festival, it has, in Kym Bonython and Max Harris, two of the most influential and progressive men, at least as far as the arts are concerned, in Australia.

I can think of no English equivalent of Bonython – war-time R.A.A.F. pilot, speedway racer, owner of a midget submarine, farmer and now proprietor of the best art gallery in the country. He has, as well, in his seaside house at Tennyson, the foremost collection of contemporary Australian painting to be seen; a stunning group of Nolan's major works, including three Ned Kelly's, Burke and Wills, and Mrs Fraser in the swamp; outstanding examples of Daws, Blackman, Boyd, Fairweather, Olsen, Lloyd Rees, Pasmore, and Cleghorn; and a variety of young sculptors and painters yet to make their name. He buys with flair and astuteness. Gallery dealers are not by nature collectors; yet Bonython, a boyish figure, never seems other than a collector first, a passionate enthusiast and promoter of what is best in the growing Australian tradition. Driving around Adelaide in his yellow Bristol, we talked alternately of cars and painting, and pulling up in the burning heat at the Speedway, which Bonython both manages and competes in, the two seemed to coalesce. For the bare red race-track with its beaky black arc-lights and outlying shanties, inhabited by aboriginals, was something that Nolan or Drysdale might well have created.

Max Harris, bookseller, publisher, editor, TV performer, poet, is a fluent more conventional kind of intellectual, whose two reviews, *Australian Letters* (co-edited with Geoffrey Dutton and Bryn Davies) and *Australian Book Review*, are admirably produced and editorially alive. The former has sponsored a dozen fascinating examples of painters being commissioned to illustrate, in full colour, groups of new poems: Pugh on Judith Wright, Drysdale on David Campbell, Cleghorn on Ray Mathew, Nolan on Randolph Stow, etc. No English review can afford such luxury, and Harris assures me that *Australian Letters* pays its way. Its support from such stores as John Martins and David Jones, from Holdens, A.B.C. Television and others is such as English magazines never get. Imagine Harrods or Whiteley's or Fortnum and Mason or the Rootes Group taking an interest in the arts! A pipe-dream.

Architecturally, Adelaide has developed less spectacularly than Sydney or Melbourne. The standard of new private building is low, the planning abominable. Of the best colonial houses few exist. What, thanks to its founder Colonel Light, Adelaide preserves still is a situation, a subtle exploitation of parks, gardens and water and a certain graciousness of outlook that its detractors regard as complacency compounded with snobbery. The city itself has little to recommend it, a few beautiful frontages in Rundle Street, cool shopping arcades, wide streets and a total absence of a prevailing style, even integrated disparate ones. North Terrace, looking towards the Torrens river, contains the University buildings, the Art Gallery, the Railway Station, and the South Australian Hotel, all buildings of solidity and substance. North of this, the trees begin and the Torrens winds through gardens and parks with the leafy prosperous streets beyond the new Australia Hotel tilting up towards the hills. A few half-built skyscrapers disfigure the Mount Lofty skyline, but the 'Australia', a cool, clean construction of concrete and glass, from whose seventh floor you can dine overlooking the Adelaide plain, is a success and the others, when they are cleaned up, may achieve an eventual harmony.

What is truly disastrous is the way that the modern suburbs, octopus-like, have strangled the original city. In every direction, like the spokes of a wheel, speculative builders have loaded the roads with a conglomeration of monstrosities that stretch for miles – gnomes in the garden, plastic flowers, bogus-Georgian, pseudo-colonial, mock-Tudor, contemporary hybrid, the lot. Down the Main South Road, bisecting the Anzac highway which runs to Glenelg, gas stations, used car lots, motor wreckers and junk yards cram together almost as far as the slopes several miles out that separate Adelaide from the superb uncluttered beaches of Port Naorlunga and Willunga. Once shaken free, the roads sweep through blonde plains, with the sea glittering beyond red serrated cliffs, and the hard sand, curved white round wide bays, is hardly dented by more than lordly gulls and a handful of people. The sense of space, with only the limitless Antarctic and the South Pole below, is headily exciting. Waves break on jagged reefs, the sand scalds, the red cliffs appear to be splitting right open, and the burning blue softens in late afternoon to metallic white.

The match against South Australia, M.C.C.'s last game before the Second Test, had various points of interest; the meeting with Sincock, the young left-hand googlie bowler whom good judges had described as something of a prodigy, another sight of Sobers, incontestably the world's greatest all-rounder (followed by Davidson, Benaud, Worrell and Dexter), a look at Brooks, Chappell and McLachlan, all possibilities for the 1964 tour of England, and finally the tidying up of the last two places in the England side. Two places were in doubt: failure by Parfitt, for all his fleetness and fine throwing in the outfield, would put his position in jeopardy, while Allen or Coldwell could replace Knight, who had bowled indifferently and made no runs for a month. Pullar was still suffering from his injured groin, but Trueman, required by his doctor to lift weights, an activity he referred to with conjecturable and withering brevity, had bowled several overs in Port Lincoln at ferocious speed and seemed to be suffering no ill-effects. Meanwhile he was to content himself with gentle spells at the nets.

The first day, after initial shocks, ended with M.C.C. 474 for 4, Cowdrey 244 not out. The temperature hovered just under the hundred, South Australia (who had defeated New South Wales, with six current test players, ten days earlier for the third successive year) were a fast bowler short – Hawke having had a car accident the week before – and Sincock was wildly erratic. But it was an absorbing day, for Sobers confirmed his remarkable qualities as two kinds of bowler, Cowdrey returned to full opulence, and Sheppard, dropped off a very easy chance when nought, revived memories of a decade ago.

Brooks, a quickish bowler with a flowing cumulative run-up, much in the manner of Lindwall – though unnecessarily lengthy – wrecked Parfitt's wicket in his second over. Parfitt since Brisbane had looked increasingly ill at ease, and his liking for opening the innings seemed scarcely justified. More even than Richardson five years ago, and Pullar now, he is an on-side player, with the bat instinctively coming down across the line. Dexter took four over the slips from Brooks and after a disconcertingly edgy innings was finely caught by Chappell at third slip off Sobers. Sheppard had been missed by Chappell at short gully off Brooks, who, like Sobers, got plenty of life off a dry pitch with more pace in it than either Brisbane or Melbourne. After forty minutes Sincock, a slight, red-haired figure with cold-cream on his nose, giving him the appearance of a circus clown, came on and his first three overs, containing some eyebrow-raising left-arm googlies, cost only seven. He has a bouncy quickening little run, as if on foam rubber, he suddenly ducks his head as he approaches the umpire, and his actual delivery, a shade reminiscent of George Tribe's, is made more square-on than is classical. His trajectory is nicely varied, but his length on this occasion was lamentable. Sheppard, having tuned himself up with some agreeable strokes off Brooks, quickly moved down the pitch to Sincock, hitting him for three successive fours, two skimming off-drives, and a pull off a full toss, with which Sincock became excessively lavish. From now on Sheppard looked light-footed and commanding, his stroking past mid-off and through the covers being delectably crisp. At lunch M.C.C. were 139 for 2, Sheppard 80, Cowdrey 41. Immediately afterwards, Sobers pitched his googly on Sheppard's leg stump and hit the top of the off.

The rest of the day belonged to Cowdrey; the timing returned as if it had never been absent, the strokes, despite rarely being more than caressive in violence, were of rippling but monumental fluidity, the mechanism, long faulty, looked restored to full efficiency. His driving was melodiously sustained, his placing to leg disturbed no fielder, he cut almost mischievously and, whenever Sincock pitched outside his legs, he followed the ball round after it had seemed to pass him to score four runs finer than even Compton ever did. He scored 100 runs in boundaries, lofted four straight sixes with the diffidence of a man tilting a top hat, and towards the end, until admonished by Graveney, hankered after giving his wicket away. He was dropped twice by Brooks, at 43 and 91, the second being deflected by the bowler to run out Barrington, backing up too far. Cowdrey at stumps was 244 not out, Graveney, who had batted pleasantly in Cowdrey's shadow, 78 not out, and M.C.C. at 474 for 4 had scored sixteen runs more than were made in one day against the Australian XI at Melbourne in November. Barrington, before fate conspired against him, achieved 52 in a fashion suggesting that only thus was he ever likely to be removed. Sincock had taken 0 for 116 in 19 overs, a demoralizing initiation.

During Sunday the temperature dropped by 30 degrees, and it was under overcast skies, with a cold wind, that Cowdrey and Graveney achieved all sorts of milestones: Cowdrey's highest-ever score, the highest-ever individual score for M.C.C. against South Australia, the record fifth-wicket partnership for M.C.C. v. South Australia (held by Braund and Joe Hardstaff Senior since 1907) and Graveney's first century of the tour. Finally Cowdrey passed Frank Woolley's 305, made against Tasmania, hitherto the highest first-class score in Australia by a touring player. Dexter declared just before lunch at 586 for 5, a juicy score on the eve of a Test match, with Cowdrey out for 307, and Graveney, who looked even more his better self, 122 not out. Titmus had not played against Victoria, and the accident of his not getting an innings here meant that he did not bat once between the two Tests.

It rained for an hour during the afternoon, after which Favell, like a revived flower, blossomed in company, first with Lill, then with Sobers. Eight years earlier, Favell, a compact bird-like person with head low on his shoulders, had scored an exhilarating century against Hutton's team. Since then he had been in and out of the Australian team, more often out, but occasionally surviving long enough to display an array of strokes brilliant as a peacock's tail. That his adventurous inconsistency led to his being superseded by more stolid performers, such as Macdonald, was predictable, but nevertheless sad, for he would have always been an adornment to Test cricket.

The principle by which Favell bats is a simple one – make the most of every ball, for the next one might get you out. He lets little go by, in consequence making numerous vain flourishes and airy passes over gully. In rich compensation he cuts with splendid finality, hooks and drives with fruitful self-indulgence, glances delicately, and buzzes up runs with the busyness of a bee round a hive. He was severe on Larter, who despite a more rhythmic approach gave away 73 runs in 10 overs, and found little to curb him from Coldwell, Titmus and Allen. Lill departed after a lackadaisical, unruffled innings of 55, Favell was out for 120, and Sobers wound up the day with a variety of ennobling strokes that hinted at permanence.

On Boxing Day, South Australia, less vividly, took themselves to within 136 of M.C.C.'s total. Sobers, slightly constrained, was caught off Barrington for 89, but he struck back in the evening when he and Brooks shot out Sheppard and Parfitt for 12. This was Parfitt's fifth first-class score of under 15 in a row, and looked likely to put a temporary end to his Test chances.

The final day, owing to Dexter's and Sobers' initiative, had all the makings of a thriller, but continual interruptions through rain tailed it off. Cowdrey was caught in the gully off Sobers from his first ball of the morning, but Dexter, hitting five fours and a six that carried to the roof of the main grandstand – only the third time this had been done in forty years – gave Adelaide a brief view of his power. He was caught off a long-hop for 37, but Graveney batted smoothly for 35, before Sincock hit his middle stump with an off-break. Sincock looked an altogether more convincing bowler after this, though his match figures of 1 for 208 were scarcely indicative of it. Barrington played in his now customary sober and acquisitive fashion for 52 not out, and Dexter declared at lunch, with M.C.C. 167 for 6.

South Australia were therefore left 240 minutes to score 304 runs. Favell and Lill were quickly out, both to Coldwell, but the baby-faced Sobers now arrived to play an innings of heraldic brilliance. He immediately spread-eagled Coldwell's attacking field, took fifteen off a solitary over from Dexter, and raced to 50. Larter disposed of Cunningham and McLachlan, but after an hour's break for rain, Sobers returned to take four successive fours off Coldwell. His hitting off the back foot and his driving past the bowlers were of astonishing force and if persistent drizzle hadn't finally halted him, anything might have happened. He batted only an hour for 75 not out, which included twelve boundaries. Both his bowling and batting in this match (he had made 99 against M.C.C. the first time round, taken five wickets and scored 100 not out in the victory over New South Wales) confirmed him once again as the best player in the game. As bowler or batsman alone he would be an immediate pick for any Test side, and as a fielder he makes hardly a mistake.

When play was abandoned an hour early, M.C.C. flew in a chartered plane direct to Melbourne. The evening before, the team for the Second Test had been announced with two changes from the Brisbane twelve: Graveney and Coldwell for Knight and Allen. The presumption was that Parfitt would be twelfth man. Trueman and Pullar had been passed fit. Australia had already named an unchanged team, predictably enough, although a third fast bowler might not have come amiss.

Christmas Day in Adelaide. The streets empty, a wind brusque enough to prohibit the beaches. Launches steamed up and down the Torrens, solitary couples strolled hand in hand past the boat houses and rowing clubs, black swans cruised idly by the fountains. The sun came and went. In the South Australian Hotel 500 people lunched in vast convivial parties, and all through the afternoon the singing went on below my bedroom. 'It's a Long Way to Tipperary', 'Loch Lomond', 'Rule Britannia' and inevitably 'Waltzing Matilda'. When I set out to drive to Springfield for dinner at seven o'clock, the foyer was once more deserted, the restaurant like a morgue.

The coastal route back to Melbourne is some hundred miles longer than the inland, the road for the first 150 miles following the Currong, a flat marshy waste, with seabirds rising out of dried-up salt creeks and the sun flattening over endless sand dunes. It's something like the Camargue, only more arid and featureless, with no settlements at all. Such traffic as there was consisted of cars pulling caravans or towing boats on trailers. A lonely place for a break down, with service stations fifty miles apart. I drove 360 miles the first day, finding the motel at Portland full, and eventually holing up at Mac's Hotel, a harbour-front building with cast-iron balconies over-hanging wooden pillars, and deflating balloons all over the dining-room.

The town itself, a miniature Southend, with long criss-crossing jetties newly built for tankers, was the first to be settled in Victoria. A fierce sea-breeze blew up the skirts of promenading girls and rocked the cluster of yachts beyond the fun-fair. A pretty church huddled above the cliffs and a lighthouse blinked out at the bleak, white-capped ocean. It was as funereal as are all resorts in blustery weather.

Earlier the car radio had reported the surprising defeat of New South Wales by Victoria – the second State defeat of the star-studded New South Wales team in a fortnight. Lawry made 133 out of his side's 230, and Victoria, with Meckiff and Guest sharing the wickets, went on to win by 8 wickets. Simpson and Harvey both failed twice, and only O'Neill, with 93 in the second innings, and Booth, with 55, of the Test players contributed anything. The Australians seem vulnerable enough to each other, if not to other people.

The ocean road from Portland to Melbourne is as packed with incident as the one from Adelaide to Portland is featureless. It is some 100 miles shorter and takes nearly twice as long to drive. Hairpin bend succeeds hairpin bend, there are few flat stretches and for much of the way the bitumen fades into deep red gravel in which the wheels drift disconcertingly. You drive in a cloud of dust and any wandering of attention would be the end of you. After Princetown, the route curves inland to Lavers Hill and then winds down again to Apollo Bay, a distance of sixty miles over which 25 mph is a fair maximum speed. Dense forests arch over and stretch away on either side of the steep gravel surface, the road itself lined by huge dust-covered ferns. A break-down anywhere here, and you would be stuck for hours. Occasionally emerging from a dark gully you climb to a narrow shoulder, with long views across tilting forests and lonely shacks glinting in oases of open country. Back on the coast the resorts, Apollo Bay, Lorne, Anglesea, open out wide surf-combed beaches at twenty mile intervals. In between, the road dips, snakes, climbs, the sea rushing in to precipitous gorges, with strange detached rocks, holed like giant pieces of sculpture, littered off-shore. You pull the wheel to its full extent one way, then back the other. The inside of the car fills up with dust. The sea is one moment roaring beneath you, the cliffs dropping shear from the gravel edge, the next you are braking under overhanging rock. The bays, when they come, are of over-lifesize generousness, wide white beaches, with a string of smaller ones on either side, stretching between the cliffs. Rivers run into them from the hills, and on one side of the road you can see men fishing from boats, on the other, tents dotted over the scrub, and surf riders coming in on the long breakers.

The Ocean Road, between Port Campbell and Torquay, is generally regarded as the most beautiful stretch of the Australian coast. The weather, unfortunately, was cloudy and humid, sky and sea grey. Without the necessary blue, the exciting harmonies are lost. Less exotic and rich in contrasting foliage, it is altogether more austere than the Mediterranean *corniches* that are its European counterpart. The towns, too, lack the mellow beauty of French and Italian stone, the historic context and grace that redeem most Mediterranean sea villages, no matter how grossly exploited. The Australians, devoid of fastidiousness, settle for caravan-sites and camping grounds, shacks and guest-houses. Sea, river, and forest are enough for them; physical activity is self-sufficient. Everyone around you is cooking, boating, catching fish, tinkering with yachts, surfing. Living largely urban lives, only thus does the old pioneering spirit, the habit of self-reliance, reveal itself.

Between Geelong and Melbourne, the four-lane highway cuts for forty-five miles through the pale stubble that stretches westward off Port Philip Bay. The palm-trees stand four square all down Racecourse road, past Flemington, and the pervasive stench of the Melbourne abattoir, and soon the oblong glass wedges, the towers and spires of the city centre reach up against the sunset.

By midnight, the England and Australian teams, flying in from all parts of the country, were securely ensconced in the Victorian grandeur of the Hotel Windsor. The Test match tension, gradually dispersed by the twenty-four-day interval since Brisbane, began to build up. The weather was sultry, with rain forecast. The pitch had had to be kept covered and not even the groundsman knew how it might turn out.

3 Melbourne: The Second Test

First Day: Walking through the Treasury Gardens in oppressive sultriness, one could smell the rain, now blown away, on plants and trees. Passing Captain Cook's cottage, it is impossible each time not to be reminded of Fred Trueman's favoured riddle: 'What Yorkshire and England Captain came to Australia and never played in a Test.' No prizes for the answer. The roads and parking spaces were crammed with Holdens, Fords, Studebakers and Morrises, with an occasional Rolls looming magisterially, a stray Jaguar nosing predatorially among them.

The Melbourne Cricket Ground was *en fête*, flag-strewn and dolled up (though despite its vast seating capacities it remains one of the least comfortable grounds to play in or work from). For this was the centenary celebration of the first visit by an All-England cricket team to Australia. In December 1861, Mr Stephenson's All-England XI, sponsored by the catering firm of Spiers and Pond, who had failed to come to terms with Charles Dickens over a projected lecture tour, arrived in Melbourne after sixty days at sea. A match was arranged against a team of eighteen Melbourne and District players (Stephenson having received a white feather through the post for refusing to play twenty-two), and it began on New Year's day. A new grandstand had been built in the lee of which were fruit and sweet stalls, roulette wheels, shooting galleries and various bars, estimated at holding 500 cases of beer. Contemporary accounts describe the Melbourne players as wearing straw-coloured shirts with red spots, round dove-coloured hats, with magenta ribbon. The All-England team wore white shirts with blue belts and white caps with blue stripes. The scene wanted only a Frith or a Sisley.

Twenty-five thousand were present when Melbourne's eighteen began their innings. They were put out for 118, Griffith and Bennett, round-arm swift, and round-arm breaks, taking seven wickets each. Mr Stephenson's XI batted for nearly two days, making 305, a compilation delayed by the frequent departure of Victorian fieldsmen for drinks. 'Terrible Billy' Caffyn, the Surrey pet, scored 79, George Griffith, the lion-hitter, 61. In their second innings, the Victorians managed only 92, ten of their number failing to score at all. The *Argus* complained about the amount of smoking that went on, in the presence of ladies in the grandstand. On the fourth day Messrs Spiers and Pond provided a balloon ascent, the balloon, inflated by Mr Hutchinson of the Melbourne Gas Co, carrying three passengers, Mr and Mrs Brown, and Mr Deans.

This scene, save for the ballooning, was now faithfully re-enacted equally as to costume, physical appearance, technique and equipment, before the more serious proceedings began. Frank Tyson played the part of Stephenson, and other be-whiskered performers included Ponsford, Iverson, Hassett, Lindwall and Johnstone.

Finally, before an audience of nearly 70,000, the two 1962 Test teams were presented to the Governor-General, the captains tossed and Benaud, winning, announced he would bat. It looked a useful toss to win.

England, if they were to strike as sharply as at Brisbane, would it seemed need to do so in the first hour. But at noon Australia were 44 for 0, Trueman, who had shot half-a-dozen beautiful out-swingers past Simpson's groping bat, was bowling off his shorter run, and Statham had come off. The thrust had been effectively, if not exactly comfortably, muffled. The rain that was hanging about before breakfast had blown away and Trueman bowled the first over under a sky that was generously blue. It was a very good one too. He rapped Lawry on the pad and rounded on an uncommunicative umpire; he beat Simpson outside the off stump, the next ball found the edge. Dexter set a long leg and deep third man for both bowlers, limiting Statham to three slips, and Trueman to two slips and two gullies. Trueman had one backward short leg, Statham a leg slip and a short square leg. Simpson was no happier at Statham's end, for he was perilously near two that lifted and twice slashed over second slip's head. Trueman solidly attacked Simpson's off stump, beating him twice more and then again finding the edge as Simpson veered away from the line. Lawry, meanwhile, remained watchful as a hawk, getting his nose over the ball, and his whole body behind it. He off-drove Trueman to the boundary and tucked Statham away off his legs. Statham was as usual magnetized by the left hander's leg stump, an addiction not profitable when bowling to Lawry. Trueman reduced his run and Simpson hit him handsomely through the covers. To prove this meant no lessening of hostility, Trueman bounced the next two unnervingly close to Simpson's rapidly withdrawn face. After four overs Coldwell replaced Statham, and Simpson appeared to find the pronounced drop in pace to his taste. Trueman came off, Statham changed ends, and Simpson slashed him again just over Graveney at second slip to the boundary. Coldwell now troubled Lawry, holding the ball up and getting it to drift away from him outside the off stump. The 50 appeared, but not long after Coldwell got one to Simpson to move a shade the other way and Smith took a comfortable catch. O'Neill settled in without apparent need for reflection, goading Lawry into a rasping cover-drive, and taking short singles on the move. Statham once found the outside edge of Lawry's bat, but Smith was rootedly slow getting across and the ball shot for four well fine of slip. Evans, or Parks for that matter, would have swallowed it.

Trueman returned, this time somewhat sluggishly, for, more than most, he needs an early wicket. Barrington bowled one over before lunch, but by now both Lawry and O'Neill gave every sign of taking their ease. By the time a brass band emerged to bounce martial airs into the arena Australia had reached a satisfactory enough 91 for 1. One sniffed a huge score.

Lawry again ensconced himself, playing more strokes than in either innings at Brisbane, or against M.C.C. here a fortnight ago. O'Neill appeared to be at his most relaxed and affirmative, but no sooner was he threatening the full annihilating repertoire, than he cut too friskily at Statham, and Graveney at second slip gratefully gobbled up a low catch. Dexter now summoned up Trueman to greet Harvey, but Trueman seemed reluctant, so Coldwell was obliged to suspend his walk to the boundary. It turned out for the best for Coldwell immediately hit Harvey's off stump with a ball of full length. Coldwell had been varying pace and direction skilfully and only that lack of final nip which Bedser possessed prevented him from being even more troublesome. Trueman now expressed himself willing to bowl at the other end, and he made the most of this indulgence by comprehensively yorking Lawry who was still in a fine tangle of legs and bat with the bails already up by Trueman's feet. At 112 for 4, three wickets having fallen for one, Australia were precariously balanced. Dexter brought long leg up to squat off the batsman's hip, for the first time in the day setting an aggressive field. Trueman demonstrated his return to affluence by throwing in left handed from the boundary to the top of the stumps, the applause for which he was exaggeratedly ready to acknowledge. Coldwell, who had bowled in considerable humidity for a whole hour, showed signs of distress and left the field. Dexter attacked the leg stump with an arc of three men between mid-wicket and mid-on.

Titmus bowled over the wicket to five men on the leg side. The pressure was off until the new ball, but neither Burge nor Booth managed to find distinguishable strokes. The audience began to demand action. Burge, growing restless, swished irritatedly across the line of flight in an increasingly crude and fruitless fashion. He put his left leg down the pitch once too often, however, and his complacent immunity against Titmus's appeal was this time abruptly shattered. Dexter gave little away, but Booth, compared with his Brisbane fluency, was curiously stilted. He moved quick enough up the wicket to

Titmus, but having got there was content to push. One ball before tea he swept at Titmus with the abandon of a teetotaller proffered a Baby Cham, and Barrington at deep long leg unwinkingly took the catch and threw it delightedly high. The afternoon had brought Australia only 71 runs, and England surprisingly enough five wickets. Thus far the faster bowlers had shared thirty-three overs as against eight by Titmus and Barrington. Dexter, bowling six overs for ten, had done a useful if pedestrian job. The final session was an important one for England since it was at this stage in Brisbane that Australia wriggled off the hook and made the most headway. Dexter began with spinners at each end, one off and one leg against two left-handers. Graveney was allowed to join in and with Davidson swinging powerfully at anything up to him and Mackay gleaning runs with unusual avidity the new ball was rapidly due. Statham took it at once, and there were then eighty minutes of the evening left. Davidson hooked him almost into the stand at square leg to raise 50 for the partnership, fielding errors, plentiful before lunch, crept in again, and England's control perceptibly loosened.

Trueman appeared out of condition, and spent, a fact he underlined by clutching his side and going down on one knee. Dexter seemed unimpressed. Trueman was put back to work and managed a rather wan bouncer at Mackay. Coldwell, now becomingly attired in a floppy church-fête hat, returned to the attack but was short of a length. During his earlier spells he had given the ball room in which to move and looked the better for it. The batting was desultory but gluey, with Mackay loping between the wickets with his bat held across his body like a loaf of French bread. He played at nothing he did not have to, leaving Davidson to flash the odd half-volley through the covers. Half an hour before the close, Trueman, whose gait was rapidly resembling a lifer's, drew Davidson forward and surprisingly took the outside edge. The seventh wicket had added 73 runs in a manner to suggest it would not stop at that. Benaud, who fancies these kind of brief postscripts against weary bowlers, drove Statham and hooked Coldwell. In the last over, Statham summoned up a final burst of speed, and Benaud, fending one off his ribs, sent a sharp catch to backward short leg where Sheppard got both hands to it, juggled, but failed to hang on. Mackay remained unconcerned, jabbing shiftily and chewing relentlessly to the end.

It was a day that had provokingly followed the pattern of the opening day at Brisbane, though this time England had cut sixty runs off the Australian total. Getting seven wickets down for 263 on such a wicket was something to be thankful for. A better fielding side would have had Australia all out. Against this, Australia threw away much of the advantage of the toss and revealed notable limitations in the process. The middle batting was remarkably uncouth, and only Lawry and to a lesser extent O'Neill and Davidson emerged unimpaired. Few of the performances on either side were, in the context of Anglo-Australian cricket, of distinction. Trueman's shock pace lasted for few overs, Statham was unflagging and unlucky, but not particularly persuasive. Coldwell, until the heat got him, bowled interestingly, but his pace is little more than, for example, Appleyard's was, with less steepness of delivery and much under Bedser's. Titmus got his two wickets from sweeps, and if he set his sights low, giving the ball little air or spin, he kept an honest length. But for long periods it might have been a club match.

AUSTRALIA – First Innings

W. Lawry, b. Trueman	52
R. B. Simpson, c. Smith, b. Coldwell	38
N. O'Neill, c. Graveney, b. Statham	19
R. N. Harvey, b. Coldwell	0
P. Burge, l.b.w., b. Titmus	23
B. Booth, c. Barrington, b. Titmus	27
A. K. Davidson, c. Smith, b. Trueman	40
K. Mackay, not out	37
R. Benaud, not out	21
Extras (b. 2, l.b., 4)	6
Total (7 wkts.)	263

FALL OF WICKETS. 1—62, 2—111, 3—112, 4—112, 5—155, 6—164, 7—237.

Second Day: More humid still, the sun swathed by puffy banks of lilac cloud. Over Sunday the Australian batting had received a critical roasting, and now Benaud and Mackay looked properly thoughtful. Dexter set Trueman going again with Coldwell partnering him, and almost at once Dexter, fielding suicidally close at forward short leg, snapped up Benaud but on the half-volley. Trueman, attacking the leg stump with some venom, found the inside edge of Benaud's bat, but otherwise Benaud, first against Coldwell, then against Statham, was precise and poised. Mackay, batting like a stand-in for himself, was little in evidence, scraping runs only under dire compulsion, and then unintentionally. The arc of his bat was limited to six inches. After forty minutes the fast bowlers seemed without further resource and Titmus replaced Trueman. In his second over, Benaud, refusing the evidence of Booth and Burge's dismissals, lunged hard across the line and Barrington, judging the catch nicely at deep square leg, took it and flung it skywards. It was the reward for much immaculate fielding and throwing by Barrington, and England's fielding generally looked altogether cleaner. Mackay now produced a cannibalistic contortion, a squatting sweep at Titmus, was struck on the lower rump and adjudged l.b.w. Titmus had 4 for 36, 2 for 5 in 4 overs since coming on. He bowled with no straight deep fielders, each batsman ignoring the empty spaces ahead of them as if they were leprosy areas.

McKenzie and Jarman, pugnacious and not inelegant batsmen, sent up 300, and were feasting on cuts, thick edges and insubordinate singles until Trueman almost fatalistically brought one back to bowl McKenzie.

England, with thirteen minutes batting before lunch, were immediately assaulted by Davidson, for whom Benaud set four slips, one leg slip, and neither third man nor long leg. Sheppard left the first ball, was beaten completely by the second, left the third, and was l.b.w. to the fourth, which dipped in to him. He had looked pathetically at sea, his open-chested stance rendering him particularly vulnerable to

Davidson. Dexter knew nothing about his third ball, which swung and darted late off the seam to frisk the off stump, but got his bat to the eighth, the only time the ball had been hit. It was a memorable over, in the classic opening manner of Lindwall and Miller in their prime.

McKenzie induced a dreadful stroke by Pullar, but Dexter and he kept out Davidson's second over and England went shakily in at 4 for 1.

Pullar twice cut McKenzie to the fence in the first over of the afternoon, then Dexter with corrective violence drove Davidson to the long-off boundary. McKenzie twice had Pullar groping at out-swingers, and Dexter, hooking at him, nearly returned a gentle catch off the splice. Now Pullar faced Davidson, who swung one of good length between bat and pad to clip his leg stump. The slips were increased to five and one could feel their buoyancy. Cowdrey, looking soberly judicial, fended a lifting one past gully and Dexter viciously pulled McKenzie from outside the off stump and not much short of a length to the square leg boundary. He turned him off his legs to the same spot a moment later.

Davidson, after three overs, switched ends with McKenzie. He pitched short and Dexter slashed him through the covers. The next ball Dexter hit hard off the back foot, to the sightscreen. Long leg and third man took up station, mid-off moved deeper. At 48, of which Dexter had made 31, Benaud almost greedily called for the ball.

But for once, he seemed an anti-climax. Dexter chopped him, Cowdrey swung a full toss first bounce into the crowd and then lay back to bisect the covers, singles were taken plentifully and imaginatively. Twenty-five came off his first three overs. Mackay relieved McKenzie, and Cowdrey charmed him away past mid-off. Dexter forced him through mid-wicket, each took casual singles to leg, drawing the field in, so that the gaps widened. Soon Dexter was cutting Benaud to the pavilion to reach 50, his third of the series in a row, and soon, with Cowdrey also cutting Benaud, the 100 was up.

Benaud's control visibly tightened, Dexter once edging him dangerously near slip, and with Mackay settling on a constricting length, pickings became few. At tea, England were 107, Dexter 53, Cowdrey 43; 103 runs had been scored in two hours for the loss of Pullar.

Simpson tried his hand, Cowdrey calling the tune with nippy singles that had Dexter struggling. He was overhauling Dexter who seemed to have momentarily run out of steam. Cowdrey reached 50, the hundred for the stand coming quick on its heels. Davidson's walk to his mark grew noticeably more languid. Dexter, pulling a long-hop from Simpson and then sending a half-volley from Davidson humming through mid-on, spurted ahead again. Simpson nearly got his googly past Dexter, which encouraged Benaud to bring O'Neill into operation – a *tu quoque* for Barrington and Graveney on the first day. O'Neill's first over was a maiden that had Cowdrey frowning; the second ball of his second, spinning away and bouncing off a shortish length, surprised Cowdrey as he shaped to cut, and Simpson at slip dropped a sharp catch he had appeared to grab. Cowdrey was 56, the score 147; it was his first detectable error. Dexter cut Simpson cruelly for four, Cowdrey twice but more persuasively cut for three. At five o'clock, with an hour to go, England were 167, Dexter 89, Cowdrey 67.

O'Neill's first ball afterwards was a full toss, which Cowdrey put away to make the partnership worth 150. He took a single and then Dexter lashed his first ball straight back at O'Neill who let it through his hands just to the left of his face. Cowdrey cut O'Neill grandiloquently for four, so it was an eventful over.

Cowdrey was now steering, gaining runs as he had done several times before from incisive singles turned into overthrows.

McKenzie flung down several overs short of a length and now the batsmen, more obviously than the bowlers, seemed exhausted. Again Dexter, looking in dire need of a gin and tonic, failed, as at Brisbane, quite to stay the course. With twenty-five minutes remaining Benaud threw one up to him on the off

SYDNEY SKETCH BOOK: THE HILL

BY RUSSELL DRYSDALE

R.D.

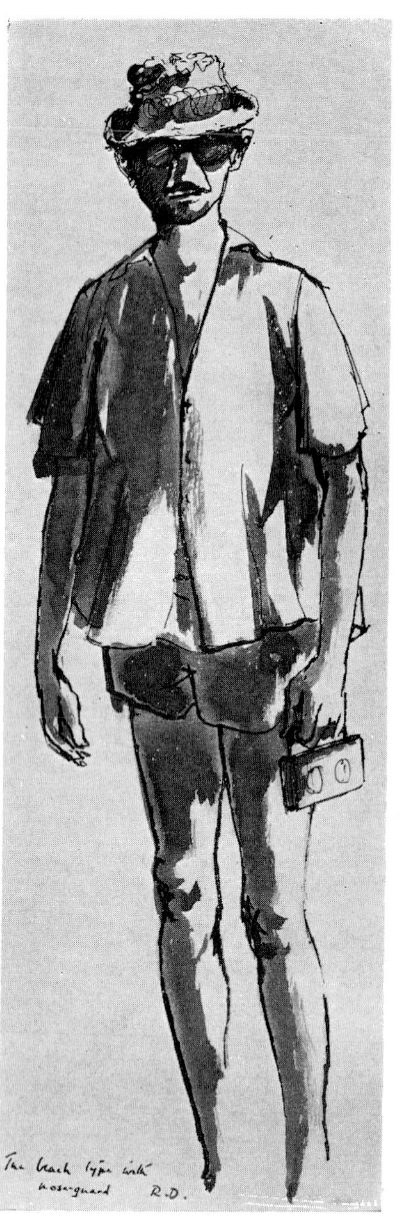
The beach type with
nose-guard R.D.

R.D.

A good days cricket. R.D.

'The Cricketers' by Russell Drysdale

The Hill.

R.D.

The painter Rapotec watching on the Hill. R.D.

The blokes from the bush. R.D.

R.D.
'Ave a go, yer mug!'

stump, it gripped, and Dexter, pushing wearily forward, edged it face high to Simpson at slip.

It had been a determined, retrieving innings, though with less flourish and finery than usual; the target and perspective had been kept in clear focus, with marginal graces eliminated. He had appeared less able than Cowdrey to conserve his energies, the final sapping of which, more than anything, cost him his wicket. He is not accustomed to playing out time, any self-imposed constraints seeming to dent his concentration.

Barrington several times stabbed McKenzie a yard short of forward short leg, but he took nine off Benaud in the last over of the day. Cowdrey, quietly reflective, was 94 not out. It had been, from his first ball, a masterly demonstration of technique, timing and control.

The new ball would be taken first thing. The situation, with England 210 for 3, was nicely balanced. The clouds had given way to serene sunshine and the 62,000 streaming away to celebrate New Year's Eve had seen something worth while.

The Fitzroy Gardens, their sprinklers silvered by the sinking sun, smelt sweet on the walk home through the cool archway of trees.

AUSTRALIA – First Innings

W. Lawry, b. Trueman	52
R. B. Simpson, c. Smith, b. Coldwell	38
N. O'Neill, c. Graveney, b. Statham	19
R. N. Harvey, b. Coldwell	0
P. Burge, l.b.w., b. Titmus	23
B. Booth, c. Barrington, b. Titmus	27
A. K. Davidson, c. Smith, b. Trueman	40
K. Mackay, l.b.w., b. Titmus	49
R. Benaud, c. Barrington, b. Titmus	36
G. McKenzie, b. Trueman	16
B. Jarman, not out	10
Extras (b. 2, l.b., 4)	6
Total	316

FALL OF WICKETS. 1—62, 2—111, 3—112, 4—112, 5—155, 6—164, 7—237, 8—289, 9—294, 10—316.

ENGLAND – First Innings

D. S. Sheppard, l.b.w., b. Davidson	0
G. A. Pullar, b. Davidson	11
E. R. Dexter, c. Simpson, b. Benaud	93
M. C. Cowdrey, not out	94
K. F. Barrington, not out	11
Extras (l.b. 1)	1
Total (3 wkts.)	210

FALL OF WICKETS. 1—0, 2—19, 3—194.

Third Day: Davidson, bowling from the opposite end, towards the pavilion, took the new ball at once. This time Benaud allowed him two spokes out of the umbrella, long leg and third man. It was grey again, but cooler, with a breeze. Cowdrey pushed a single, Barrington cut wristily to beat third man, and then played Davidson back past his umpire. Eight runs came off the over. McKenzie was off length. Barrington drove him through the covers and Cowdrey turned a full toss to mid-wicket to reach his 100. Eight years earlier on this ground he had saved Hutton's bacon with 102 after Miller had threatened to plunder the entire English batting.

Davidson, too, wasted the new ball, overpitching and looking far from the torrid bowler of the day before. Barrington, reaching out, played an out-swinger beautifully wide of mid-off, so Benaud took short leg to extra cover, himself moving from third slip to gully. Barrington drove Davidson's next ball to the sightscreen.

Benaud replaced McKenzie after two overs for 10. He began with a maiden to Cowdrey, but during the next Cowdrey hit successive balls off the back foot to the off boundary, and Barrington scooped a short one for three to square leg. That was 50 for the partnership, Barrington having made 34 of them.

Benaud brought back McKenzie for Davidson, and Cowdrey in his first over pulled a long-hop hard but straight into the hands of Burge standing by the square leg umpire. It was an unthinking reflexive stroke to a ball that perhaps came quicker off the pitch than he expected. In his next over McKenzie brought one sharply back at Barrington who after an agonizing delay was given out l.b.w. The innings, promising so strongly, was suddenly broken-backed. Titmus was caged in by three rudely predatory short legs, and looked likely to prove immediate fodder for any one of them. Graveney eased matters by pulling Benaud for two successive fours, and Titmus, encouraged, smote a full toss from McKenzie to the fence at long-off. Graveney drove Benaud through the covers, a stroke of reassuring elegance and conviction, and Titmus cut McKenzie with a ferocity denying all intimidation. Next he turned him to the long leg boundary, whither one short leg now departed.

Davidson relieved Benaud, whose five overs cost 27, and Graveney drove his first ball uppishly but just wide of the bowler for three. Titmus, appearing to have weathered the worst, played some unruffled strokes into the covers, but when he had begun to look there for lunch he touched a lifting one down the leg side from Davidson, and Jarman was quickly across to it. England, with four wickets left, were still 24 behind.

Eleven of them came off three balls in McKenzie's next over. Graveney twice steered him past second slip and then McKenzie, bouncing one at Smith, cleared both batsman and wicket-keeper. These two hung on until the interval, with Graveney 40, Smith 1, and England two short of Australia's 316.

The first ball of the afternoon saw the end of Graveney. He played McKenzie fine of Harvey at cover, called euphorically, in an effort to keep the strike, for a second, and was run out by a fast low throw which Jarman swept up on the half-volley.

Trueman, with two disapproving thumps at McKenzie, took England into a precarious lead, which they had managed in eleven overs, and an hour, less than Australia. Unfortunately, having tasted blood after a dour beginning, Trueman chose to swing at a good length ball from Davidson, delivering it in a gentle parabola to Booth at short extra. Statham lost his middle stump to Davidson with little dignity. Coldwell was caught in the gully, and England, throwing away their last seven wickets for 77, had utterly surrendered their strategic advantage. Davidson, who picked up four wickets for 12, finished with 6 for 75, an analysis he earned more at the beginning of the innings than at its end.

Simpson and Lawry set off at a lively rate, going out for their shots and driving at anything over-pitched. The bowling looked comfortably within their compass, and they appeared to be under instructions to get busy. Trueman swung a few past Simpson, but not as many as usual. The 30 was rapidly hoisted, at which point Trueman brought one back at Simpson who played no stroke, and can only have been centimetres off being l.b.w. It took a piece out of the pitch and Simpson went out and patted it down. The next ball swung late into him, he played over it, and his middle stump went sailing. Dexter crowded O'Neill, bringing up two short legs. Trueman's first ball to him pitched on the off stump, leaving him late and lifting angrily. It flew off the splice and Cowdrey at first slip took a brilliant catch low to his right. So Harvey, pale and subdued, walked slowly in to face a hat trick and a pair. He survived these, and Australia at tea were 39 for 2.

Immediately afterwards, Lawry drove Trueman to mid-off where Pullar let the ball through his legs. They took two. Lawry drove Trueman harder and wider and Pullar fielded the ball on the boundary edge. Harvey meanwhile was coming back for a fourth. Pullar, with a good 90 yards to throw, reached Trueman at the stumps first bounce and Trueman, taking the ball above his head, beat Harvey to it by a fraction. 46 for 3.

Lawry remained meditative and seemingly impregnable, while Burge, save for a hook or two at Coldwell, was scowlingly constrained. Twenty runs ticked up. Statham then pitched one short at Burge, who shaped to hook. It kept low, and Burge, these days too frequent a hitter across the line, found himself unable to change his stroke and was bowled off his pads.

Statham kept up a sustained attack, hurrying several through to Booth, who jabbed down on them convulsively. Trueman, having entertained his sector of crowd by flicking casually and repeatedly from the boundary to the top of the bails, re-

AUSTRALIA

First Innings		Second Innings	
W. Lawry, b. Trueman	52	not out	41
R. B. Simpson, c. Smith, b. Coldwell	38	b. Trueman	14
N. O'Neill, c. Graveney, b. Statham	19	c. Cowdrey, b. Trueman	0
R. N. Harvey, b. Coldwell	0	run out	10
P. Burge, l.b.w., b. Titmus	23	b. Statham	14
B. Booth, c. Barrington, b. Titmus	27	not out	19
A. K. Davidson, c. Smith, b. Trueman	40		
K. Mackay, l.b.w., b. Titmus	49		
R. Benaud, c. Barrington, b. Titmus	36		
G. McKenzie, b. Trueman	16		
B. Jarman, not out	10		
Extras (b. 2, l.b. 4)	6	Extras (b. 4, l.b. 3)	7
Total	316	Total (4 wkts.)	105

FALL OF WICKETS. *First Innings:* 1—62, 2—111, 3—112, 4—112, 5—155, 6—164, 7—237, 8—289, 9—294, 10—316. *Second Innings:* 1—30, 2—30, 3—46, 4—69.

ENGLAND – First Innings

D. S. Sheppard, l.b.w., b. Davidson	0
G. A. Pullar, b. Davidson	11
E. R. Dexter, c. Simpson, b. Benaud	93
M. C. Cowdrey, c. Burge, b. McKenzie	113
K. F. Barrington, l.b.w., b. McKenzie	35
T. W. Graveney, run out	41
F. J. Titmus, c. Jarman, b. Davidson	15
A. C. Smith, not out	6
F. S. Trueman, c. O'Neill, b. Davidson	6
J. B. Statham, b. Davidson	1
L. J. Coldwell, c. Benaud, b. Davidson	1
Extras (b. 4, l.b. 4, n.b. 1)	9
Total	331

FALL OF WICKETS. 1—0, 2—19, 3—194, 4—254, 5—255, 6—292, 7—315, 8—324, 9—327, 10—331.

turned for a final fling, with Titmus bowling for the first time half an hour from the end. Graveney, chasing one in the deep, pulled a muscle and left the field.

The first ball of Trueman's last over found the edge of Lawry's bat, but though Sheppard, at second slip where Graveney would have been, stuck out his left hand he could not hold it. It was a sharp chance of the kind that Sheppard had been dropping distressingly often, and a fielder of quicker reactions should have taken it. On such stolen opportunities do Test series hang.

Lawry appealed against the light and, after allowing four more balls, the umpires upheld it.

Fourth Day: A bruised, threatening sky, under which Trueman bowled three testing overs to Lawry who began uneasily. Coldwell contained Booth no less firmly, so that an hour of unrelenting defence brought Australia a bare twenty runs, dryly appreciated. Coldwell, after five overs for four runs, made way for Titmus. Booth moved down the pitch and drove him through the covers, the first positive stroke of the morning. It was half an hour before the crowd, mute with stupor, saw another one. Again it was by Booth, this time off Barrington, who had replaced a persevering but unpenetrative Statham. After ninety minutes, Lawry had prodded eight, Booth twenty-one. It was like watching two caged hamsters pedalling a tread-mill. Lawry got wedged on 49, for half an hour, eventually indulging in a single off a begging long-hop. His 50 had taken over four and a half hours. Booth, who now caught up with him, was a mere two hours less over his. Titmus bowled seven overs for nine runs. Dexter in evident frustration called for the ball himself. The last ball before lunch he hurled down round-arm at great pace, it shot almost along the ground, and uprooted the dismayed Lawry's middle stump. Apart from a couple of drives by Booth, it was the sole incident in two hours' unbridled sterility.

Fine drizzle delayed things for half an hour, then shirts were ripped off again in the Outer, the beer cans were set up, and play proceeded at snail's pace under pale skies. Dexter bowled steadily, aiming for the disruptive spot, and Statham, rapping Davidson about the pads, asked twice with some hopefulness. Benaud's strategy seemed basically for his batsmen to go plodding on, waiting for the wicket if not for time to operate in their favour. Davidson was in ruminative mood, the hour after the rain producing a leisured thirty. Titmus returned, and now he spun one outside Davidson's off stump to find the edge. Trueman, who had been, because of the wet ball and the prospect of the second one, sparingly treated, took the new ball with Coldwell ten minutes before tea. He had time for one over at Mackay, getting the seventh to cut in at him and catch him in flagrant protection.

Statham had borne the brunt of the afternoon's work and it was again Coldwell who bowled with Trueman. Booth snicked him for four off the inside edge, and was then beaten by one that went the other way. Benaud was foxed by a similar ball he was lucky not to touch. This was swing bowling of the kind Statham does not often manage.

Trueman now found one to swing and lift at Benaud. It took the shoulder of the bat and Cowdrey, flinging himself to his right, hauled the ball back and up as it seemed to scud past him. He rolled like a seal, the ball held inches off the grass. In the same over Trueman made a fair mess of McKenzie's stumps.

Booth meanwhile proceeded through the nineties. He managed the strike, picking up singles here and there. He was 99 when Trueman, getting an over at Jarman, swung one late, but this time the ball shot between first and second slip for four.

Off Statham, Booth reached a century that had taken five hours of the closest concentration. It was an innings devoid of embellishment but based securely on first principles. He moved solidly behind the line, early in position for anything that kept low. Without him, Australia would scarcely have progressed at all.

Jarman put a healthy broad bat to the ball, and Trueman, after five overs which had brought him 3 for 16, retired in favour of Coldwell. Coldwell bowled one over, drinks were taken, and Trueman, watered, returned. But Jarman was not to be shifted, and it was Booth in the end who went. Statham pitched one short, Booth hooked and Trueman, circling shakily at square leg, eventually got under a skier.

The last pair, perched not uncomfortably for forty-nine minutes, had put on 20 runs. Trueman's bag was 5 for 62. Dexter had saved him for the new ball, a decision that left Coldwell, Statham and himself with the task of curtailing and conceivably striking. As it happened, they curtailed, but could not strike effectively enough.

England, needing 234 to win, had thirty-five minutes batting. Pullar took five off an exploratory looking over from Davidson, getting down off the last ball to the other end. McKenzie's first ball to him pitched on his legs, he flicked it, and Jarman, hurtling across, plucked the ball up. The Australians swarmed gleefully to him, as well they might.

Davidson bowled two good ones at Sheppard in light grown indifferent. Between overs he and Dexter consulted, the umpires conferred, and play seventeen minutes early was suspended.

The Australian batting, laboriously paced almost throughout, had threatened a fruitless day. But Booth's stoical persistence, Trueman's spell with the second new ball, and the two scorching catches by Cowdrey and Jarman had rescued it.

It was absolutely anyone's match.

AUSTRALIA

First Innings		Second Innings	
W. Lawry, b. Trueman	52	b. Dexter	57
R. B. Simpson, c. Smith, b. Coldwell	38	b. Trueman	14
N. O'Neill, c. Graveney, b. Statham	19	c. Cowdrey, b. Trueman	0
R. N. Harvey, b. Coldwell	0	run out	10
P. Burge, l.b.w., b. Titmus	23	b. Statham	14
B. Booth, c. Barrington, b. Titmus	27	c. Trueman, b. Statham	103
A. K. Davidson, c. Smith, b. Trueman	40	c. Smith, b. Titmus	17
K. Mackay, l.b.w., b. Titmus	49	l.b.w., b. Trueman	9
R. Benaud, c. Barrington, b. Titmus	36	c. Cowdrey, b. Trueman	4
G. McKenzie, b. Trueman	16	b. Trueman	0
B. Jarman, not out	10	not out	11
Extras (b. 2, l.b. 4)	6	Extras (b. 4, l.b. 5)	9
Total	316	Total	248

FALL OF WICKETS. *First Innings:* 1—62, 2—111, 3—112, 4—112, 5—155, 6—164, 7—237, 8—289, 9—294, 10—316. *Second Innings:* 1—30, 2—30, 3—46, 4—69, 5—161, 6—193, 7—212, 8—228, 9—228, 10—248.

ENGLAND

First Innings		Second Innings	
D. S. Sheppard, l.b.w., b. Davidson......	0	not out.................	1
G. A. Pullar, b. Davidson..............	11	c. Jarman, b. McKenzie	5
E. R. Dexter, c. Simpson, b. Benaud.....	93	not out.................	3
M. C. Cowdrey, c. Burge, b. McKenzie..	113		
K. F. Barrington, l.b.w., b. McKenzie...	35		
T. W. Graveney, run out..............	41		
F. J. Titmus, c. Jarman, b. Davidson.....	15		
A. C. Smith, not out..................	6		
F. S. Trueman, c. O'Neill, b. Davidson...	6		
J. B. Statham, b. Davidson.............	1		
L. J. Coldwell, c. Benaud, b. Davidson...	1		
Extras (b. 4, l.b. 4, n.b. 1)...........	9		
Total..........................	331	Total (1 wkt.).........	9

FALL OF WICKETS. *First Innings:* 1—0, 2—19, 3—194, 4—254, 5—255, 6—292, 7—315, 8—324, 9—327, 10—331. *Second Innings:* 1—5.

Fifth Day: Rain had fallen plentifully during the night, enough to take thirty runs off the pace of the outfield, and again before breakfast. The clouds remained low, with a cooling breeze. It looked a day to bowl in, just heavy enough for Davidson without being oppressive.

Benaud, as he had done the night before, set third man and long leg for both bowlers, with only two slips and a gully. Attack was being realistically tempered with caution. McKenzie began with an aggressive over to Dexter, rapping him on the thigh and beating him twice outside the off stump. Sheppard took a single off Davidson, and Dexter, contemptuously almost, hit a half-volley to the long-on fence. Davidson now set his sights outside the off stump, a disappointing reaction, which obliged Dexter to let the next over go by or reach for the cut. When two overs later Davidson again pitched on the stumps Dexter loftily thumped him through the covers. McKenzie bowled Sheppard a full toss which he placed uppishly wide of Harvey at square leg. McKenzie, too, kept his attack wide of the off stump. Harvey misfielded badly in the covers and his irritated throw cleared Jarman by yards for two overthrows.

Benaud replaced Davidson after four overs, and Dexter,

cutting at a top spinner, scraped it inches past his off stump. Benaud, having bowled a taxing maiden to Dexter, who at this stage was noticeably more edgy than Sheppard, changed ends, going round the wicket. Sheppard hammered his first ball to the fence between cover and extra, and England were 50 runs on their way. Dexter cut Benaud past slip, and the second wicket had passed 50 in eighty minutes. Benaud made frequent minute adjustments of field and the absorbed silence, with for the first time no one bare-chested in the Outer, was vibrantly audible. Benaud kept Dexter at full stretch, but he was settling and when once Benaud overpitched Dexter put him efficiently away.

Mackay came on and Sheppard, having cut him late, leaned out to drive him beautifully to the extra cover boundary.

Benaud went over the wicket. Mackay bowled confiningly at Dexter, to a ring of three on the leg side, and Dexter, after a fretful period, looked relieved to swing a long-hop from Benaud for four. Sheppard moved out to Benaud, taking three between mid-wicket and mid-on, but when Davidson came back before lunch he found himself stabbing down on several that dipped late into him.

McKenzie bowled the over before lunch, Dexter slashing the last ball past Mackay, who on the third man boundary blindly darted the wrong way as if pursuing a falsely-laid scent. England finished the morning 96 for 1, Sheppard and Dexter 44 each.

Benaud reverted to his original end, Sheppard hitting his first ball through the covers and then chopping him past slip to reach 50. Dexter drove at Davidson's out-swinger and Benaud at short gully nearly hauled it out of the sky. He threw himself at it, got both hands there, but the force spun it away. Sheppard moved down the pitch to Benaud and his flowing drive exactly bisected cover and extra. He was drawing away from Dexter now, who seemed pleased to let him.

Simpson replaced Davidson and Sheppard carted a stiff long-hop first bounce to the fence. Davidson returned at

Benaud's end, Benaud switching his attack desperately to break the strangle-hold. Dexter turned Davidson off his pads to reach his own 50, taking twenty minutes longer over it than Sheppard.

Both were now going well, Sheppard relaxed and fluent, Dexter tautly watchful. Then at 129 Sheppard, pushing Simpson to Benaud at short cover, called for an implausible run. Dexter did his best, but was just short when Jarman whipped across Benaud's underhand throw. It was an act of sudden folly, bringing Australia unexpectedly back into focus.

Benaud brought back McKenzie, crowded the batsmen for the first time, and the fielding increased in relentlessness. This was more the Australian style. Davidson, cutting the ball at medium pace, settled on a nagging length, Cowdrey looked all pads and inhibitions. The impetus had gone.

At length Sheppard fastened on a half-volley from Davidson to beat mid-off and England were again on the move. Drinks were taken at twenty to three, England needing 94.

The sun came out and Lawry, at forward short leg, seemed to be scrutinizing Cowdrey's trousers for stains. Cowdrey surfaced to loft Davidson back over his head. In the next over he tried to steer McKenzie and Davidson at second slip put down a not difficult catch, straight to him. Sheppard flicked now at Davidson, Jarman got a glove to it and diverted the ball through Simpson's hands. Had these two catches been taken, with Cowdrey 7, and Sheppard 78, the match might have swung decisively back to Australia.

Cowdrey cut Davidson, drove McKenzie through the covers, and stability was restored. Sheppard turned McKenzie off his legs and when at length Benaud, after eight doggedly accurate overs by Davidson, returned, Sheppard cut him past cover and danced out to swing him wide of mid-on.

Benaud pitched short to Cowdrey who lay back and carved past cover. At tea England, 188 for 2, wanted 46. Sheppard was 96, Cowdrey 26.

Mackay bowled after tea, and one sensed now that, at last,

Benaud had given it away. He had tried everything, from either end, but England, unlike the Australians, had displayed the strokes and drawn the reward.

In Benaud's first over of the evening, the ball thrown up, Sheppard came down the wicket and drove towards the sight-screen. The crowd rose to him and he stood there bareheaded, his bat raised high. He had batted four hours twenty minutes, a trumpeting recall to achievement on the brink of withdrawal, for a failure here would have cost him his Test place.

Benaud gave Davidson the new ball at once, and a packed slip field, but it was a gesture only. Davidson could scarcely raise a gallop. Cowdrey hooked his first ball in almost kindly fashion to the fence, twice more in the same over turning him into the deserted outfield. Benaud charitably released him after one over, and it was against Mackay and McKenzie, on a suddenly golden evening, that Sheppard and Cowdrey with a flood of elegant strokes were sailing home. But there was a final retributive twist. With the scores level Sheppard called Cowdrey for a sharp single off McKenzie's last ball. Lawry, racing in from short third man, threw the wicket down and Sheppard was about as short of his ground as had been Dexter. So Booth bowled to Cowdrey, centurion to centurion, and Cowdrey, having played one ball with exaggerated circumspection, cut the second to the boundary. There were seventy-five minutes left for play.

Retrospect. It had been a thrilling, convincing win, after a match throughout which, despite frequent fluctuation, England had called the tune. Australia had batted twice with niggardly lack of ambition, showing no imagination and little technique. They had degenerated steadily from aggressive stroke makers into back-foot pushers. They had lessons to learn in plenty, with only Booth's steadfastness and Davidson's fine early spell on the second morning to show for five days struggle.

For England, Dexter, over and above his own two defiant and dominating innings, lifted England by his self-confidence and determination to new levels. He kept a tight hold on proceedings, his fielders rose to the occasion, and the bowlers, with Trueman in full magnificent flow, answered each call on them. That the Australians allowed them to bowl as tightly as they did was, as much as anything, the reason for their downfall.

Finally, England, on this mellow evening, batted with a grace and affluence that seemed to have deserted the Australians. The batting of Sheppard, Dexter and Cowdrey stemmed from an amateur, classic tradition, its origins and outlines firmly delineated. Once again, and nobody could be sorry for it, the making of fastidious and firm strokes had proved, even on a pitch which Benaud had wrongly conceived to be prohibitive to them, of conclusive relevance. It had, in the last resort, been Sheppard's day. Before this innings few would have given him a couple of overs against Davidson. But he made up his mind early to get on to the front foot, combating the swing, so that even if it took the edge his reach was sufficient to steer it past gully. In consequence he was no longer at the mercy of the late in-swinger, of the type that had got him in the first innings. He saw the new ball comfortably off and no sooner had Benaud come on than he moved down the pitch to hit through the covers with flowing and opulent follow-through. Benaud was forced to bowl quicker and flight the ball less, a policy which, on a wicket which the continual humidity had bound together, denied him lift and turn. It was an astonishing resurrection, this of Sheppard's, for he had looked to be steadily sinking.

But for four hours he played with the assurance of one who had heard an old nostalgic tune, its melody as it made itself familiar recalling forgotten and delightful associations. His stroke play acquired a dream-like smoothness, all angularities and awkwardnesses smoothed away. When it was over, he was near collapse, but the song's echoes were of the kind that linger indelibly.

Dexter, too, could look back on this match as a turning-point in his captaincy. He demonstrated what had, since the days of Bradman and Hammond, tended to be forgotten, that number 3 is the key position, whatever the context. It was typical of him that, with Pullar quickly out, the light bad and only a few overs left to play on the fourth evening, it never occurred to him to send in a night-watchman. For too long our best players have shielded themselves from the new ball. But Dexter, by his sense of near infallibility, his assumption of responsibility, changes any situation before it can develop. He cracked anything within reach with a brutality that induced Davidson to waste the new ball fruitlessly wide of the off stump. He cast a cold, contemptuous eye on Mackay. Against Benaud he was sagely wary, waiting for the untidy ball and then thumping it.

On the field, too, he showed concerned responsiveness towards his bowlers which, if it fell short of Benaud's exuberant demonstrativeness, had previously been quite alien to him. Some had criticized his sparing use of Trueman in the second innings, but his strategic insight and his controlled assessment of possibilities remained plainly in evidence. He had set his bowlers precise tasks which they achieved. Coldwell, with his subtle changes of pace, worried the left-handers. Statham, even if at times he gave the impression of a mechanism slowly running down, kept at it with a wholehearted perseverance only just short of penetration. Titmus, flighting the ball cleverly, played up to the prevalent Australian indulgence in the sweep.

The fielding, too, was clean and swift, Barrington in the covers or at long leg picking up quite beautifully. Cowdrey's two slip catches were collector's pieces. Dexter himself pounced on the ball with a ferocity that rippled from man to man.

It is rare to see Benaud discountenanced as he was on this last day. He pulled the strings as tautly and as calculatingly as usual, but the responses were increasingly less magical. Australians rarely disintegrate, but the feeling gradually spread that this time no miracle was going to save them. Davidson had been ground down, Benaud had no tricks left. His leading stroke-players, O'Neill, Harvey, Simpson, Burge, had each failed him twice, and the gluey consistency of what was left could only be a lowering substitute. Why had he not made plain to them what was required during that penultimate morning and afternoon? It seemed that some real miscalculation of the wicket, and of England's possible response to it, had dictated an uncharacteristic caution that in the end cost him dear. It was hard to believe he would ever let it happen again.

The takings for the match were £A51,018, a record for any Test.

'. . . and forgive him his dropped catches . . .'

SEE OVER FOR FINAL SCORE CARD

AUSTRALIA

	First Innings		Second Innings	
W. Lawry, b. Trueman		52	b. Dexter	57
R. B. Simpson, c. Smith, b. Coldwell		38	b. Trueman	14
N. O'Neill, c. Graveney, b. Statham		19	c. Cowdrey, b. Trueman	0
R. N. Harvey, b. Coldwell		0	run out	10
P. Burge, l.b.w., b. Titmus		23	b. Statham	14
B. Booth, c. Barrington, b. Titmus		27	c. Trueman, b. Statham	103
A. K. Davidson, c. Smith, b. Trueman		40	c. Smith, b. Titmus	17
K. Mackay, l.b.w., b. Titmus		49	l.b.w., b. Trueman	9
R. Benaud, c. Barrington, b. Titmus		36	c. Cowdrey, b. Trueman	4
G. McKenzie, b. Trueman		16	b. Trueman	0
B. Jarman, not out		10	not out	11
Extras (b. 2, l.b. 4)		6	Extras	9
Total		316	Total	248

FALL OF WICKETS. *First Innings:* 1—62, 2—111, 3—112, 4—112, 5—155, 6—164, 7—237, 8—289, 9—294, 10—316. *Second Innings:* 1—30, 2—30, 3—46, 4—69, 5—161, 6—193, 7—212, 8—228, 9—228, 10—248.

ENGLAND

First Innings		Second Innings	
D. S. Sheppard, l.b.w., b. Davidson	0	run out	113
G. A. Pullar, b. Davidson	11	c. Jarman, b. McKenzie	5
E. R. Dexter, c. Simpson, b. Benaud	93	run out	52
M. C. Cowdrey, c. Burge, b. McKenzie	113	not out	58
K. F. Barrington, l.b.w., b. McKenzie	35	not out	0
T. W. Graveney, run out	41		
F. J. Titmus, c. Jarman, b. Davidson	15		
A. C. Smith, not out	6		
F. S. Trueman, c. O'Neill, b. Davidson	6		
J. B. Statham, b. Davidson	1		
L. J. Coldwell, c. Benaud, b. Davidson	1		
Extras (b. 4, l.b. 4, n.b. 1)	9	Extras (b. 5, l.b. 3, n.b. 1)	9
Total	331	Total (3 wkts.)	237

FALL OF WICKETS. *First Innings:* 1—0, 2—19, 3—194, 4—254, 5—255, 6—292, 7—315, 8—324, 9—327, 10—331. *Second Innings:* 1—5, 2—129, 3—233.

Bowling Analysis

ENGLAND

	First Innings				Second Innings			
Trueman	23	7	83	3	20	1	62	5
Statham	22	2	83	1	23	1	52	2
Coldwell	17	2	58	2	25	2	60	0
Barrington	6	0	23	0	6	0	22	0
Dexter	6	1	10	0	9	2	18	1
Titmus	15	2	43	4	14	4	25	1
Graveney	3	1	10	0				

AUSTRALIA

	First Innings				Second Innings			
Davidson	23.1	4	75	6	19	2	53	0
McKenzie	29	3	95	2	20	3	58	1
Mackay	6	2	17	0	9	0	34	0
Benaud	18	3	82	1	14	1	69	0
Simpson	7	1	34	0	2	0	10	0
O'Neill	5	1	19	0				
Booth					0.2	0	4	0

UMPIRES: C. Egar and W. Smyth
Total Attendance: 247,831
Total Receipts: £A51,018

4 From a Journal II: Melbourne - Canberra - Sydney

The Australian team for the Third Test shows one change: Guest, a strong, lively Victorian bowler, who uses the new ball better than most, in place of Burge. Guest, who had no great success against M.C.C., has a wristy action, which seemed on superficial acquaintance not beyond suspicion. We shall see.

This was a logical change, in the sense that it allows Davidson to be kept for short bursts and gives Benaud more breathing space generally. On the other hand, it was the batting that basically let him down; the assumption perhaps is that one batsman less might work wonders for the initiative of the others. Harvey must be on the brink of withdrawal; O'Neill and Simpson play Trueman with evident distaste. There remains the nightmare recollection of M.C.C.'s last performance at Sydney.

Over in Tasmania what promised to be a routine courtesy call took on an explosive aspect. The Australian selectors imported Lawry, O'Neill, Booth and Shepherd to bolster up the locals and to give needed batting practice to O'Neill, though surely not to Lawry who will be present in all the first-class matches M.C.C. have still to play. It seemed a bit thick.

Fred Trueman does not often exert himself on these occasions. This time, however, sickened possibly by the selection of Lawry and stimulated by offers of beer crates by Tasmanian brewers, he decided to let fly. Maybe, with the weather close and sultry, he simply sniffed wickets, a question of conditioned reflexes.

Anyhow, the upshot has been that, after M.C.C. had declared at 331 for 7, Sheppard, Barrington, Knight and Illingworth each passing 60, Trueman tore into action and within half an hour had ripped the batting apart. After five overs he had dismissed Lawry, Connor and Booth for three runs. He sent the ball flying about O'Neill's head, making plain that if he needed batting practice, he had come to the wrong place. Parfitt, Sheppard and Dexter took fine catches close to the wicket. Finally, Larter stepped in, mauling the stumps of sundry lethargic practitioners, and the Combined XI were put out for 77.

Sheppard, when M.C.C. batted again – Dexter sociably accepting the obligations of entertaining 6,000 assorted farmers – played his third dashing innings in three days. Parfitt, too, at long last looked like emerging from total seizure, but was checked by prolonged and thickening drizzle.

The Sunday, devoted to fishing, was again wet, and it was not until 2.30 on the final afternoon that further progress could be made. Dexter declared, getting his spinners quickly to work on a pitch too wet for Trueman to bowl on. The Combined XI, having shown their distaste for speed, now weakly surrendered to spin. In ninety minutes they were hustled out for 57, Allen, who hit the stumps of both O'Neill and Booth, taking four wickets, Illingworth three. The four Test stars, Lawry, O'Neill, Booth and Shepherd, whose appearance cost the Tasmanian authorities £A300, again individually and in bulk failed to earn their keep. The wicket, though damp and with hot sun on it, never became truly sticky. From an Australian point of view it was an humiliating performance.

Weather again disappointing for the drive to Sydney. Clouds everywhere and the threat of rain. Long, dreary suburbs – how Australian cities sprawl – before entering Gippsland at Dandenong. The railway follows the road for most of the way. Mostly this is mining country, with scattered farms and islands of forest alternating over gently tilting plains. Greener than anything I've driven through so far, it is also less characteristically Australian. The hills to the north seem here intensifications of cloud. This is the peak holiday season, nearly every car beyond Bairnsdale towing a caravan or a boat. Suddenly, round a steep bend, Lakes Entrance lies below, a series of connecting wooded lakes separated from the ocean by sand bars into which the streams of the Great Dividing Range empty themselves. The pale evening sun illuminates still blue waters, sailing boats, fishing trawlers and speedboats moving over them like toys. Seawards a narrow strip of yellow sand, the surf crashing beyond, curves for ninety lonely miles. In the port, a smell of fresh fish, the bare thighs of uniformly plump girls in bathing suits goose-fleshed with cold. As usual, the genuine prettiness of the place is wrecked by caravan sites, camping grounds, old car dumps. What Australia needs is a dictator of aesthetics.

At Nowa Nowa, in a clearing cut among the eucalypti, a cricket match is in progress. It might almost be in England, on a village green, except that the losing side is composed of elderly Aborigines. Young ones, with haunting lost faces, look sullenly on. On the tiny wooden pavilion someone has scrawled in chalk, 'Nowa Nowa Ruffians v. Lake Pansies'.

At Orbost, a township out of a wild west epic, the drunks are reeling out of ancient pubs. The motels are full. I decided to drive out to Marlo, a secluded fishing village ten miles away, and hope for the best.

The place is exquisite, a solitary pub, a general stores, and a jetty reaching into a narrow, sandy inlet overhung by trees. I sleep in a tiny monks' cell, with no hot water, and the roar of the surf thundering through the night.

Next day I continue through vast forests penetrated by shafts of weak sun. Log-strewn creeks intersect the road, willows and fern trees scattering their shadows over blackish water. Soon I cross into New South Wales, the car thick with red dust. At Boydtown, where I lunch, a fabulous site on Twofold Bay, comprising an inn, a ruined overgrown church and a telephone box in the form of a lighthouse, is grotesquely disfigured by the customary paraphernalia of tents, rubbish and caravans.

Only the sand, glistening round an empty bay, whose trees stalk the water's edge, remains pure and unsullied. The Seahorse Inn, built by convict labour for Benjamin Boyd in 1843, is Sam Lord's Castle in Barbados gone badly to seed. Gothic arches, grandfather clocks, hand covered doors, brass locks and a shell museum. Boyd set up a whaling fleet here in 1842, a project that languished for ten years and expired with his murder. The clouds pile up again and by the time I turn down towards Merimbula it's pelting.

Merimbula, the choicest spot on the Sapphire Coast, is a more sophisticated version of Lakes Entrance. A beautiful beach, a lagoon flanked by sand dunes and elegant villas embedded in woods, a well-designed and comfortable motel, the Black Dolphin. But, being Sunday, I can't get a drink. Victoria issues no Sunday papers and Sydney is too far away.

The rain lets up after dinner, the lagoon, with fishing boats drifting in a rose and saffron sunset, flickers with lights. It might be Japan. On the distant seaward edge of the lagoon a miniature Coney Island swings and throbs faintly in the darkness. I dine, spiritless, on oysters and snapper.

The Snowy Mountains Highway, spiralling 3,500 feet up from the coast to Nimmitabel, beyond Brown Mountain, must be scenically among the most spectacular drives in Australia. The surface is red gravel, which after a few miles coats the engine, your eyes, the inside of the car and the inside of your mouth, and for over two hours it is rarely possible to accelerate beyond 35 mph. Blind corner follows blind corner, steeply tilted up or down. The hills are choked with trees as far as the eye can see. No sun could penetrate them. Near the road giant ferns splay their paler leaves against the blue, and bird notes, clear as bells, echo in the conservatory shade. Waterfalls splash down black gullies, cleansing the ferns and stirring the creeks beneath them. As the road winds, ochre hills swing into view.

The damp cool, with everything moistly sweating, empties

into sudden heat. Towards the top the trees give out, litters of huge druidical stones, circular and phallic, lying among dead eucalypti. At cloud level you look back over miles of spilling foliage, close curled as a negro's skull. Heat and shade alternate, with Mt Kosciusko soaring above the Murray river westward, and the peaks of the Great Dividing Range stretching like a fever chart to the north-east.

Beyond Cooma the road dips more gently, the forest thins out as if gutted by some urbane landscapist. It is vaguely reminiscent of Natal, with rounded mamillary hills like kopjes, and the same rusty earth underlining luxuriant valleys.

The road becomes bitumen, a sign announces Australian Federal Territory, and one bowls smoothly along a succession of genteel highways into the heart, if it can be said to have one, of Canberra.

The descent from Utopia to Sub-topia is steep and short. Walter Burley Griffin's plans for Canberra, shelved during two wars and a world depression, are, it is true, being resuscitated, but in the meantime the original vision has been smeared beyond repair. Griffin's basic conception, a series of concentric circles triangularly grouped, with city and Government both separated and unified by a vast bridge-straddled lake, remains integral, though the lake over the unsightly Molonglo river-bed is still, after fifty years, unrealized. This has at last been taken in hand, so that within the next twelve months the present forsaken rubbish dump should be replaced by water, and probably mosquitoes.

It is unfair to judge a new city in mid-construction. Canberra, forced into existence by inter-State jealousies in 1911, has everything against it, except the natural beauty of its site – a gently rolling plain in a crust of hills. It has no links with the sea, which is nearly 200 miles away; it is off all main routes of communication; there is no basic reason for it to exist at all. Not surprisingly, it has the air of an oasis, isolated from the real world. However much the uncontrolled damage done to

Griffin's scheme can be repaired, Canberra can never hope for more than an artificial coherence.

Looking at it now, the effect is of a garden suburb lovingly prolonged and tenderly cultivated. Man has been made subservient to trees and cars, becoming a dwarf in the process. The excess of space, detrimental to architecture throughout Australia, reaches its apex here, where hideous bungalows line all the main highways into the city and such unity of vision as once existed in theory has been obliterated by undistinguished sprawl.

The civic centre, so called, is a monument to the automobile. Neo-Manhattan skyscrapers, wedged round fountained piazzas, may eventually raise the eye from the Spanish-mission style crescents at present distractingly in evidence, but it is plain that the lavish and undisguised car parks, nakedly adjacent to each section of the business and shopping blocks, will win in the end.

The diplomatic avenues, radiating from Capital Hill, are inescapably dull, such efforts at national distinctiveness as have been made never properly surfacing above the prevailing and derivative uniformity. Generally speaking, a city so generously planted with trees should please, but somehow the neatly marching platoons of cedars, gums, elders, ashes and oaks, here and there interrupted by a gingko or a Japanese pagoda, convey merely the uninspired servility of the municipal mind.

In the end, of course, a city depends on the quality of its buildings and Canberra, sad to relate, has neither contemporary excitement nor colonial grandeur. The idioms of each exist here in imitative adaptations and nothing short of scrapping the lot and starting again could save it.

With its 2,000 acre lake and complacent trees, its feeling of space and its rim of mountains, Canberra when it is finished may have some of the qualities of a placid, scaled-down and debilitated Geneva. But that would be flattering it.

Necessity, in terms of urban creation, must always be preferable to artifice. Canberra, whose present population of 60,000 is expected to reach 100,000 by the end of the decade, will depend inevitably on its people making the best of a bad job. Too much is being risked on it now for it ever to stagnate, but a bad job it is disappointingly likely to remain. Diplomats, Government officials, university students and businessmen may, in their growing numbers, offset gracious mediocrity with intelligence and competitive vitality, but the omens, study them how you will, are not good.

Cities acquire character by tough historical and commercial processes, by the traffic of ships and aircraft, the junction of railways. Canberra was never conceived as a metropolis but as a Federal Capital; dumped in the bush, without tradition or unity of architectural conception, she has a thin chance of engendering love.

Sydney is four hours' drive. The sun gleamed fitfully on the grey ripples of Lake George, the Federal Highway, curving through elegant but uncultivated and unsettled countryside, slowly thickened with cars. Beyond Goulburn the roads were lined with stalls advertising fresh peaches and plums, apples hung on orchard trees like unlit bulbs.

Over the red roofs of Sydney the blue extended its hard familiar pressure. Ferries chugged manfully towards the North Shore. Segments of sea glinted between harbour-side buildings. Palm-trees splayed against the dipping sun. Soon King's Cross was winking its neon and siphoning its fountains under a sky charged with chunky stars. Smells of coffee and garlic, of flower shops and scent stores, spilled among marauding sailors, their arms round blondes in matador tights. Jazz throbbed underground. It was like returning to life.

5 Sydney: The Third Test

M.C.C., on the crest of the wave, flew in from Hobart the day before the Test. The team, announced in Tasmania, showed one change from Melbourne: Murray in place of Smith, with Allen added to the twelve. Tom Graveney had arrived in Sydney earlier for treatment to a muscle, but by the time the others had joined him he was maddeningly laid up with a virus attack. Parfitt, who had scored 120 in a two-day match against Tasmania, was therefore recalled. Allen, after inspection of the pitch, became twelfth man. It was a curious decision, for the wicket, lushly grassed the night before – the curator assuring Keith Miller that it would remain so – had since been razored, its grey surface like a worn carpet bearing faded, scarcely distinguishable patterns. Australia were to select their side on the morning of the match.

First Day: The traffic was thick along Anzac Parade long before breakfast. There were clouds in plenty, but they were high, with sun widening the blue. By half-past ten the Hill was a blob of faces, no grass visible anywhere. Australia left out Mackay, rejected after a run of thirty consecutive Tests. His scores in this series had been 86 not out, 49 and 9, but with Lawry and Booth he had turned Australia into a team of procrastinators. The other change from Melbourne was that Shepherd came in for Burge.

A band was pounding away in front of the Noble stand, the flags flapped noisily from the green domes and pagoda turrets of the pavilion, and when Dexter came out to toss with Benaud the outfield shone like satin. Dexter called correctly and chose, though perhaps not without misgivings, to bat.

Sheppard, in ripening form, was quickly reduced, no less

than in the first innings at Melbourne, to indecisive innocence by Davidson. He appeared to have forgotten any resolutions about playing off the front foot. By the time Davidson, within the space of two overs, had got several to lift and swing both into and away from him, he scarcely knew whether he was coming or going. He pushed weakly out at a good length ball in his third over and McKenzie at second slip took, not too certainly, a lowish catch.

Dexter reached for and laid into Davidson's first ball, Harvey at wide mid-off catching it first bounce above his head. The counter-attack was under way. Pullar, having learned his lesson at Melbourne, looked witheringly at McKenzie's leg side attack, but pushed Davidson fruitfully off his legs.

Dexter, moving quickly into line, made mellow resonant sounds, cutting Davidson through the slips and turning him to the square-leg boundary. He was all elegant assurance, the refinements of his technique reinforced by latent power. Twice he hit with sudden savagery, Shepherd at gully and O'Neill at cover bringing off swivelling one-handed stops. Pullar, catching some of Dexter's gloss, if not his authoritative delicacy, drove and placed with maturing ease. Davidson withdrew, Guest bowled his first, rather vague Test overs, and McKenzie, still pitching short, changed ends. The fielding was shark-like. At 54 Benaud came on, switching Guest to Davidson's original end. Dexter once or twice drove uppishly, but the temper of the batting was pleasantly even.

Pullar fetched a full toss from Benaud from outside the off stump, but driving never quite got his foot there. Dexter, having cut the quick bowlers with scrupulous care, now tried to force Benaud off the back foot. Incontestably short, the ball must have bounced higher and slower than Dexter expected. Lawry at short third man cupped his hands under a quiet, curving catch, immaculateness having slipped in mid-stroke into improvident untidiness.

It was a wicket thrown to the wolves. Benaud's length remained erratic, Cowdrey receiving an odd assortment of long-hops and full tosses. Davidson came back for two overs before lunch, Pullar making airy non-committal passes at him. England were 73 for 2, Pullar 30. The morning had perceptibly gone Australia's way.

The crowd, tryingly, squashed like sardines, squabbled among themselves, while Cowdrey leaned Davidson through the covers and Pullar lay back to cut Benaud past gully. Cowdrey, hesitating over a short single, earned five in overthrows, the first error in fielding after nearly three hours' meticulousness.

The batting now developed a post-prandial lethargy. Pullar found piercing the gaps temporarily beyond him; Cowdrey, reflective and urbane, was without severity. He batted as a man smokes a cigar, taking his ease and looking placidly around him. Guest bowled some accommodating overs, only his concealed slower ball earning attention.

Pullar surfaced to hit Benaud to the long-on boundary, sending up the hundred, but for the most part his timing was not such as to carry to the fence. Cowdrey, too, found the outfield slow, requiring more force than he cares to exert. Benaud gave Simpson a try, a move Pullar immediately justified by swatting a long-hop hard and low to Benaud at mid-wicket.

Barrington in his first over drove McKenzie past mid-off and cut him audaciously late for four, two strokes of signal relish. Cowdrey began now to sharpen his caress, both Simpson and Davidson suffering. The batting acquired lustre and edge. Barrington swept at Simpson, Cowdrey eased him between mid-off and cover. The odd one stopped, an occasional leg-break turned, enough anyway to encourage Benaud's return for the final speculative over of the afternoon. England, 161 for 3 at tea, had gained back some ground.

Cowdrey twice roughly cracked Guest, whose length and direction never settled, through the covers; Benaud at the other end was all over the place, eleven coming off his first over. He bowled as if bent on hastening the new ball. Simpson tried again, quite as generously. Benaud plied Cowdrey with full tosses which Cowdrey, as if gobbling spaghetti, disposed of obligingly. The 200 went up, Cowdrey having absorbed 28 in twenty minutes. Simpson bowled yet another long-hop, but this time Cowdrey, surfeited with driving, went to cut. It kept low, hustled through, and Jarman snapped up a catch off the bottom edge. It was a trivial end to an innings of ripeness and polish. The indulgent prodigality of the last few overs had threatened drama with farce, creating an illlusion of false prosperity.

Perspective was quickly restored, for Benaud, hedging Parfitt about with close fielders, had Lawry at leg slip pluck the ball almost out of his pocket. Twice in an over Parfitt had pushed precariously down the pitch; the third time he went. Simpson had taken 3 for 33.

Davidson, much against the loudly voiced wishes of the Hill, was now given the new ball. His first over with it, the ball curving in prodigiously late like a boomerang, silenced his critics. Barrington slashed despairingly at McKenzie's third ball, a widish half-volley, and Davidson at second slip, though he got both hands there, failed to hold it. It was no great loss, for soon afterwards Davidson swung one in viciously and Barrington, with both legs in front of his stumps, had scant chance of escape. The next ball, to Murray, swung even more sharply, the umpire's hand this time going up after some deliberation.

The innings now in ruins, Trueman strode in to an emperor's reception, though the context – of saving the hat-trick – was less than noble. This he managed, glaring down the pitch with the baleful gaze of one rudely disturbed from merited rest. For twenty minutes he pushed self-denyingly down the line, earning a single at the end of them. Davidson pitched one short at Titmus, who hooked it high to leg. Booth, just in from the boundary, reached it but it swerved out of his hands.

Titmus, playing with some fluency, encouraged Trueman to display his strokes, shyly hoarded hitherto. Guest was restored and Trueman swatted him straight, before more decorously turning a full toss to the mid-wicket boundary.

Benaud, with a quarter of an hour left, brought back Simpson. Titmus lay back and cut his first ball to the pavilion, a stroke of pure disparagement. Trueman now scowled his intention of hanging on, come what may. He thrust his bat defiantly out, with no hint of lasciviousness. Benaud had to call it a day. These two had seen off the new ball and muffled the spinners for forty-five minutes.

All the same, Benaud had reason for pleasure. England, at 201 for 3, had appeared to have righted themselves, after an indifferent start. Simpson then had wormed through the middle, pitching his leg-breaks less inaccurately than Benaud, and opening the way for Davidson with the new ball. Davidson, both early and late, bowled beautifully, Benaud being able to unload some of the odd jobbing on Guest. Neither Guest nor McKenzie, though, had much to offer, while Benaud himself bowled with bewildering looseness.

The wicket had been on the slow side, not always of predictable pace, with a very few scuttling through. For the third time running seven wickets had fallen on the first day. Now it was England's less accustomed bowlers who would have the chance to exhibit redemptive batsmanship.

54,476 people had watched, paying over £A12,500, a record taking for any single day on the Sydney ground. They had seen spectacular swing bowling, one innings of honeyed, if delayed, sweetness, and voracious ground fielding.

ENGLAND – First Innings

G. P. Pullar, c. Benaud, b. Simpson	53
D. S. Sheppard, c. McKenzie, b. Davidson	3
E. R. Dexter, c. Lawry, b. Benaud	32
M. C. Cowdrey, c. Jarman, b. Simpson	85
K. F. Barrington, l.b.w., b. Davidson	35
P. H. Parfitt, c. Lawry, b. Simpson	0
F. J. Titmus, not out	28
J. T. Murray, l.b.w., b. Davidson	0
F. S. Trueman, not out	16
Extras (l.b. 3, w. 1)	4
Total (for 7 wkts.)	256

FALL OF WICKETS. 1—4, 2—65, 3—132, 4—201, 5—203, 6—221, 7—221.

Second Day: Trueman, his features arranged so as to dispel any notions of comedy, began on the self-evident principle that the longer he batted the less he would need to bowl. Davidson opened with a maiden to Titmus, who played him with the calculating condescension of one long habituated to this kind of thing. Brass bands and crowds of 50,000 are meat and drink to Trueman, who immediately put on display a cover drive and a slash off the back foot to the pavilion that were of classic orthodoxy. He took measured short singles off Davidson with a puritanically straight bat, overhauling Titmus and hoisting 50 for the partnership. But habit will out, and suddenly he swatted at a yorker from Simpson as if it were a mosquito and lost his leg bail. Statham cut at the next ball and Benaud at short slip took a superb one-handed catch high to his left. Titmus, in danger now of being left high and dry without adding to his score, drove Davidson past mid-off, ducked under a bouncer that was signalled as an overhead wide, and, finally, trying to force an in-swinger away, was bowled neck and crop. England in forty minutes had added 23. Davidson's four cheap wickets, achieved in short spells, emphasized the value to Benaud of an extra seam bowler, indifferently though Guest performed. Simpson's five were simply out of the hat, but he had shown that, when the wickets are not coming Benaud's way, he can haul them in himself.

The Australians started quietly. Dexter, according to his custom, gave both bowlers long leg and third man, and Statham at once brought one sharply in to rap Simpson's pads. Then he beat him with one that moved off the seam, fizzing over the shoulder of his bat. Lawry, facing Trueman, got low down over the ball in the position of one suffering continual attacks of gripe. After three overs each Dexter decided to switch ends, replacing Trueman temporarily with Coldwell. Coldwell's second ball pitched on Lawry's leg stump, Lawry flicked at it, and Murray, diving across, took a fine catch as he thudded to the ground. He was helped up, ruefully rubbing his shoulder. Trueman returned to set about Harvey, O'Neill having been dropped down to five, and immediately he got one to lift and find the edge. The ball flew to the left of Cowdrey at first slip who got both hands to it but could not hold it. Harvey stabbed down on one from Trueman that skidded inches wide of the leg stump. Trueman in a magnificent over beat both Simpson and Harvey with out-swingers, Simpson getting the faintest of touches, but the ball just not carrying to Cowdrey. Murray, in obvious discomfort, had now to retire, Parfitt taking over. It was cruel luck. Simpson underlined it by glancing Trueman wide of Parfitt for four. Australia at lunch were 39 for 1, Simpson 24. England had deserved better of their seventy minutes' assault.

The hour after lunch produced forty-eight runs, mostly by way of deflections and quickly-run singles, more than one of which would have put paid to Harvey if the throw had hit the stumps. Coldwell was accurate, Statham steady, but Simpson, chastened by his Melbourne experiences, made fewer flourishes outside the off stump. Harvey, shadowy and imprecise, once glanced Statham fine enough to find the sightscreen; otherwise he settled for disarming pushes on either side of the wicket, unkindly exploiting the most cumbersome movers. At 72 Titmus bowled for the first time, his field split five and four with no one more than thirty yards from the bat. Simpson popped up a couple and the odd one hurried through. The bowling was commendably tight, the batting unimaginative. The Hillites, squashed together like specimens ripe for canning, grew fidgety. It was not surprising because little happened to make them sit up in nearly two days. If anyone shifted position, or stretched, a rain of beer cans from behind descended on him. Parfitt, who very often looked on the verge of tears, had few ideas about the duties thrust on him and the fielding suffered in consequence. Barrington, coming on at three o'clock, began untidily; and Simpson, breaking loose at last, struck both him and Titmus resoundingly to the fence. This seemed to stir old echoes in Harvey, who came down the pitch to Titmus in emulation. He was 32 when he drove a half-volley at comfortable height to Sheppard at extra cover. It fell out as if struck with Lindrum-like back spin. Dexter covered his face with his hands.

Harvey, visibly startled, swished Barrington with the spin, the stroke seeming to search out Sheppard, at long leg. Sheppard circled, unaccountably stopped, and the ball plopped like a cockroach five yards short. Nothing went right now. Harvey, timing hopelessly awry, spooned the ball up between fielders and Barrington twice almost had him picked up at leg slip. A fight broke out on the Hill. Dexter, understandably crestfallen, did his best to restore morale by his own energy at cover, but Simpson, moving his feet, was cruising contentedly. Australia, in the two hours of afternoon, scored 105 runs, Harvey having needed and enjoyed the luck of the devil.

Trueman, to whom Dexter had given the afternoon off, resumed at his most modest pace, suggesting that greater expenditure of effort at this stage would be unprofitable. Harvey drove Titmus more persuasively through the covers, Dexter finally sealing the gap by placing himself and Barrington at silly mid-off. He tired of this soon; creating a deeper, more comprehensive ring in its place. Harvey, heedless of it, mishit Titmus straight to Barrington at cover. A catch was finally held. Harvey, who can do nothing ungracefully, had salvaged respect but in general this patchy and fortuitous innings, skeletal in substance, evoked more sadness than nostalgia. Three runs later Simpson, curiously still without a Test 100, made overmuch room in an attempt to cut Titmus and was bowled. It had been a sound, restorative innings, his most composed so far, if somewhat limited in scope. Simpson's batting has a disregard for the expansive manner that is truly Scottish. The new ball was only 23 runs off, but Dexter had little alternative but to keep Statham, already over-committed, going at Booth and O'Neill, both newly arrived. He shaved the stumps of each in turn, while Titmus at the other end had O'Neill, breathing defiance, pushing forward just square of where Barrington was posted at short mid-on. The scoring had dried up completely, the batsmen on a high wire. O'Neill, fretting, moved out now and swung across a curving half-volley from Titmus, his mind seemingly made up before the ball was bowled. It drifted from outside his legs. He hit over it and his middle stump drooped. Three wickets had gone for thirteen, all to Titmus. This was O'Neill's fourth failure in five Test innings. Statham's length remained so immaculate and Titmus was so precisely on the spot that it looked as if Trueman would not, after all, get the new ball before morning. With twenty minutes left, and Australia six short of the 200, Dexter called up Barrington to hasten things on. His first three balls to Shepherd were all long-hops. Shepherd hit the first fiendishly hard along the ground to mid-wicket, the second and third had Sheppard, halfway to the boundary, leaping vainly like a goalkeeper as they cleared him by a yard or so.

Shepherd fastened on two more long-hops, which bounced just right, and twenty runs, which was more than Dexter can have bargained for, had been served up on a plate. He changed his mind about taking the new ball, letting Titmus bowl the last over. Booth, crowded out, groped forward at the second ball. It took the inside edge and dropped like a dead partridge into Trueman's lap at backward short leg. Titmus, bowling unchanged for three hours, had in his last eight overs taken 4 for 5. It was a singular achievement.

Almost single-handed, with his jerky Chaplinesque gait and control of flight, he had rescued a match that seemed to be drifting far out of England's reach. He turned few, but his taut, strung-up action, with its curving delivery and changes of pace, had kept the Australians tied miserably to their crease. He rarely managed, in the manner of earlier off-spinners like Laker and Tayfield, to get the ball to go with the arm, but if his range showed limitations, he nevertheless, with cockney tenacity, made the best of them. Without him, and Statham's untiring support, Australia would have been in a commanding position. Dexter might well regret, it seemed, the exclusion of Allen. But, despite it, and without Murray, suffering a possible dislocation of the shoulder and unlikely to return, he could take comfort over the weekend in having made Australia, 174 for 1 at a quarter to five, glad to settle for 212 for 5.

ENGLAND – First Innings

G. A. Pullar, c. Benaud, b. Simpson	53
D. S. Sheppard, c. McKenzie, b. Davidson	3
E. R. Dexter, c. Lawry, b. Benaud	32
M. C. Cowdrey, c. Jarman, b. Simpson	85
K. F. Barrington, l.b.w., b. Davidson	35
P. H. Parfitt, c. Lawry, b. Simpson	0
F. J. Titmus, b. Davidson	32
J. T. Murray, l.b.w., b. Davidson	0
F. S. Trueman, b. Simpson	32
J. B. Statham, c. Benaud, b. Simpson	0
L. J. Coldwell, not out	2
Extras (l.b. 3, w. 2)	5
Total	279

FALL OF WICKETS. 1—4, 2—65, 3—132, 4—201, 5—203, 6—221, 7—221, 8—272, 9—272, 10—279.

AUSTRALIA – First Innings

W. M. Lawry, c. Murray, b. Coldwell	8
R. B. Simpson, b. Titmus	91
R. N. Harvey, c. Barrington, b. Titmus	64
B. C. Booth, c. Trueman, b. Titmus	16
N. O'Neill, b. Titmus	3
B. Shepherd, not out	18
B. N. Jarman, not out	0
Extras (b. 6, l.b. 6)	12
Total (for 5 wkts.)	212

FALL OF WICKETS. 1—14, 2—174, 3—177, 4—187, 5—212.

Third Day: The second ball of the morning, bowled by Trueman, went for four byes through Parfitt's gloves, an unkindly early underlining of Murray's ill-fortune. Trueman decided on the new ball and about the rest of the over Shepherd knew little. Dexter called up Coldwell to share it, Statham walking somewhat sadly down to third man. Jarman played the first one off his pads and Sheppard, at forward short leg, stretched out an elastic left hand, in the same movement throwing the wicket down. Jarman, intending no malice but overbalancing, found himself out. He departed thoughtfully, meditating perhaps on the consequences of the day of rest.

Davidson, within inches of being run out before he had scored, showed immediate signs of pugnaciousness. Twice he cut Trueman with resounding thuds, though in the next over he was properly at sea to him. Coldwell, after three overs for five, gave way to Statham, put on his mettle. The Hill was already as packed as on Saturday, although quieter. A fresh breeze blew under a mackerel sky. Dexter began to switch his bowlers, finding nothing quite to his taste. Statham bowled one over downwind, Coldwell two against it. Titmus, with rapid, tiny steps, hurried up to relieve Statham, opening with a maiden. Twenty-nine runs came in the hour, 14 to Davidson, 8 to Shepherd. The batting was putting on weight, as it were, relaxing rather than striving. Shepherd looked solid, Davidson had exchanged flourishes for copybook forward strokes.

Drinks arrived, seeming to go straight to Davidson's head. He danced out to Titmus, was not quite at the pitch, and the ball, taking the outside edge, dollied up to Trueman at short extra. This was the second ball of Titmus's third over, one run only having come off him. Australia were 37 behind, three wickets in hand.

Shepherd pulled Titmus to the mid-wicket fence, his first aggressive stroke of the morning. Benaud, from the start, made it plain he meant business, galvanizing Shepherd into firmer deflections and a startling cut off Statham. Dexter, treating Trueman as if he were as delicate as Mistinguette, gave Statham the brunt of the bowling at a moment when some of Trueman's undisguised hostility would have been more to the point. Statham found no edges and Benaud and Shepherd, with the field sufficiently deep, began to push and run every ball.

With Australia only five short, Titmus threw one up to Benaud who crashed it back waist high. It would have gone through him if he hadn't got his hands there. But he did, with no more fuss than a man doing up a button.

Titmus now brought one rudely back at McKenzie who looked offended at such complexities. He was rapped on the pads and hurried from the pitch as if late for pleasanter appointments.

Shepherd, fetching Titmus from outside the off stump, reached 50, a phlegmatic, calculated innings, nicely paced according to context. Australia, 290 for 9, went in for lunch eleven runs on.

It took England another three quarters of an hour to break it up. Guest produced a firm, ascetic forward prod, from time to time unbending enough to sweep Titmus or cut Trueman. Shepherd, in no trouble at all, looked there for the day, if Guest would keep him company. Trueman had to give them best. Shepherd swung Titmus for a huge six over long-on and Australia's lead had spurted to 40. Finally Guest, relenting, allowed Statham to bowl him off his pads. Titmus, in 37 overs, had taken 7 for 79, an analysis bettered by an English spinner in Australia only by Braund, Rhodes and J. C. White, a leg-spinner and two left-handers. Trueman and Statham, bowling 41 overs between them, took 0 for 68 and 1 for 67 respectively. It had not been their day.

England, for the fourth time in a row, began disastrously. Hardly had the crowd reflected the situation, stretched and re-settled than Davidson had rattled Pullar's stumps. The ball was Davidson's second, and Pullar, jabbing wretchedly across it with no movement of the feet, dragged it from outside the off stump on to his wicket. It was a thoroughly bad stroke, the head nowhere near the line. England's last four opening partnerships now read 0, 5, 4, 0.

Dexter hurried out as if he could scarcely wait to get at Davidson. He struck him past mid-on for three, glanced him to long leg and looked in customary challenging mood. Sheppard hit a full toss from Davidson to the pavilion, drove him hearteningly past cover, cut McKenzie square.

But Davidson this time was not to be thwarted. He bowled Dexter three beauties in a row, each cut sharply from leg and beating the forward push. Then, with the sixth ball of his second over, he finally took the shoulder of the bat, Dexter not properly over it, half-way between steering and defending. It flew wide of first slip, but Simpson, moving quickly with it, grabbed it in both hands. It had been Dexter's most fallible innings yet.

Sheppard, giving glimpses of Melbourne grandeur, fell abruptly from grace. The first ball of Davidson's fourth over pitched on a full length around the off stump. Sheppard, much as he had done in the first innings, failed to kill the swing decisively, and the ball, skewing away to first slip, gave Simpson a second, more comfortable catch.

It was too late for contrition. Three wickets had gone to strokes with in each case the feet wrongly placed, the intentions ambiguous. Davidson, getting life from the wicket of a kind Statham and Trueman never hinted at, swung away from and into Barrington like a magnetic compass gone berserk. It was bowling altogether unnerving in its vitality, its violent lateness of movement.

Benaud decided to bowl the last over before tea. His first ball to Cowdrey turned and bounced. Cowdrey, hypnotically following the spin, merely helped it on its way via the wicket-keeper to slip, where Simpson tumbled dog-like for his third catch. Surrender had become unconditional.

Benaud seemed intent now on humiliating Parfitt. He ringed him with three short legs, insultingly close, and Parfitt, reaching forward, edged him to each in turn. Barrington, struck about the thighs by Davidson, was stung finally into a rasping square cut, followed by a pull off Benaud that banged the pickets angrily.

McKenzie came on, and Barrington, giving himself an unnecessarily long look at a half-volley, was bowled playing back. England, with the top five wickets gone, were a paltry thirteen to the good.

Parfitt, finding no further sense in passively suffering contempt, hit Benaud over long-on and in the same over through Benaud's own outstretched hands. Defiance at this juncture had a pathetic, forlorn ring to it.

Benaud entrusted O'Neill with an over or two of googlies, Titmus cutting him correctively for four. But he next pushed blindly out at a top-spinner and Booth at leg slip caught him.

Benaud brought Davidson back to bowl at Murray, bravely, but it seemed pointlessly, coming in at his usual number. Murray, able to do little than push forward, kept Davidson out, Benaud having further need of O'Neill. The crowd, fobbed off with precious little, were streaming away. Parfitt drove Simpson high for four, then did the same to Benaud. Murray had six men round him, as if expecting him to faint. He remained upright. Enough drama had been wrung from the day, almost all of it by Australia.

It was tragic that Titmus's great effort had gone so bewilderingly to waste. But Davidson, yet again, showed that, fresh and with the new ball, he remained the master. No bowler of pace has so swung the ball since the war nor cut it so sharply off the seam. England, after the false serenity of Melbourne, were again fathoms out of their depth.

ENGLAND

First Innings		Second Innings	
G. A. Pullar, c. Benaud, b. Simpson	53	b. Davidson	0
D. S. Sheppard, c. McKenzie, b. Davidson	3	c. Simpson, b. Davidson	12
E. R. Dexter, c. Lawry, b. Benaud	32	c. Simpson, b. Davidson	11
M. C. Cowdrey, c. Jarman, b. Simpson	85	c. Simpson, b. Benaud	8
K. F. Barrington, l.b.w., b. Davidson	35	b. McKenzie	21
P. H. Parfitt, c. Lawry, b. Simpson	0	not out	26
F. J. Titmus, b. Davidson	32	c. Booth, b. O'Neill	6
J. T. Murray, l.b.w., b. Davidson	0	not out	0
F. S. Trueman, b. Simpson	32		
J. B. Statham, c. Benaud, b. Simpson	0		
L. J. Coldwell, not out	2		
Extras (l.b. 3, w. 2)	5	Extras (b. 2)	2
Total	279	Total (for 6 wkts.)	86

FALL OF WICKETS. *First Innings:* 1—4, 2—65, 3—132, 4—201, 5—203, 6—221, 7—221, 8—272, 9—272, 10—279. *Second Innings:* 1—0, 2—20, 3—25, 4—37, 5—53, 6—71.

AUSTRALIA – First Innings

W. M. Lawry, c. Murray, b. Coldwell	8
R. B. Simpson, b. Titmus	91
R. N. Harvey, c. Barrington, b. Titmus	64
B. C. Booth, c. Trueman, b. Titmus	16
N. C. O'Neill, b. Titmus	3
B. Shepherd, not out	71
B. N. Jarman, run out	0
A. K. Davidson, c. Trueman, b. Titmus	15
R. Benaud, c. and b. Titmus	15
G. D. McKenzie, l.b.w., b. Titmus	4
C. Guest, b. Statham	11
Extras (b. 10, l.b. 11)	21
Total	319

FALL OF WICKETS. 1—14, 2—174, 3—177, 4—187, 5—212, 6—216, 7—242, 8—274, 9—280, 10—319.

Fourth Day: The last rites, before a surprisingly involved crowd of 20,000, were not unduly protracted. Murray was again unchivalrously encircled, nine men staring him out from a distance of a few yards, but considering his imposed limitations he dropped down on the ball with enhancing correctness. It was Parfitt who went first, after twenty minutes tucking McKenzie off his hip into O'Neill's hands at backward short leg. Trueman belligerently lapped Benaud twice in an over to the mid-wicket fence, but then, playing a genteel, front-parlour kind of glance, was caught by Jarman on the leg side.

Davidson, hoarded for fifty minutes, was eventually allowed to bowl and his first ball predictably removed Statham's middle stump. Coldwell in the same over sliced a catch to Shepherd in the gully. Davidson, to his three annihilating wickets of the afternoon before, had added two more with almost casual detachment. His final figures were 5 for 25, McKenzie's 3 for 26. England, in an hour, had painfully scored 18 runs, Murray being undefeated. That, one-handed, he should have survived altogether for an hour and a half was in its way the cruellest comment of all on England's batting.

Australia, held up for half an hour by drizzle, scored the necessary runs without flourish. The atmosphere was like an undertaker's parlour. Trueman, pitching into the rough from around the wicket, yorked Lawry at 28, bowler and batsman equally surprised, if not exactly moved one way or the other. Harvey, batting as if with amnesia, showed moments of recollection before he played absently at Trueman and was l.b.w.

With three runs wanted, hundreds of children, over-anticipating the coming hit, invaded the pitch, removing a stump and swallowing up the players. By the time they had been dispersed, it was raining heavily. Dexter bowled the final ball at twenty-past two, exactly a day-and-a-half remaining.

ENGLAND

First Innings		Second Innings	
G. A. Pullar, c. Benaud, b. Simpson	53	b. Davidson	0
D. S. Sheppard, c. McKenzie, b. Davidson	3	c. Simpson, b. Davidson	12
E. R. Dexter, c. Lawry, b. Benaud	32	c. Simpson, b. Davidson	11
M. C. Cowdrey, c. Jarman, b. Simpson	85	c. Simpson, b. Benaud	8
K. F. Barrington, l.b.w., b. Davidson	35	b. McKenzie	21
P. H. Parfitt, c. Lawry, b. Simpson	0	c. O'Neill, b. McKenzie	28
F. J. Titmus, b. Davidson	32	c. Booth, b. O'Neill	6
J. T. Murray, l.b.w., b. Davidson	0	not out	3
F. S. Trueman, b. Simpson	32	c. Jarman, b. McKenzie	9
J. B. Statham, c. Benaud, b. Simpson	0	b. Davidson	2
L. J. Coldwell, not out	2	c. Shepherd, b. Davidson	0
Extras (l.b. 3, w. 2)	5	Extras (b. 2, l.b. 2)	4
Total	279	Total	104

FALL OF WICKETS. *First Innings:* 1—4, 2—65, 3—132, 4—201, 5—203, 6—221, 7—221, 8—272, 9—272, 10—279. *Second Innings:* 1—0, 2—20, 3—25, 4—37, 5—53, 6—71, 7—90, 8—100, 9—104, 10—104.

AUSTRALIA

First Innings		Second Innings	
W. M. Lawry, c. Murray, b. Coldwell	8	b. Trueman	8
R. B. Simpson, b. Titmus	91	not out	34
R. N. Harvey, c. Barrington, b. Titmus	64	l.b.w., b. Trueman	15
B. C. Booth, c. Trueman, b. Titmus	16	not out	5
N. C. O'Neill, b. Titmus	3		
B. Shepherd, not out	71		
B. N. Jarman, run out	0		
A. K. Davidson, c. Trueman, b. Titmus	15		
R. Benaud, c. and b. Titmus	15		
G. D. McKenzie, l.b.w., b. Titmus	4		
C. Guest, b. Statham	11		
Extras (b. 10, l.b. 11)	21	Extras (b. 5)	5
Total	319	Total (2 wkts.)	67

FALL OF WICKETS. *First Innings:* 1—14, 2—174, 3—177, 4—187, 5—212, 6—216, 7—242, 8—274, 9—280, 10—319. *Second Innings:* 1—28, 2—54.

Bowling Analysis

AUSTRALIA

	First Innings				Second Innings			
	O.	M.	R.	W.	O.	M.	R.	W.
Davidson	24.5	7	54	4	10.6	2	25	5
McKenzie	15	3	52	0	14	3	26	3
Guest	16	0	51	0	2	0	8	0
Benaud	16	2	60	1	19	10	29	1
Simpson	15	3	57	5	4	2	5	0
O'Neill					7	5	7	1

ENGLAND

	First Innings				Second Innings			
	O.	M.	R.	W.	O.	M.	R.	W.
Trueman	20	2	68	0	6	1	20	2
Statham	21.2	2	67	1	3	0	15	0
Coldwell........	15	1	41	1				
Titmus	37	14	79	7				
Barrington	8	0	43	0				
Dexter..........					3.2	0	27	0

UMPIRES: W. Smyth and I. Rowan
Total Attendance: 166,626
Total Receipts: £A38,974 17s.

Retrospect: Which of Melbourne and Sydney had been the dream, which the reality? Whatever the answer, it had taken Australia only ten days – to be more specific, one hour – to reinstate themselves. England, having emerged from one nightmare, Benaud, were deep in another, Davidson. This Australian triumph had not essentially been a team one; it belonged to Davidson alone. Australia, though they had fielded magnificently, had batted little better than at Melbourne; they had Simpson's innings, and the sturdy promise of Shepherd, to show for it, nothing else. O'Neill had lost further face, Harvey's decline from eminence persisted. Lawry and Booth, tangled up in their own protective wrappings, exuded boredom, mercifully cut short.

England, batting twice, had one hour's stability, no more. The largest crowd ever to watch a cricket match in Sydney had few images to carry away: four batsmen of arguable greatness, Dexter, Cowdrey, O'Neill and Harvey, had been on view, and between them they had scarcely produced a recallable stroke. Dexter, so coldly determined at Melbourne, had flirted perilously here in a fashion neither glamorous nor sensible. He had failed to get on top quickly or satisfyingly, and in each instance had been the victim of his own impatience. Four times now in a row he had come in with the new ball less than five runs old; twice he had carried the fight, twice had been worsted. There are no half-measures with him. Davidson, his prestige suffering badly at Dexter's hands, reasserted himself, first morally and then by completely unhorsing Dexter when it most mattered. He came within inches of bowling him for nought at Melbourne, but was roundly rebuffed. Now he could take him on again with honour satisfied. He has only a few overs these days in which to strike and he had done so.

Just as in Melbourne the middle England batting had flourished in Dexter's wake, now it shrivelled up. Graveney's absence, Murray's injury, had been bitter blows. But the gloss had simply peeled away. Parfitt fell an easy victim to simple traps, Barrington never managed to impose himself.

He looked a consolidater, not a revivalist. Titmus and Trueman had moments, but it is only in the central positions that England have any advantage. The beginning and the end live on their nerves alone.

6 From a Journal III: Sydney

Starting coincidentally with the last ball of the Test, heavy sub-tropical rain has poured down most of the week. Had England lasted another hour, it could have saved them. Sydney suddenly contracts, the harbour a churned grey, the north shore obliterated. Ferries emerge like ghosts from the mist, convoyed by gulls. The litter of sailing boats at Rush-cutter's Bay, liners at Central Quay, aircraft-carriers, freighters at Woolloomoolloo, reel under the deluge, decks awash. Later, palm trees drip, the steep streets of Paddington run like canals. Wrought-iron gleams as if newly painted. Exotic scents waft through freshened air, Rose and Double Bay full of birds and fragrantly green.

The mist lifts, and by midnight the stars crackle over a harbour glossy with reflected orange, green and red lights.

A party given eleven floors up by Qantas for the Test teams. Benaud in a Simpson's check sports coat that would enhance any English Colonel. Trueman fuming at having to go as twelfth man to Newcastle. Murray is recovering well, and should be fit for Adelaide, as also will Graveney. Mounds of oysters in crushed ice, pyramids of lobsters and prawns. Sydney a spray of neon and water.

South Australia, clearly leading the shield table, are in Sydney to play New South Wales, winners for the past nine years. The rain lets up and South Australia, put in on a wet wicket, fall to the leg-breaks of Martin and Benaud. On Saturday Harvey, in an innings of dreamlike charm, races to 231, his highest score in first-class cricket. His cutting and driving were of a precision and grace that belonged to an impressionist painting. Rumour has it that he should bat in glasses, but whether he should or not he seemed from the first to see the ball like a balloon. He despatched Sobers with the new ball and demolished Sincock, bisecting the covers as if by radar. Sincock, apart from a massive off-break that pitched outside the wretched O'Neill's off-stump and knocked down the leg, was again all over the place. He has amended his action, stooping less in delivery and aiming more consistently at the off stump. But full tosses and long-hops were dispensed with uncontrolled lavishness. Martin is a more organized cricketer altogether.

Thomas, opening the N.S.W. innings with Simpson, batted with refreshing aggression, keeping pace with Harvey. If only such as he and Favell, who batted gloriously in the second innings, could acquire a workable consistency, how much more enjoyable Test matches would be. As it is, selection for international cricket is based on quantity, not quality.

The papers are full of O'Neill's nervous tension, his need of tranquillizers; as always he looked a fine player until he got out. Nothing is wrong with technique or timing and twenty minutes from him is worth several hours of most others. He is simply out of luck.

Benaud, who has been bowling at a handkerchief in the nets during lunch, says he has got his bowling back. How much more determinedly Australians apply themselves than do the English, always practising, experimenting, adjusting. They mean to improve. The English, wearily complacent, look as if they take net practice as a chore.

Saturday night at King's Cross. Neon lights winking, the sky stabbed with green, mauve, red. Sunday papers, loud with murders, are already on sale. Jazz thumps dimly from night clubs, juke-boxes and espresso bars, dark as caves in which Central European faces swim out of the shadows. People moon past, gazing in as if at aquariums. Long brown legs everywhere, the day's sun-soaking like make-up on the skin. Midnight cinemas begin, the stars crackle, fountains spray. The air is warmly caressive, Neapolitan.

Sunday, and the beaches, Bondi, Manley, Camp Cove, are more flesh than sand. The harbour is bridal with sails. Cricket matches, with the sea beyond the boundary, compete in whiteness. The New South Head Road thickens with girls carrying tennis rackets, beach towels; everything is within reach. There's no need ever to think, the body takes over.

Towards evening the light grows syrupy, ferries, freighters, yachts glowing in orange liquid as if in some magical preservative. Wherever one drives palms rear up dark against blue sea, lemon-green sky, the pink curve of the bridge. The ocean is like an octopus reaching into everything.

Later, dining by the water, the stars seem close enough to touch, a mere extension of the skyline. The sea washes gently under the hulls of moored boats, its surface splashed with light. Tomorrow is another day.

Sid Barnes, in his 'Like It, or Lump It' column in the *Sydney Sunday Telegraph*, sets about Keith Miller for attributing O'Neill's and Harvey's Test failures to Bradman's dressing-room interference. 'I played cricket with Keith Miller', Barnes writes, 'and in those days Sir Donald also used to call in and have a yarn with us. He was our skipper. He was very much less a nuisance than the tribe of bookies, jockeys and other such personalities who used to visit Mr Miller in the dressing room.'

Barnes also asserts, 'Sir Donald does not advise batsmen, bowlers, or captain Richie Benaud unless he is asked to do so. Then he will talk *ad infinitum* if necessary. . . .'

Today, both Neil Harvey and Alan Davidson announced their retirement from first-class cricket. It is nearly fifteen years since Harvey, then nineteen, made a century in his first Test against England. Cardus called him Mozartian. He was certainly the most unobtrusive of the great post-war batsmen. He never seized the imagination, or button-holed the onlooker. He lacked magnetism and aggressiveness. One could forget he was on the field – until the ball went to him. But once in action, the grace, the physical co-ordination, the footwork, the brilliance of execution, revealed him indelibly. His throwing from cover was beautiful and deadly. Batting, strokes streamed from him almost as if he had not made them himself. His quickness into position, his instinctive judgment and eye, tended to simplify the whole art of batting, so that one was conscious of ease and felicity, never of struggle. When he was out of touch he could look more fallible than most, but this was simply because his methods were based on instinctive appreciation, on fluid principles that never congealed. I cannot ever remember being bored by Harvey. At his best, he had a magical fluency, a lightness of touch that, even on bad wickets, prevented him from getting bogged down. Perhaps he was Mozartian, if by that one means effortlessness and virtuosity, a control that had long since progressed beyond the mere mastery of techniques. The good player makes one conscious of his methods, of the skeletal origin; the great one leaves one admiring and exhilarated, the bone filleted. Harvey made no demands on the spectator; he beguiled him, occasionally astonished, but it was with diffidence, with tact and courtesy.

Davidson, for long deprived of the new ball by Lindwall and Miller, both for New South Wales and Australia – for Australia Bill Johnston also got earlier use of it – emerged finally as the greatest exponent of fast left-arm bowling since the war. During his Test apprenticeship he fielded at leg slip so magnificently – his particular yen was for Hutton, whose leg glances he intercepted from positions that seemed in no way involved – and batted at number 8 with such dash that it seemed of little consequence whether he bowled or not. In fact, he was always primarily a bowler and once Lindwall and Miller were out of the way he quickly established himself. He learned from Johnston the angles at the disposal of the left-hander, the use of the crease and the way to slant the ball across the body or cut it off the seam. But where Johnston bowled with nagging accuracy at fast-medium, Davidson was able, over short periods, to produce bursts of real speed. He had a nasty bouncer, his in-swing was late and sharp, he got the ball to go with the arm outside the off stump and lift devastatingly.

No more than Harvey was he a flamboyant character. His manner was thoughtful, his behaviour introspective. He gave the appearance at times of hypochondria, so constant was his attention to muscular twinges, pains or malaises, revealed by flexings of the knee or rubbings of one kind or another. Fast bowlers tend to enjoy such focusings of concern, testimony as it were to the hazards of their occupation.

Davidson seemed frequently listless, ineffectual; then just when the burdens of life appeared too heavy even for his stoical shoulders, he would suddenly shrug off the years, the mood, the anxiety, and emerge – as at Sydney last week – altogether lethal. It was as if some ballistic problem he had been ruminating for weeks had magically resolved itself. The bowler stood revealed in the full mastery of his art.

7 Adelaide: The Fourth Test

The weather in Sydney looked to be breaking, but, as we flew towards Adelaide, the blue threw wide curves around the Viscount, the red plains below alluring and flat as if they'd been rolled. Flying, even more than driving, one is made conscious of the Australian immensity, the passive indifference of the land, the separateness of man from man.

Rivers, snaking pallidly through the red emptiness, appeared almost to lose heart, but wound on unattended. Scattered towns, their roofs seen from above glinting like broken glass, formed neat squares, then gave out. Heat and sheer space defeated them. There was too much of everything, too little of it productive.

At Sydney airport the Duke of Norfolk, returning from snow-bound London, took over from Billy Griffith. Three hours later, in Adelaide, he answered a barrage of questions, re-affirmed his optimism, and drove off with Dexter and Cowdrey.

England had already announced twelve names for the Test; Illingworth, Graveney and Smith coming in for Murray and Parfitt, both unfit. Allen was again overlooked.

Australia had dropped Guest and Jarman, Mackay and Grout, both nearer forty than thirty, returning. McLachlan of South Australia was in the twelve, but after a bad match against New South Wales looked certain to be twelfth man.

Both teams had work-outs at the Oval, over-watered pitches making net practice impracticable. The Governor gave a party at Government House, the Australians, as is their eve-of-test custom, dined together, the Duke of Norfolk and Ted Dexter, sharing a table at Ernest's overlooking the river, ate to soft lights and sweet music. It was symptomatic, somehow, of a difference in approach.

First Day: Oven-like heat, the sky cloudless, the Mount Lofty Hills muffled in haze. By breakfast, queues stretched through the Creswell Gardens, traffic began piling up over the Bridge.

At half-past ten the Police Band struck up, the England players turned their arms over in the nets. Statham flattened Sheppard's off stump. Trueman puffed at a cigarette and said he felt fabulous.

Benaud and Dexter walked out to toss and Dexter, throwing his arms up, signalled the worst. The ground hummed, the pitch looked perfect. Coldwell and McLachlan were left out of the respective twelves.

Trueman bowled the first over to Lawry, whose bat seemed stuck to the crease. Simpson glanced Statham's fourth ball and Smith, diving, caught it. The gift seemed too good to be true, but Simpson was walking away, nevertheless. Lawry, even more constipated than usual, prodded at Trueman and the ball flew from his bat on to his pads and over Titmus's head at forward short leg. Twice Trueman beat Harvey outside the off stump and an over later Harvey turned Statham off his legs, Dexter at leg slip getting a finger nail to it. Sweat poured from the bowlers, the batsmen seemed mummified.

After forty-five minutes, with Australia 15 for 1, Dexter brought on Illingworth in place of Trueman. Lawry, like a hypnotized stoat, made virtually no movement of his bat and was bowled by one that floated in between bat and pad. Illingworth, bowling round the wicket to three short legs, was meticulous in length. The Australians were under siege.

Harvey at last lifted it, driving first Statham then Trueman through the covers. He now drove at Illingworth, mishit, and Cowdrey at short slip dropped the catch. Harvey swung across the line of the next ball, and it went straight into and out of Sheppard's hands at short fine leg. There was a stunned silence. Harvey, then 11, hung his head on the handle of his bat. Sheppard looked as if he wanted the ground to swallow him. The fielders turned away, beyond pity.

Harvey, sensing that no harm could come to him, cut

airily and drove. Booth settled in, coming down the pitch to Illingworth, but finding no gaps. Illingworth pitched outside Harvey's off stump and Harvey, lying back, slashed him wide of short third man.

Dexter relieved Trueman forty minutes before lunch. Booth drove his first ball to the cover boundary, placed him to leg. Fifty went up. Harvey, 26, drove at Dexter, got the finest edge and the ball went through Cowdrey's hands at first slip, waist-high. There seemed some demon abroad, guiding Harvey's elbow, nudging everyone else's. It was as if England, half-doped by sun, were blatantly conspiring to make Harvey's last Adelaide appearance memorable, come what may.

Now both Harvey and Booth in turn moved out to Illingworth and drove past mid-off. Harvey cut Dexter to the cover boundary. Booth steered him, but was beaten twice outside the off stump, once nearly bowled. At lunch Australia were 82, Harvey 45, Booth 27. What it could have been was too painful to contemplate.

The band returned, the temperature climbed towards ninety, the palm-trees drooped. Picnics were spread under striped parasols, the grass banks were a sprawl of bare legs and arms.

Dexter afterwards assumed some of the burden himself, bowling round the wicket, with Trueman toiling at the other end.

Harvey passed 50, but showed no self-approval. Booth looked stringily secure. The fielding grew grotesquely inept. After half an hour Statham and Titmus took over. Titmus's first ball pitched on Booth's off stump, drifting across. Booth pushed out and Cowdrey at slip clutched the ball to his middle, putting it in his pocket. The crowd looked puzzled. Booth departed.

O'Neill, three short legs brazenly close, played most of that over with his pads. He was wearing his lucky lemon socks. He was also troubled by flies and after five minutes changed his gloves. Statham bowled at him with neither long leg nor third man, using three slips and two backward short legs. O'Neill went to force Titmus off his legs and Dexter, the middle of the short legs, could have caught him had he not turned his head. In the next over O'Neill viciously swept and cut Titmus, Dexter this time having good reason to duck.

O'Neill, looking the better for these, drove Illingworth to the sightscreen, slicing the next ball over Cowdrey at slip for four more. Harvey, seeming sleepy, sent for his cap, affording him total disguise, as well as shade. O'Neill jumped out to Titmus, clipping him past extra cover. He was in focus now, full of animal magnetism and aggression. Twice more in an over he took fours off Titmus, driving him past the lumbering Sheppard at mid-on and cutting him fine of cover. While Harvey dozed, O'Neill went, with panther-like quickness, from rout to orgy. Harvey, refreshed, hit Titmus twice to the sightscreen and in the same over to the extra cover boundary. Neither Titmus nor Illingworth had a length left, so swift were the batsmen's advances, so crisp their cutting. Dexter left them on together a shade long, their fields inadequately spread, so that boundaries soared while singles dwindled. Coming on himself before tea he halted O'Neill in his tracks, nearly yorking him twice in one over.

O'Neill reached 50, Harvey his 100. Quality was finally redeemed, the nonentities placed into perspective. The 100 partnership had taken ninety-six minutes, the two hours of afternoon bringing Australia 120 runs.

The band reappeared, playing *Waltzing Matilda* with something like relish. The crowd stretched, breathing contentment.

The new ball was no deterrent, extra slips quickly departing to the outfield, while O'Neill cut and Harvey glanced. It was power as against fluency, rhythm against melody.

Illingworth tried at medium pace, but he was short of a length and Harvey disposed of him behind square leg, and past cover. Dexter was tidier, getting occasional lift and keeping O'Neill on the bit; Harvey, however, could no longer be contained. Graveney, Illingworth and Sheppard each misfielded in turn and only Titmus and Barrington preserved illusions of attentiveness.

Harvey began to tire, retreating into his cap. O'Neill, lately taking stock, moved gently to his century. Having reached it he waved his bat wearily at Dexter and was caught at slip. He had made his point.

Harvey, joined by Davidson, went to his 150 by way of four overthrows that also took Australia past 300. He then drove Dexter to Statham at mid-off, raised his bat in farewell and withdrew. Two wickets had gone to exhaustion, but if anyone had earned them Dexter had.

It was not a great innings, nor should it have been an innings at all. No batsman, even Harvey, can count on three lives before thirty. But it kindled nostalgia, and once established he showed the old range of stroke, an authority never contrived or stilted. Where others flag and bog down Harvey keeps on the move. From this stems both his charm and his uncertainty.

It had been a long, tiring day. Once again England had only themselves to blame that it had not ended more agreeably. As so often in this series, the sweet smell of success was snuffed out before its bouquet could be savoured. They missed their catches, they were slow and ungainly in the deep, they fumbled close in. If England were to save the match now, they would have to do it the hard way.

AUSTRALIA – First Innings

W. M. Lawry, b. Illingworth	10
R. B. Simpson, c. Smith, b. Statham	0
R. N. Harvey, c. Statham, b. Dexter	154
B. C. Booth, c. Cowdrey, b. Titmus	34
N. C. O'Neill, c. Cowdrey, b. Dexter	100
A. K. Davidson, not out	16
B. Shepherd, not out	4
Extras (b. 1, l.b. 3)	4
Total (5 wkts.)	322

FALL OF WICKETS. 1—2, 2—16, 3—101, 4—295, 5—302.

Second Day: It was a morning for picture hats, parasols and iced hampers, a day for sea or river, not for fast bowling on a perfect wicket. The frieze of palms and eucalyptus below the heat-muffled hills were as still as if they had been painted. Nevertheless, once the national flag had been hoisted by the Duke of Norfolk in honour of Australia Day, the anniversary of Phillip's landing in 1788, and the gloomy dirge associated with it sung, Trueman and Statham each bowled several overs of impressive fieriness. Trueman softened up Shepherd with three that reared up nastily and then Statham disposed of him, taken in the gully by Trueman. This was Statham's 237th Test wicket, overhauling Alec Bedser's eight year-old world record. But it had taken him sixty-six Tests as against fifty-one. Trueman, still in the chase to beat both, now found a good one for Mackay. It took the outside edge and Smith caught him low down in front of first slip. Mackay had barely time to get through a dozen chews but he made up for it on the way in. Dexter came on after fifty minutes, and Benaud, whose technique makes a mockery of his position in the order, played two immediately identifying strokes to the cover boundary.

Dexter had quick revenge, however, getting one to whip back off the pitch and knock down Benaud's leg stump. Benaud looked offendedly up as if in their relationship such things were his privilege. Davidson, thoughtfully promoted overnight to give him the longest possible rest between batting and bowling, defied these good intentions by playing in the fashion of one not to be fobbed off with charity. He should have gone at 40, though, Titmus refusing a comfortable return catch. He responded with an off-drive that mercifully cleared Sheppard half way to the boundary, but an over later had his off bail flicked by Statham. It had been a quiet, introspective innings, spread over two-and-a-quarter hours. McKenzie, searching out Sheppard on the mid-wicket boundary, now swung prodigiously at Titmus. The ball soared as high as the adjacent spire of St Peter's Cathedral and Sheppard, a foot in from the ropes, cupped his hands under it, and miracle of miracles, it nestled.

Thus his guilty run of six successive droppings had ended. Australia, adding 71 in exactly two hours for the loss of five wickets, were all out for 393. It was a lot less than one had feared.

England, altogether brisker in the field after Friday's dopey slovenliness, had come out of the morning well. So to martial music, lunch and the renewal of anguish. Benaud gave Davidson his most aggressive field for some time; neither long leg nor third man, three slips, gully, leg slip and backward short leg. McKenzie, bowling from the Cathedral end, had much the same. His first over came near to reward, for he beat Sheppard outside the off stump, had him steer an out-swinger a yard in front of Benaud at gully, and then glance an in-swinger uppishly past leg slip for four. Pullar against Davidson was mildly encouraging: he turned him twice off his legs, placed a full toss to mid-wicket for three, and then drove him straight. Davidson, digging the ball in, strove for lift rather than swing, and Sheppard played a short one down only just out of point's reach. McKenzie, bowling with greater control than of late, was getting the ball to fly off a length. But Pullar, bowled by the sixth ball of his second over, had no such excuse. He shaped to push forward, changed his mind, and finally, offering no stroke at all, had his off stump hit by a ball that cut back a bare couple of inches.

Barrington came next, the familiar yellow tape across his bat, and his opening strokes belonged to some gothic fantasy devised with no respect for custom. Davidson, intent still on penetrating the wicket's geological foundation, dug in four in a row. Swivelling at the first, Barrington hooked it off the top edge over Grout for four. He slashed the second wide of cover's left hand to the ropes. He swished at the third and fourth, which came back at him from well outside the off stump, and cleared the slips with ease. The ball bounced happily into the crowd. Davidson, midway through his fourth over, was 0 for 30. It was too much for him. One sensed the consequences, and soon he clutched at his thigh and limped off to the dressing-room.

Barrington, who had not displayed such desperate euphoria since Hall and Watson knocked the sawdust out of him in the West Indies, sobered down at the prospect of Mackay. McKenzie changed ends and Barrington cut him for his fifth boundary in twenty runs. As if this was not drama enough, a violent fight broke out on one of the slopes, alcohol and heat producing a bare-knuckle bout worthy of the Ned Kelly era. Beer cans rained, but order was quickly restored. Mackay's bowling can reduce even the wildest of colonial boys to apathy.

Benaud quickly discarded Mackay, himself opening with a maiden to Sheppard before Barrington pulled a long-hop to the fence. McKenzie came off after seventy minutes lively bowling, much of it short but never comfortable to play. Mackay replaced him and Sheppard, driving at his first ball, sliced it over third slip for four. No one could complain that the batting lacked originality. Sheppard next came down the pitch to Benaud and drove him sweetly through the covers. Barrington, less puppet-like and jerky now the fast bowlers were tamed, played Mackay smoothly on both sides of the wicket. It had seemed that the tremors had finally subsided when, twenty minutes before tea, Benaud threw one up to Sheppard, flighting it beautifully. Sheppard, rising as innocently as a trout to the most bewitching fly, came after it, found himself well short, and was stumped by a yard. It was almost too casually done. The score at tea was 87, the temperature 92°.

Dexter, after his considerable bowl, wisely kept his feet up, and it was Cowdrey, on the ground where he had last topped 300, who joined Barrington. He at once pulled Benaud first bounce into the stand at mid-wicket and generally gave off an air of affability and ease, if not of command. It is the absence of a will to dominate, allowing the bowlers to take pleasure in themselves, that holds Cowdrey back from greatness.

Barrington drove Benaud hummingly to the sightscreen and, chopping him past slip, reached 50. His bat now was as straight in defence as if his arms were in splints. He slashed Benaud along the ground past cover and his general acquisitiveness approached the obsessive. McKenzie, meanwhile, searched for yorkers, Barrington scooping them out with evident difficulty. At 117, forty minutes after tea, Simpson relieved Benaud, sea-gulls suddenly circling behind him. They settled, were dispersed, and finally spread themselves in committee. Barrington moved out to his first ball, was beaten in the flight as he made to push it to leg, and was bowled. He looked back as if his ears as well as his eyes had deceived him. Two runs later Cowdrey, driving at McKenzie, who had been brought back for Dexter, was given out caught at the wicket. He made no move to go and seemed surprised at the decision. Dexter and Graveney each played handsome strokes wide of mid-on, but for some time Dexter was pinned down by Simpson, who had fastened on to a fretting length. Simpson has little of Benaud's rhythmical and lilting poise in delivery but he adds to a well marked googly greatly improved control and a variousness of flight. Dexter was bound soon to take out this enforced curtailment on someone and Mackay suited him nicely. He swung him contemptuously to the palings at square leg and running down the pitch to the next ball crashed it against the sight-screen.

There was a repressed fury to these strokes that made Graveney, when he twice beat the field with off drives, seem gently sensuous in comparison. Dexter could not suggest languor if he tried and when Simpson pitched short he struck him with cross-batted savagery towards the marquee at long-on. Next he drove past extra cover with imperial splendour. It was exciting rather than soothing to watch, for, despite the evident disdain, his rapid movements up and down the pitch left little margin for error. All the same, it was Graveney, looking the more relaxed and secure, who went. McKenzie managed to get one to kick, and Graveney, fending it off his chest, quietly found Booth at backward short leg off his glove. Dexter, as if in irritation, ran out to Simpson and twice in three balls hit him high and straight for six. It was a lavish retort, and no other batsman in the world, in such a context and with only twelve minutes left, would have contemplated it. Benaud returned and Dexter hammered him to the cover boundary. He glanced McKenzie, who still had energy to rap Dexter on the fingers, to reach 50 and it had taken him only seventy-five minutes. No innings of more impeccable judgment, nor purer antagonism, had yet been played in the series.

It had been a good day, not exactly favourable to England, but with point and sparkle. Wickets had fallen, strokes had been made. The ball had scarcely turned, and the pitch was such that it was not likely to. Still, there had been Dexter's innings, with two sixes and six fours in fifty runs, and that was worth anyone's money. McKenzie, deprived of Davidson, had bowled 17 overs with remarkable spirit and stamina, always attacking. He had served Benaud well. Much would depend on the new ball, due early on Monday, on Dexter's resistance to it and the fidelity of the others. Had Harvey gone when he should, it might have been altogether different. But the match was alive, the weather, with the sky yellowing over the river and the sun plunging the ocean, promising. It was, in the circumstances, as much as we could hope for.

AUSTRALIA – First Innings

W. M. Lawry, b. Illingworth	10
R. B. Simpson, c. Smith, b. Statham	0
R. N. Harvey, c. Statham, b. Dexter	154
B. C. Booth, c. Cowdrey, b. Titmus	34
N. C. O'Neill, c. Cowdrey, b. Dexter	100
A. K. Davidson, b. Statham	46
B. Shepherd, c. Trueman, b. Statham	10
K. D. Mackay, c. Smith, b. Trueman	1
R. Benaud, b. Dexter	16
G. D. McKenzie, c. Sheppard, b. Titmus	15
A. W. T. Grout, not out	1
Extras (l.b. 5, w. 1)	6
Total	393

FALL OF WICKETS. 1—2, 2—16, 3—101, 4—295, 5—302, 6—331, 7—336, 8—366, 9—383, 10—393.

ENGLAND – First Innings

G. A. Pullar, b. McKenzie	9
D. S. Sheppard, st. Grout, b. Benaud	30
K. F. Barrington, b. Simpson	63
M. C. Cowdrey, c. Grout, b. McKenzie	13
E. R. Dexter, not out	50
T. W. Graveney, c. Booth, b. McKenzie	22
F. J. Titmus, not out	2
Extras (b. 1, l.b. 2)	3
Total (5 wkts.)	192

FALL OF WICKETS. 1—17, 2—84, 3—117, 4—119, 5—165.

Third Day: The Sunday had been cloudy, with agreeable junketings at Yalumba, the Smith vineyards in the Barossa Valley. Much of the settlements there are of long-standing German origin, tiny wooden churches nestling among hills, much as along the Rhine. Only here palms line the red soil, the villages have pillared pubs that could only be Australian, and the space oppresses.

Overnight the rain drifted steadily up and by morning the swish of cars on the roads told their story without need for confirmatory glances skywards. Until nearly lunch time it persisted, the hills blanketed, the trees dripping. Crowds sat in the stands like waxworks, absorbed by nothing. The news was that Davidson would not field, and would bat only in emergency. The band marched, piping to keep their spirits up.

At a quarter to two the teams came out, the sky still blueless and threatening. Seagulls sought sanctuary by the sightscreen, ignoring the damp. McKenzie and Mackay bowled, the new ball denied them. There was a certain unreality about it, as if the plot was over. But in fact there was time enough, as far as England were concerned, for disaster if not dynamite.

Dexter in any case was in no humour for fireworks. He played with the correctness and remote courtesy of an Italian nobleman entertaining tenants. Just as his demeanour was irreproachable, so was his technique. His withdrawal seemed almost religious, the sadist turned mystic.

Titmus, on the other hand, was chirpy, good-humoured,

quite evidently flourishing. If Dexter chose to deny himself, he would, like Horatio in Hamlet's absence, assume the stage. He cut, he deflected, and when after forty minutes Benaud came on, he drove opulently.

Dexter showed signs now of renewed appetite, but he had fasted too long. McKenzie pitched short to the off, Dexter voraciously flashed, and Grout, far back, fastened on it as it shot high to his right. It was a ball that – if one can apply such obtuse terms to Dexter – need not have been played, perhaps a shade too close to the body and lifting too steeply for cutting. Dexter had looked in the mood for a long innings.

Illingworth played Benaud at full stretch, but calmly. He hooked once and swept, making contact. Against McKenzie he looked fragile, soon to be brushed aside. McKenzie, having been given the new ball, got one to leave him, Illingworth touched it, and Grout threw it up.

Titmus struck Mackay twice through the covers, was dropped off McKenzie by O'Neill at second slip, and gently prospered. McKenzie, cooled by refreshing drizzle, showed even after two hours no loss of pace or lift. He strode his nine lengthening paces, opened his shoulders, and let go. Smith knew little of several, Titmus not much more. By tea, when England were 263 for 7, McKenzie had bowled eleven overs, taking 5 for 74 in all.

He bowled again afterwards, a rainbow on the hills beyond him, the outfield awash with non-playing, non-paying gulls. Smith, made hideously inept by McKenzie, lifted Mackay over his head, snicked him past slip. The gulls squawked. Smith tried again but, though he achieved height, he lacked distance. Lawry at deep mid-off caught him, giving Mackay his first wicket of the series. Titmus in the same over chastened him, hitting to the cover boundary and pulling him next ball for four to square leg. The recording of these took him to 50, an innings bright as a button.

Trueman thrashed McKenzie through the covers, an intimidatory stroke that suggested business. Benaud offered himself as replacement for Mackay, a move Trueman acknowledged by carting his first ball to long-off for six. He hit the third first bounce to the same place, and now Benaud dropped a man back. Trueman did not score off the next three, but pulled the last with fine discrimination between mid-wicket and long-on. Benaud pitched short in the next over and Trueman humped him down to long leg. He satisfied himself that the next was ripe for plunder, swung and was decently caught by a man in the first row of the stalls.

Titmus took accommodating singles and Trueman swatted Mackay over long-on. He had grown heady with success now, scornful of length; he reached at a wider, shorter one and Benaud got under a skier at mid-off. Trueman withdrew, muttering imprecations. But 52 had been added, his own share 38.

Depressed by Trueman's dismissal, the umpires conferred, deciding that if Trueman could not see, no one could. It was odd logic, for the light was reasonable. They called a halt forty minutes early, leaving the gulls and perambulating girls in uncontested possession.

Australia had lost, England gained, rather over three hours. Titmus 57 not out, had, with Trueman's bludgeoning support, taken England within striking distance.

Near enough, it seemed, at least for the match not to be lost.

AUSTRALIA – First Innings

W. M. Lawry, b. Illingworth	10
R. B. Simpson, c. Smith, b. Statham	0
R. N. Harvey, c. Statham, b. Dexter	154
B. C. Booth, c. Cowdrey, b. Titmus	34
N. C. O'Neill, c. Cowdrey, b. Dexter	100
A. K. Davidson, b. Statham	46
B. Shepherd, c. Trueman, b. Statham	10
K. D. Mackay, c. Smith, b. Trueman	1
R. Benaud, b. Dexter	16
G. D. McKenzie, c. Sheppard, b. Titmus	15
A. W. T. Grout, not out	1
Extras (l.b. 5, w. 1)	6
Total	393

FALL OF WICKETS. 1—2, 2—16, 3—101, 4—295, 5—302, 6—331, 7—336, 8—366, 9—383, 10—393.

ENGLAND – First Innings

G. A. Pullar, b. McKenzie	9
D. S. Sheppard, st. Grout, b. Benaud	30
K. F. Barrington, b. Simpson	63
M. C. Cowdrey, c. Grout, b. McKenzie	13
E. R. Dexter, c. Grout, b. McKenzie	61
T. W. Graveney, c. Booth, b. McKenzie	22
F. J. Titmus, not out	57
R. Illingworth, c. Grout, b. McKenzie	12
A. C. Smith, c. Lawry, b. Mackay	13
F. S. Trueman, c. Benaud, b. Mackay	38
J. B. Statham, not out	0
Extras (b. 5, l.b. 5)	10
Total (9 wkts.)	328

FALL OF WICKETS. 1—17, 2—84, 3—117, 4—119, 5—165, 6—226, 7—246, 8—275, 9—327.

Fourth Day: England lasted another seven minutes, scoring three runs. Then Statham, aiming to steer Mackay, was triflingly bowled. Titmus was left to meditate on the consequences of first principles being so wilfully disregarded. Mackay loped off with three wickets.

The clouds were puffily black, but higher. The seagulls looked surly, as if after a bad night. Trueman bowled a good over at Lawry, beating him and getting one to hop off his glove just short of gully. Statham prepared to bowl, and now gusts of drizzle blew in from the sea. It had not happened in Adelaide, they said, during forty years of Test cricket.

There was time to reflect on the disfigured skyline, the beauty of mackintoshed girls, the stateliness of the Moreton Bay figs massed below the cathedral. Australia, with a lead of 62, had, rain permitting, five or six hours to increase this to 350 before Benaud, with a lop-sided attack, could hope to declare. He would be hard put to get England in before nightfall, should victory still be in his mind. It was soon evident it was not.

At noon, with twenty minutes lost, Statham finished his over. The rain had given way to glare, with patches of blue emerging. Trueman was fiery, Lawry like some beaky bird swaying on its perch. Simpson drew back as if stung from one that flew past his face, and then took one above the elbow, throwing his bat down in pain. Trueman affected to comfort him, then bounced the next ball over his head. Such is brotherly love.

For some time both batsmen were more concerned to protect their bodies than their stumps. Trueman cut his run after half an hour, during which two runs had been scored off him in five overs, and went round the wicket to Lawry. Dexter brought up two backward short legs, himself in front and almost in the shadow of Lawry's cap. Lawry snicked Trueman to the long leg boundary, and in the same over sliced a drive to Graveney at second slip. He seemed to disown both strokes, remaining rooted to the spot, until discharged.

Dexter bowled in Statham's place, but was wide and short. Trueman from long leg overthrew, so used his left hand, adjusting the range. Dexter rested Trueman, and Harvey drove Statham to the cover boundary. He played forward somewhat loosely in the same over and Barrington in the gully took a casual catch. Australia, 37 for 2, were 99 ahead.

They looked in no hurry to add to this after lunch. Trueman and Statham, their edge gone, bowled accurately at not much over medium pace for forty minutes. Simpson seemed sleepily, Booth, jerkily content. The crowd dozed, aware that, temporarily anyway, the game was floundering. Simpson, every so often, tested the alertness of the fielders, tapping the ball a yard or two, and scampering. He was altogether too nippy. Booth stabbed and jabbed his way to 10 after an hour.

Titmus, bowling with no one deep, was more to Booth's liking and twice in an over he ran out and drove him past mid-on. Simpson, though coming well down the pitch, declined to do this, pushing the ball back to Titmus. Dexter bowled for the best part of an hour, neither achieving much, nor giving much. Booth, eyeing the open spaces, swung Titmus for six to long-on. Dexter's placing of fields bore no close relation to the saving of runs. The batting, perhaps, had drugged him. Simpson reached 50, in three hours, as inexpressive an innings as a clock without hands. He, like time, existed, that is all one could say; and human frailty in the machinery was not evident. By tea Australia were 128, Simpson 57, Booth 45. It had been a dull business.

Benaud, it seemed, was content that wickets should not be lost, rather than the tempo accelerated. Simpson, save for one square cut off Statham, went placidly on. Booth, savouring the delights of Illingworth, at last given a bowl instead of Titmus, used his feet to drive, and when Illingworth dropped shorter, pulled and cut. He had taken thirty runs between mid-on and square leg before Dexter sealed the boundaries.

Booth, flourishingly ahead now of Simpson, hit Dexter low to Barrington's left hand at mid-wicket and got away with it. Simpson flicked at the next ball and was taken at the wicket. Dexter greeted O'Neill with a spirited bouncer, then was cut for a single. Booth edged him past slip for four, ducked under another bouncer. Dexter dug the last ball in outside the leg stump, Booth glanced, and Smith was across to catch it. It had been an eventful over; there were stirrings now of interest.

Dexter modestly took himself off, bringing back Trueman. The first ball flew past Shepherd's head, so did the last. Dexter decided after all to preserve these energies for the new ball and returned himself. He kept O'Neill impressively quiet, and Shepherd, showing signs of belligerence, soon mishit him to extra cover.

Allen fielded there in Sheppard's absence, suffering from sore throat. Illingworth, too, had recently retired, with similar symptoms.

With half an hour left Dexter brought Trueman back for the new ball. He bowled two with the old and Mackay, dabbing at the second, was neatly taken by Graveney at second slip. Trueman took the new one, but Benaud, edging Statham twice through the slips and then swinging him to long leg, roughed it up. O'Neill played two beautiful square cuts to remind one of his presence, and then, after one ball of Trueman's last over, Benaud speculatively appealed against the light. He was allowed his way, though it seemed scarcely justified.

Australia were 291 runs on. They had gone warily, stoically putting up with much short bowling, but never pressing. There was a fatalistic air about all the batting, as if Benaud placed his reliance on England getting themselves out, saving the game without chance of winning it. Certainly, he showed no inclination for spending longer in the field without Davidson than he had to.

It was understandable, but made for drab cricket.

AUSTRALIA

First Innings		Second Innings	
W. M. Lawry, b. Illingworth	10	c. Graveney, b. Trueman	16
R. B. Simpson, c. Smith, b. Statham	0	c. Smith, b. Dexter	71
R. N. Harvey, c. Statham, b. Dexter	154	c. Barrington, b. Statham	6
B. C. Booth, c. Cowdrey, b. Titmus	34	c. Smith, b. Dexter	77
N. C. O'Neill, c. Cowdrey, b. Dexter	100	not out	22
A. K. Davidson, b. Statham	46		
B. Shepherd, c. Trueman, b. Statham	10	c. Titmus, b. Dexter	13
K. D. Mackay, c. Smith, b. Trueman	1	c. Graveney, b. Trueman	3
R. Benaud, b. Dexter	16	not out	13
G. D. McKenzie, c. Sheppard, b. Titmus	15		
A. W. T. Grout, not out	1		
Extras (l.b. 5, w. 1)	6	Extras (b. 1, l.b. 3)	4
Total	393	Total (6 wkts.)	225

FALL OF WICKETS. *First Innings:* 1—2, 2—16, 3—101, 4—295, 5—302, 6—331, 7—336, 8—366, 9—383, 10—393. *Second Innings:* 1—27, 2—37, 3—170, 4—175, 5—199, 6—205.

ENGLAND – First Innings

G. A. Pullar, b. McKenzie	9
D. S. Sheppard, st. Grout, b. Benaud	30
K. F. Barrington, b. Simpson	63
M. C. Cowdrey, c. Grout, b. McKenzie	13
E. R. Dexter, c. Grout, b. McKenzie	61
T. W. Graveney, c. Booth, b. McKenzie	22
F. J. Titmus, not out	59
R. Illingworth, c. Grout, b. McKenzie	12
A. C. Smith, c. Lawry, b. Mackay	13
F. S. Trueman, c. Benaud, b. Mackay	38
J. B. Statham, b. Mackay	1
Extras (b. 5, l.b. 5)	10
Total	331

FALL OF WICKETS. 1—17, 2—84, 3—117, 4—119, 5—165, 6—226, 7—246, 8—275, 9—327, 10—331.

Fifth Day: The heat came back with a vengeance, and it was as if it had never rained at all. The sky vacantly blue, a few white

1. The first wicket to fall—Lawry, c. Smith, b. Trueman, 5. Australia—5 for 1. Trueman, using the crease, slanted the ball skilfully across the left-handers' bodies.

2. (*left*) Statham bowls Harvey on the first day with one that came back at him. Rarely did Statham move the ball off the pitch like this.

3. (*below*) Booth, the safest player of off-spin among the Australians, swings Titmus to leg during his long, face-saving innings.

WATCHING BENAUD BOWL

Leg-spinners pose problems much like love,
Requiring commitment, the taking of a chance.
Half-way deludes; the bold advance.

Right back, there's time to watch
Developments, though maybe too late.
It's not spectacular, but can conciliate.

Instinctively romantics move towards,
Preventing complexities by their embrace,
Batsman and lover embarked as overlords.

Alan Ross

5. (*left*) Dexter, in an even duel that lasted the series, hits Benaud into the covers. Throughout, it was the English, rather than the Australian batsmen, who went through with their strokes.

6. (*below*) Statham bowls to Lawry in the Second Test. Lawry, prodding off the front foot, seized up almost completely as the summer advanced.

7. (*right*) Burge, sweeping at Titmus, is l.b.w. This fondness for the sweep cost Burge his Test place.

8. (*below*) Dexter, c. Simpson, b. Benaud, 93. After Brisbane, Benaud took few wickets, but Dexter was usually one of them.

9. (*above*) Graveney, back at his beguiling best, pulls Benaud for four. This was the beginning of Graveney's spirited return to form.

10. (*left*) Australia, cruising comfortably in their second innings, were halted by Trueman. Here he uproots Simpson's middle stump; next ball O'Neill was caught at slip.

11. (*above*) Mackay l.b.w. to Trueman with the new ball. He was altogether out of his depth.
12. Benaud caught by Cowdrey off Trueman with the new ball. This was the finest catch in a series that saw both great and disastrous catching.

13. Sheppard, driving Benaud, reaches his hundred with a stroke that was also a sharp return catch to the bowler.

14. The match-winners of the Second Test. Trueman, Dexter, Sheppard, Cowdrey. A fortnight later the bubble had burst.

15. (*above*) The Selection Committee in session at Sydney.

16. The Third Test. Sheppard, c. McKenzie, b. Davidson, 12. Davidson cut the ball across Sheppard's body and Sheppard, pushing out inside the line, got a thick edge.

17. (*above*) Dexter drives Davidson past mid-off. Early on he hit Davidson back with great ferocity, but Davidson, in the second innings, got his revenge. Later, Dexter dropped down to number five when a quick wicket fell.

18. Cowdrey batting against Davidson during his innings of 85. Cowdrey's technique against the ball leaving him, head well over the line, was the safest among the English batsmen.

19 and 20. Two pictures of Simpson's fluent first innings of 91. *Above*, he is cutting; *below*, he has made so much room to cut that he is out of the picture as he is bowled by Titmus.

21. (*above*) Cowdrey, c. Simpson, b. Benaud, 8. Benaud got this both to turn and bounce. With Cowdrey's dismissal, England's hopes of adequate recovery in the Third Test disappeared.

22. (*below*) Alan Davidson's follow-through. Murray backs up.

23. (*above*) Murray, batting with an injured shoulder, made a valiant effort to save the Third Test for England. McKenzie bowls. Seven Australian fieldsmen cluster around.

24. (*below*) Davidson removes Statham's middle stump to clean up England's second innings.

25. (*above*) A premature end to the Third Test. Excited schoolchildren swarm on to the pitch before the winning stroke has been made.
26. (*below*) Harvey dropped at 11 by Cowdrey off Illingworth on the first morning of the Fourth Test. Had Cowdrey, at short slip, caught this after knocking it up, Australia would have been 35 for 3.

27. (*above*) O'Neill, during his first innings of 100, sweeps Titmus. Dexter, who consistently fielded too close to the bat to catch anything except snicks off the pad, ducks.

28. (*right*) Barrington, promoted to first wicket down for the last two Tests, hits a ball from Benaud for four during his century in the Fifth Test. He scored his vast number of runs largely by cuts and sweeps.

29. (*above*) Titmus, whose partnerships with Trueman were invaluable to England, steers a ball from Davidson past McKenzie for a single.

30. (*left*) The final stand of the series which England could not break. Here Cowdrey dives but fails to hold a chance given by Burge off Allen.

puffs over the hills like gunshot. Illingworth and Sheppard, the pharyngitis victims, remained in their hotels, awaiting summons.

Benaud had announced overnight that he would bat out the innings. In fact, helped along by their own woeful catching, it eventually became in England's interest to let Benaud continue as long as possible. He did just that, getting out himself in the last over before lunch.

He should have gone in the first over. Trueman's seventh ball to him pitched short on the leg stump and he turned it quietly to Titmus at backward short leg. Just as quietly Titmus put it down, as if not interested in such simple stuff.

Trueman, in his next over, got one to lift outside O'Neill's off stump. O'Neill got the finest of edges and Cowdrey at first slip caught him unconcernedly.

Benaud, reprieved, now batted as if in front of a mirror, narcissistic but scornful of runs. McKenzie drove Trueman to the sightscreen and was generally no less formal than Benaud. The bowlers treated their opposite numbers with faultless courtesy.

Dexter bowled after forty minutes and Benaud cut him, not offensively but as if regrettably left no alternative. It was, after all, a very short ball. Trueman came off after fifty-five minutes, a decent spell, but not in a context calculated to fire him. He looked loose and free, a picture of a fast bowler going through the motions without animosity.

Statham relieved him and McKenzie, playing inside the line, was caught at the wicket. The first hour had brought Australia thirty runs. Davidson, accompanied by Simpson, limped stiffly out, a martyr to affliction. Not always the best judge of direction, he raised his bat and had his off-stump knocked back. The cortège retreated at funereal pace.

Grout had other ideas, covetous perhaps of Lawry's position. Indeed, it might have been the opening pair in action. Trueman bowled again at half-pace and Benaud met him with a forward stroke of irreproachable correctness. Grout imitated him, almost mimicking. It had become a *pas de deux*, demonstrably pleasant for the participants, puzzling for onlookers. Those in the sun clapped ironically; Benaud showed studied indifference. Grout, less aloof, lofted Titmus to long-off where Pullar dropped him. Grout did better two balls later, clearing him comfortably. Benaud, it was clear, would not declare. Dexter intimated that it was all right by him. Trueman bowled the last over before lunch, and Benaud, on 48, lashed him to cover where Barrington took a fine catch. The applause for Benaud was scant: the bars buzzed with disgruntled imbibers. Australia's lead was 355, with four hours left. It was no score to chase, though if Titmus had not despised his catch, it could well have been. Such idle pottering deserved an idle answer.

Sheppard, looking pale, and with a temperature, came out with Pullar, and soon over-leisurely lunchers were prised out of detachment by two roars, hard on each other. Sheppard drove weakly at Mackay's first ball, it flew to Benaud at second slip, was juggled there, and as it fell a second time was finally grabbed over Simpson's body by Grout. Pullar drove inside a half-volley from McKenzie in the next over and Simpson at first slip took a sharp catch. England were 4 for 2.

McKenzie went off for boot repairs and Benaud bowled with Mackay. Cowdrey struck his first ball for four, looking replete and serene. Barrington, jumpily at first, should have been caught at gully off McKenzie, but Benaud had set third man instead. Already he had turned his back on victory. Barrington prospered, hammering Mackay into the covers. Cowdrey cut and drove Benaud, who bowled without guile. Soon O'Neill was on, and Cowdrey, forcing off the back foot, edged him wide of slip.

Barrington entered now one of those plushy Edwardian periods when the bowlers, like serving wenches, seemed desirous merely to please him. He swept to the square leg boundary, he cut, he despatched full-tosses, off-drove half-volleys. At the end of each over he collected a single for the strike. Then again he swept and cut. One moment 20 to Cowdrey's 30, he was soon humming past 60, hell-bent. Cowdrey was put out to grass, as it were. He got out of touch, and also, it appeared, out of condition. For Barrington, having put O'Neill's throwing from cover more than once to the test, called him for a sharp one, Cowdrey started sluggishly and O'Neill's throw, like its predecessor, came in like a bullet.

It was senseless, and Cowdrey's face showed it. Barrington cut Simpson again, and O'Neill, throwing from the fence, had him scrambling home for his second. It was preciously close. England at tea were 112 for 3, safe enough it seemed; an illusion Benaud looked keen to propagate, understandably in the circumstances.

But Dexter, shutting up shop, went quickly, scooped off the grass by Simpson at short slip as he pushed forward at Benaud. Now Benaud had 100 minutes left, six wickets to get. The match, apparently gone off the boil, was gently bubbling again.

McKenzie bounced several at Graveney, then one fairly leaped off a length to crack him on the elbow. It was a nasty delivery, more so even than that which took Graveney's wicket in the first innings. Graveney had need of drink, and a rest, and when he had recovered McKenzie knocked the bat from his hand with a high full toss. He let fly again, hitting Barrington in the kidneys. Barrington cut him for four. It was aggressive, discomforting bowling, produced with the minimum expenditure of effort.

Benaud brought back O'Neill and Barrington swung a long-hop for four. Graveney swept Benaud to long leg, drove O'Neill expressively through the covers. At five o'clock, with an hour left, England were 155, Barrington 92, Graveney 17.

O'Neill produced two more long-hops and Graveney put both away. Simpson bowled, and Barrington, opening his shoulders, swung him high to long-on for six. It took him to his 100, half of it in boundaries, made in just under three hours.

Benaud went round the wicket, the seagulls circled, their wings taking the late sun. Barrington, idling after his 100, swung Simpson for another six, pulled him for four.

Benaud, with half an hour left and the new ball seven runs

off, enticed Graveney with full-tosses but he wasn't having any. He called up Lawry, who bowled left-handed. Barrington watched him in disbelief. So Grout let go eight byes, four of them wide.

At twenty to six, somewhat spendthrift, McKenzie took the new ball. He could scarcely get to the wicket, though twice he earned the edge of Barrington's bat. The police took up station on the boundary, McKenzie managed a bouncer, the crowd, all but a few sunbathers, drifted away.

AUSTRALIA

First Innings		Second Innings	
W. M. Lawry, b. Illingworth	10	c. Graveney, b. Trueman	16
R. B. Simpson, c. Smith, b. Statham	0	c. Smith, b. Dexter	71
R. N. Harvey, c. Statham, b. Dexter	154	c. Barrington, b. Statham	6
B. C. Booth, c. Cowdrey, b. Titmus	34	c. Smith, b. Dexter	77
N. C. O'Neill, c. Cowdrey, b. Dexter	100	c. Cowdrey, b. Trueman	23
A. K. Davidson, b. Statham	46	b. Statham	2
B. Shepherd, c. Trueman, b. Statham	10	c. Titmus, b. Dexter	13
K. D. Mackay, c. Smith, b. Trueman	1	c. Graveney, b. Trueman	3
R. Benaud, b. Dexter	16	c. Barrington, b. Trueman	48
G. D. McKenzie, c. Sheppard, b. Titmus	15	c. Smith, b. Statham	13
A. W. T. Grout, not out	1	not out	16
Extras (l.b. 5, w. 1)	6	Extras (b. 1, l.b. 4)	5
Total	393	Total	293

FALL OF WICKETS. *First Innings:* 1—2, 2—16, 3—101, 4—295, 5—302, 6—331, 7—336, 8—366, 9—383, 10—393. *Second Innings:* 1—27, 2—37, 3—170, 4—175, 5—199, 6—205, 7—228, 8—254, 9—258, 10—293.

ENGLAND

First Innings		Second Innings	
G. A. Pullar, b. McKenzie	9	c. Simpson, b. McKenzie	3
D. S. Sheppard, st. Grout, b. Benaud	30	c. Grout, b. Mackay	1
K. F. Barrington, b. Simpson	63	not out	132
M. C. Cowdrey, c. Grout, b. McKenzie	13	run out	32
E. R. Dexter, c. Grout, b. McKenzie	61	c. Simpson, b. Benaud	10
T. W. Graveney, c. Booth, b. McKenzie	22	not out	36
F. J. Titmus, not out	59		
R. Illingworth, c. Grout, b. McKenzie	12		
A. C. Smith, c. Lawry, b. Mackay	13		
F. S. Trueman, c. Benaud, b. Mackay	38		
J. B. Statham, b. Mackay	1		
Extras (b. 5, l.b. 5)	10	Extras (b. 4, w. 5)	9
Total	331	Total (4 wkts.)	223

FALL OF WICKETS. *First Innings:* 1—17, 2—84, 3—117, 4—119, 5—165, 6—226, 7—246, 8—275, 9—327, 10—331. *Second Innings:* 1—2, 2—4, 3—98, 4—122.

Bowling Analysis

ENGLAND

	First Innings				Second Innings			
	O.	M.	R.	W.	O.	M.	R.	W.
Trueman	19	1	54	1	23.3	3	60	4
Statham	21	5	66	3	21	2	71	3
Illingworth	20	2	85	1	5	1	23	0
Dexter	23	1	94	3	17	0	65	3
Titmus	20.1	2	88	2	24	5	69	0

AUSTRALIA

	First Innings				Second Innings			
	O.	M.	R.	W.	O.	M.	R.	W.
Davidson	3.4	0	30	0				
McKenzie	33	3	89	5	14	0	64	1
Mackay	28.5	8	80	3	8	2	13	1
Benaud	18	3	82	1	15	3	38	1
Simspon	8	1	40	1	10	1	50	0
O'Neill					8	0	49	0
Lawry					1	1	0	0
Harvey					1	1	0	0

UMPIRES: C. Egar and A. Mackley
Total Attendance: 131,403
Total Receipts: £A33,733

Retrospect: It had been, all along, a match of wasted opportunities. Dropped catches galore, Davidson's injury, finally three hours of rain, unheard of during Test week in Adelaide. Benaud, from Davidson's withdrawal on, turned a blind eye to victory. It was unlike him. For, allowing even for Mackay having to share the new ball, he could, without risk, have declared and given England half-an-hour before lunch. He set defensive fields, even after England had lost 2 for 4, which probably cost him Barrington's wicket. Possibly he could not have won; though even that is not certain. But his attitude was almost churlish in its intransigence, his refusal to accept what came. It was as if, having set his sights on Sydney for the grand finale, he was not going to risk it going off at half-cock.

That was how it seemed; but, of course, it was not like that. Benaud decided, rightly or wrongly, that without Davidson he could not win. Believing that, he was not prepared to lose, and took care not to do so. There was no more to it, once sized up in black and white. But it looked timid, and allowed a match to peter out that need not have done quite so blatantly.

Dexter, on the receiving end, could only wait on events. England had a wonderful chance on the first morning, and threw it away in a fashion almost unique in Test matches. They then got into trouble themselves, rescued eventually by Dexter's innings on the second evening, and by Titmus and Trueman's ninth wicket stand. England had another chance on the last morning, but Titmus's dropping of Benaud, as easy a catch as any in the series, put an end to it.

Again, not many had come out of the match with credit. For Australia, Lawry had played two more dismal innings, Mackay had looked pathetic, Shepherd indifferent. O'Neill at last had shown his hand, and it had been a fine one. Harvey, riding his luck, had batted lyrically after the first hour. The spinners had disappointed rather, and McKenzie, plugging away up till the very last, had alone shown much heart for bowling. It had been a fine match for him. His methods are simple, but his strength, directness and stamina make him a tough customer. Like Miller, only as yet without Miller's variety and swing, he runs no more than he needs, using his hips and shoulders. Where Miller ran loosely, McKenzie is tautly to the point, strung like an archer. The final pivot and spreading of the back are everything.

Mackay, pitching consistently short at a modest pace, was no kind of partner for him. Whether Davidson was fully fit or not, someone else would have to be found for Sydney. But Hoare, the most obvious choice, was out of action; Guest had done nothing in the third Test; neither Meckiff nor Rorke were worth the scrutiny. Hawke and Brooks, of South Australia, looked the best of a moderate bunch.

Simpson had played one compact, sound innings, Booth twice had taken the sting out of fast bowlers encouraged by successes against Lawry. Lawry, attacked short of a length by

Trueman, especially on the leg stump, seemed to be atrophying under one's very eyes.

Benaud, however, could take comfort in the fielding, which, apart from one dropped slip catch by O'Neill, was faultless. O'Neill himself had fetched and thrown beautifully; Grout had kept wicket with fine economy and skill, taking two brilliant catches and making his stumping with a viper's swiftness. The whole business was carried out with style and precision.

Dexter could console himself only with the thought that, catching and running between the wickets apart, England had at least given as good as they got. The bowling had been steady, he doing as well as anyone in allowing the fast bowlers to rest, and making their job easier by picking up useful wickets in each innings. Statham had shown more life; Trueman, though looking below his physical peak, had as usual had his moments. Illingworth bowled admirably on the first morning, but once his chances had been frittered away, lost direction. O'Neill and Harvey together tore into Titmus, but he kept going without loss of face.

Nothing could be said about England's opening pair. Pullar had a disastrous match, devoid of any kind of merit. Sheppard batted agreeably in the first innings, but never suggested he would stay long. Barrington's move up to three worked well, after initial hazards. His 132 was gratuitously pugnacious and spirited in the circumstances. Cowdrey got a bad decision first time, and was run out the second when well set. Dexter, a shade reduced in stature at five, was nevertheless full of menace when it mattered most, and in most ways he had a satisfying match. All that remained ahead of him was the one long innings, due, one hoped, at Sydney.

Once again Titmus and Trueman held up the Australians at an important stage; the tail might have lengthened at the top, but it had shortened at the bottom. Titmus at the beginning of the series was almost bullied out by Benaud, who ringed him with fielders in insulting fashion. He still tended to scuffle about on bent knees when faced early on by leg-spin but generally speaking the praying mantis had given way to a species of Troubadour. Trueman's renewal of interest in batting made a big difference. He fancies himself against Benaud, his methods alternating between funfair rumbustiousness and exaggerated politeness. Success goes to his head, however, and the mounting dizziness that demands fours and sixes off every ball instead of one an over undoes him. If he could be chaperoned, his twenties and thirties could turn into fifties.

There were problems enough on both sides. Two weeks remained for re-thinking and adjustment. However, they were solved, what was most urgent was that Sydney saw a head-on clash, not a delaying clinch. The time for marginal skirmishing was long past.

If the fifth Test fulfilled its promise, then it might be said to have been well stage-managed. Dexter had declared that Test matches must be viewed, not as individual games, but as part of a series. One saw what he meant, and sympathized, though Benaud, with far less justification, had spoken to the contrary.

Anyone who could see all five Tests might agree with Dexter; the casual spectator, free for a day or two, would not. Still, they could not complain about Dexter himself, either individually or tactically. He made the most of what he had. No captain can perform miracles when his opening batsmen get shot away time and again for nothing, when his fielders drop catches so openhandedly, even the best of them, at such insufferable moments.

8 From a Journal IV: Melbourne - Sydney

Flying from Adelaide to Melbourne one moves from placid aridity to unpredictable humidity. It had taken me nearly two days hard driving a month earlier; now in ninety minutes one exchanged gin and tonics on a sun-baked lawn in Menindie for afternoon tea amongst dolled-up old ladies in the Hotel Windsor. The Adelaide heat was scarcely reduced by the usual Melbourne wind, though a day later the inevitable cool change arrived and the weekend, spent at a beach-house at Aspendale, was blustery and grey, sand whipping up against the plate glass, and the sea pounding a beach circled by screeching gulls. The Antarctic seemed unusually close.

The Victorian match would be M.C.C.'s last first-class game before the final Text. It was of interest, mainly, for the batting form of various marginal M.C.C. batsmen, and as a sounding board for Allen. Australia, on their side, were looking for a third fast bowler, and there would be Guest, Meckiff and Connolly on view.

Dexter's calculations were upset somewhat by circumstances. Sheppard and Illingworth had been left behind in Adelaide to recover from pharyngitis; Cowdrey arrived off the train with an eye closed up by an insect sting, necessitating a minor operation; Murray was still unfit. In addition, Pullar, having survived less than an over against Meckiff in the first innings, pulled a muscle fielding and had to withdraw from the match. It could have been a blessing in disguise.

The match itself, narrowly saved by Victoria on the last evening, was fairly uneventful. Lawry sent M.C.C. in, and by the end of Meckiff's first over both Parfitt and Pullar were out. 5 for 2, the scoreboard showed, and it might have been a Test match. Barrington made 33, in his more jittery manner, before flicking at an outswinger and being caught at slip. Dexter played several beautiful strokes past mid-off and then was bowled by Connolly's slower ball. Knight, attacked short of a length on his body, stabbed Connolly to short leg. M.C.C. were 96 for 5. At this point Titmus joined Graveney and for two hours the afternoon was made golden by Graveney's elegance. He got quickly into position for the hook, a rare occurrence for him, he stroked the ball expressively through the covers, he banged it past mid-off and mid-on. He was dropped off a sharp chance to slip at 26, but when he was out on Monday morning for 185 he had played one of the adorning innings of the tour. His second innings of 38 not out had no less bouquet and watching him was like finding a long-fancied wine, disappointing over the years, suddenly come to full maturity. It was the batting of a great stroke player, the machinery of art invisible in the polished fluency of the execution.

Smith revealed some carefully-hoarded shots in a useful partnership with Graveney, and M.C.C. finally managed 375.

Victoria, with Lawry out for 13, though this time showing some strokes, replied with 307. Allen, initially using the two short mid-on field experimented with in Perth, took five wickets, and was the most searching, as well as accurate, of the bowlers. M.C.C. in their second innings declared at 218 for 5, Dexter making 70 and Barrington 66. Parfitt opened the innings with Knight and they scored 21 and 8 respectively.

Victoria, set 287 to win in 250 minutes, reached 188 for 9, the last pair hanging on together for a quarter of an hour. Allen, taking 3 for 24 in 13 overs, again looked the likeliest of the England bowlers.

The Australian selectors could have gained little from the match. Meckiff, regarded by the Victorian public as one crucified by the Press, took seven wickets in the match, each applauded with almost religious fervour. Any time Meckiff beats the bat, bowls a bouncer or hits a pad the crowd rise as if at a revivalist meeting. He bowled at modest pace throughout, the degree of sudden elbow-straightening in his delivery varying from ball to ball. At its worst, it is very marked indeed. What affects the batsman most is the unpredictable trajectory and the consequent difficulty in picking up the flight of the ball. In 1959, when Meckiff and Rorke shot England out for 87 in the Melbourne Test, he made much greater haste off the pitch, and was virtually unplayable. But for anyone sceptical of the difference to a batsman between a ball thrown and a ball bowled it is necessary only to stand behind a net and watch bowlers throwing the ball off a short run. You need only watch it once.

Guest, with his swerving run, as if pummelled by beam winds, moved the new ball, but lacked penetration. Connolly, despite an ungainly, flailing approach, was livelier, without suggesting he was of Test class.

Generally, the Australian critics, O'Reilly and Miller among them, were of the opinion that Mackay and Shepherd would be ditched for Sydney, Burge and Hawke, a twenty-four year-old South Australian all-rounder, brought in. The real anomaly about Meckiff was that, while everyone that mattered agreed about his action, the Victorian selectors, one of whose members, Jack Ryder, is a Test selector, continued to pick him. Once only, in the Victoria-South Australia match a few weeks earlier, had he been no-balled for throwing.

In Sydney the weather at last settled. The sun beat on the harbour, a cool breeze ruffled the palms, the days faded out in a syrupy flood of colour. Swimming at Camp Cove, where the bikinis reach their ultimate, one looked across at the wooded North Shore, the ferries crossing to Manly, the sailing boats tacking, the liners making for the Heads and the open sea. The recent savaging of a young actress by a shark had emptied the beaches and except at weekends one swam in the cold water, which never reaches Mediterranean temperatures, almost alone. At night we ate oysters, prawns or lobsters, overlooking the coloured water, going on later to see Carmen Macrae singing at Chequers, or Mamie Van Doren oozing at the

Chevron-Hilton. After midnight King's Cross swarmed with bronzed girls in shorts or tight pants, the stars glittered as low as a canopy, and the cicadae hummed in the fig trees along Point Piper and Rose Bay. The hardness of the Australian light, the crude red of Sydney roofs, melted into the caressive dark, and one was conscious only of stars, water, tall flats like illuminated brigantines gone aground, and the soothing warm.

Four days before the Test the weather again broke. Ships' sirens bleated in the harbour, mist and rain limiting visibility to a cable's length. The beaches, full of oiled, bronzed bodies the week before, were emptied, driftwood lying like bleached bones on the swept sand. Boats in Rushcutters Bay jostled in ghostly proximity. Newsprint announcing murders, rapes, espionage ran on sodden posters. I drove along a foreshore changed mysteriously out of recognition, the extrovert brashness of Sydney given melancholy depth. Darling Point, Point Piper, Rose Bay, Vaucluse, Neilson Park, Camp Cove, the Gap, with the Pacific breaking up on unyielding, cracked rocks. The districts of Sydney – Paddington, with its sloping terraced houses, the painted wrought-iron dripping; Woolloomooloo with its smell of sacking and tar; the Moreton Bay figs on the steep lawns behind the Seven Shillings and beaches of Double Bay; the moored seaplane off the Pier restaurant; the cassata green of the naval buildings near Inner South Head – have an inerasable nostalgia about them, and the names on any city map conjure up, in hauntingly vivid fashion, crucial eras of colonial history. Cook and Bligh, Phillip and Macquarie, Leichardt and Bourke. The surf beaches form a litany of their own, Manly, Curl Curl, Deewhy, Collaroy to the north, Bondi, Tamarama, Coogee, Bronte and Maroubra to the south. On a dark English winter's day it is necessary only to name them, to hunt out a wine-stained Esso map and let the eye rest on La Perouse, Botany Bay, Shark Point, Palm Beach, Randwick and Hornby Lighthouse. The images, like transfers, solidify in the memory: boats and sprawling bodies; white spinnakers bellying out over blue, octopus-tentacled waters probing into beaches and inlets; glossy horses and jockeys in striped silks; cricket matches being played against a back cloth of yachts and sea; the sun spilling on moored ferries at Kirribilli as the bridge takes the last rose layers on its silver; pink verandahed houses glowing amongst hibiscus and frangipani; palm trees blackening under the stars. The short perspective of Australian history contracts into a focus in which the commonplace ingredients, explorers and convicts, colonial governors and radicals, Bush balladists and opera singers, cricketers and lifesavers, find some composite identity that both touches the heart and triggers the memory. Lawson, Patterson, Greenway, Melba, Roberts, Streeton, Glover, Hughes, Nolan, Lawlor, Drysdale, White; and among cricketers Murdoch, Darling, Trumper, Noble, Hill, Armstrong, Bardsley, Collins, Bradman, McCabe, O'Reilly, Miller, Lindwall. These are syllables that have a poetry expressive beyond mere recitation or anecdote.

Two days before the Test the tension began to build up. Davidson's final try-out in the nets was watched over not only by two selectors, Bradman and Seddon, but by an imposing array of reporters and camera men. After twenty minutes at half-pace Davidson took off his sweater, measured out his full run and bowled twenty balls at his normal speed. The stumps flew. He dug in a bouncer half-way through, stamping the injured right leg. It was the crucial delivery and Davidson smiled his gratification that all was well. The selectors pronounced themselves satisfied. It was an impressive trial, as beautiful to watch in its cumulative rhythm as a Derby candidate galloping on the Epsom downs.

The remaining Australians batted and bowled in two adjacent nets. Bradman and Benaud sprawled together on the grass in solitary discussion. Hawke and Burge, as anticipated, were in attendance, as was Mackay, likely to be twelfth man.

Cowdrey, surrounded by movie cameras and photographers,

batted in the end net against the robot bowler invented by an Adelaide engineer called Black, a small gnomish figure with a thin Disney moustache. The robot acquitted itself well, but looked tame after Davidson.

The Curator worked on the Test wicket, covers strewn around him. The Australians came in from their practice and gossiped in the bar. The portraits of the legendary great looked down from their frames. I went with Arthur Mailey to inspect the mural he had recently painted for the boardroom, a rural scene with shadows of gum trees lengthening across the grass and the fielders trooping off at the day's end.

In the Long room behind the bar players famous in their prime posed for the camera. The photographs, but not the active images, had grown old with them. Here were Jardine and Chapman in their youth; Duckworth, Geary and Larwood in a group; Bedser, the sweat still on his brow; P. F. Warner standing at the wicket, left elbow stiffly thrust; Duleepsinhji acknowledging applause. Hung at each end, above the others, Trumper and Bradman looked across the years in eternal acknowledgment of immortality.

Outside, the sun lowered itself behind the pavilion's domes and turrets, all crisply green as the grass. The giant scoreboard, ignorant of what music was to be played on it, remained tightly shuttered. It was a question now only of waiting.

9 Sydney: The Fifth Test

First Day: The weather, without having settled, improved. Heavy showers, which had interrupted practice the day before, died out. The morning of the match was sultry, the sky pale and flecked with saucepan-coloured cloud. Pullar, selected originally in England's twelve, was finally withdrawn, leaving England with three off-spinners, Illingworth picked virtually as a batsman. Parfitt, despite his indifferent form, seemed to have been the more logical choice. Not for the first time in Australia since the war England were committed to playing a bowler in the primary role of batsman. It was an unhappy prospect. Australia left out Mackay. Dexter won the toss and it was announced that England would bat. Sheppard's name went up and then, after a painful interval, Cowdrey's. The band in their red coats thumped away unnoticed, the sun emerged, and soon Davidson and Harvey, arms round each other's shoulders, led Australia out.

Davidson bowled to Sheppard at exploratory pace; four went by outside the off stump, two swung in viciously late. Off the last ball Sheppard took a single past gully. Benaud this time dispensed with third man and long leg. Sheppard pushed McKenzie again past gully and Cowdrey played out the over. It was all strangely quiet, like an orchestra tuning up. Davidson, in his second over, had Sheppard reaching and the ball took the edge and bounced in front of slip. Standing as square-on as he did he could scarcely avoid playing across the line of Davidson's delivery. McKenzie now almost bowled him. For Cowdrey Davidson had Hawke at forward short leg; otherwise two at backward short, four slips, O'Neill at cover and Harvey at mid-off. Cowdrey followed one that swung in and gained a run to square leg. After two overs

Hawke replaced McKenzie. He began short but despite his moderate pace got two to lift at Cowdrey's ribs. Davidson, in his fourth over, pitched the fourth short at Cowdrey, it reared up, and Cowdrey, fending it off, was caught by Harvey diving forward at backward short leg. It was the ritual combination, the familiar pattern. England, after half an hour, were 5 for 1. Cowdrey, once more, had allowed the bowlers to encroach upon him to a degree that flattered them inordinately and inhibited him. Self-denial thus early clogs the machinery fatally. If the risk of sending Cowdrey in first was calculated, the consequent tactics were not. He should have been there to take charge, not prop. Otherwise he were better kept back.

Davidson came off after five overs, McKenzie relieving him. Sheppard pushed him to mid-wicket, then was beaten outside the off stump. Hawke brought two back sharply at Barrington. Sheppard had the red-coated band moved from behind the bowler's arm. After an hour, when Mackay brought out drinks, England had scraped to 16. The rhythm was disastrously wrong.

McKenzie bowled a maiden to Barrington, who jerked like a puppet being reluctantly manipulated. Then Davidson returned at the Hill end, with Hawke replacing McKenzie. The batsmen were not in the game at all. Hawke got appreciable movement inwards and Barrington, having twice turned him off his legs, scooped out three yorkers in a row. After eighty-five minutes of this, with England no more than 25, Benaud took a hand. He fed Barrington on a surfeit of half-volleys, the last of which Barrington got through the covers for the first boundary of the day. Sheppard a moment later drove Hawke past mid-off and McKenzie, flagging, just failed to stop it on the boundary edge. In the next over Sheppard mistimed and pushed slightly across an in-swinging full toss and Hawke, diving over to the off, took a nice return catch. Dexter, passing Sheppard without a glance, strode out looking properly fed up. It was twelve minutes before lunch. He cut Hawke with some relish, leaned McKenzie, whom Benaud had brought on for himself, fine of cover, and the agonizing sense of martyrdom and struggle dispersed. Benaud bowled at Hawke's end, and Dexter played a respectful maiden. Benaud's switching of his four bowlers was the main activity of a morning that had brought England 49 runs off 27 overs, 8 to Dexter, and no credit. The pitch had been slowish throughout, with little lift.

Dexter, as if determined to put bowling, pitch and batting into something like proper perspective, struck Benaud's first ball of the afternoon to the cover boundary. He cut Davidson beautifully past gully, a stroke inscribed in air with the fluency of line Picasso achieves on paper.

But Barrington, at his most intransigent, thwarted him. In four overs, during which Barrington batted as if nursing a grievance, Dexter received three balls. Barrington broke silence eventually by sweeping Benaud and then glancing McKenzie for four, but he had incurred much ironic displeasure meanwhile. What's more, he had becalmed Dexter. McKenzie, oddly lifeless, gave way to Hawke, whom Barrington cut and Dexter pulled. Benaud, after 7 overs for 16, allowed Simpson an over before drinks but, though he was more variable in length than Benaud, Dexter found the escape routes still frustratingly sealed. Fretting visibly, he moved out and drove a half-volley shoulder-high a foot to Simpson's right and a yard to the left of Davidson at mid-on. Having got this identifying gesture off his chest, he relaxed. O'Neill beat Barrington with a leg-break of perfect length, which made some haste. Dexter twice cut Simpson through the covers, but without animosity. O'Neill again beat Barrington as he stretched forward, nearly caught and bowled him in the same over, and looked more probing than either Benaud or Simpson. Dexter hit Simpson skimmingly to the extra cover boundary, at last a stroke of antagonism. O'Neill changed ends, bamboozling Barrington twice in an over. He then twice beat Dexter in successive balls. The batsmen looked relieved to get in to tea. They had scored 78 in the afternoon, but it had been a streaky, unsatisfying business.

Hardly had the general interval scuffling and clatter died

down than Dexter, pulling off his gloves, was walking away from the wicket. He had pushed half forward at O'Neill, the ball spun from the edge and Simpson, diving to his right, took a low catch one-handed. It was the fourth time Simpson had caught him, three times off leg-spinners. O'Neill nearly bowled Barrington with his googly in the same over, so that what little dignity had been salvaged between lunch and tea quickly dwindled. Barrington now found obscure avenues down which to steer and tickle O'Neill, once carting a long-hop from Benaud, one of the few all day, but almost wilfully starving Graveney of the strike. Davidson returned, testing his thigh with a bouncer that dwarfed even Graveney. Benaud turned one sharply at Graveney, who edged it just short of Simpson at slip, getting two runs as Simpson fell. They were the last he got for half an hour. Simpson bowled from one end, McKenzie from the other. Both were a shade short, the ball came slowly on to the bat, the field was dropped deep enough to make breaking it require more power of stroke than anyone had yet shown. All the same, the net was of England's own construction.

For twenty minutes Australia bowled under black cloud. Barrington appealed, but was turned down, possibly harshly. During this time Graveney, having stared accusingly at the umpires when McKenzie, pitching short, hit him, glanced McKenzie and Harvey, at leg slip, took a magnificent one-handed catch low to his left. The ball never rose six inches and it went fast. Eight years earlier Davidson, in much the same position, had caught Hutton off Lindwall; the stroke as controlled, the catch no less thrilling.

England, 177 for 4, should have lost another wicket immediately. Barrington, then 93, swept across Simpson's leg-break and Booth, running in from square leg, juggled and dropped it. Barrington hit Simpson back over his head to reach 99, in the same over pushing him into the covers for a single. Disenchanted spectators streamed from the ground, the slopes clear for comfortable reclining. The wind changed, it grew gusty and unpleasant. With ten minutes left Barrington, having denied himself for over five hours, slashed senselessly at Benaud and Harvey caught him at cover. Barrington looked justifiably contrite, but it was too late. England had shown neither imagination nor technique, and now they were paying for it. Benaud had used six bowlers, and five of them had taken a wicket for much the same amount of runs. Hawke, whose action suggests the schoolboy net bowler, bowled his medium-paced in-swingers from the full width of the crease, but while his movement inwards was generally predictable he was always at the stumps and every so often got one to dart the other way. He lacks that extra bit of pace from the pitch that the best of his kind need, but he gave little away. Certainly, he was an improvement on Mackay.

ENGLAND – First Innings	
D. S. Sheppard, c. and b. Hawke	19
M. C. Cowdrey, c. Harvey, b. Davidson	2
K. F. Barrington, c. Harvey, b. Benaud	101
E. R. Dexter, c. Simpson, b. O'Neill	47
T. W. Graveney, c. Harvey, b. McKenzie	14
R. Illingworth, not out	10
F. J. Titmus, not out	0
Extras (l.b. 2)	2
Total (5 wkts.)	195

FALL OF WICKETS. 1—5, 2—39, 3—129, 4—177, 5—189.

Second Day: It had taken two hours and cost two wickets to get to 49 by lunch the day before. Now, in the first hour, 40 were acquired for the loss of Illingworth. Five runs short of the new ball at the outset, Benaud gave O'Neill a couple of overs and himself one. Illingworth, who had batted quietly for the last half hour of Friday, hit O'Neill through the covers off the back foot and then pulled a long hop just wide of Davidson at mid-wicket for four. So Davidson took the new ball, and Illingworth and Titmus were able to give some inkling of how either might have fared in Cowdrey's shoes. Davidson swung several in pretty late and once Illingworth edged one that lifted nastily over Lawry's head at backward short leg. But by and large they were an improvement. Illingworth too often pushed out on the off with his left leg down the line of the leg stump but he is not alone in doing this and he at least suggested runs. He drove McKenzie pleasantly past mid-off, and Davidson straight, and it finally took a good one that cut sharply off the seam to remove him. It found the outside edge and Grout, who had been strangely untidy against the spinners, caught an awkward catch low to his right. Despite this neither Davidson nor McKenzie, in the fifty minutes Benaud gave them, bowled with much animation. The weather with a low ceiling of puffy black cloud was dispiriting, the wicket again stagnant. Trueman, promoted after services rendered, came in under the false banner of Smith and he scowled at the scoreboard until the correct name was substituted. The expected applause followed and Trueman, his status recognized, condescended to take guard. His appearance brought an immediate improvement in the running between wickets, and Titmus, able now to exploit the short single Illingworth had denied him, blossomed. Trueman took matters gravely like a specialist in consultation, even when Benaud appeared. The crowd openly lusted for violence; Trueman was content to display a bedside manner. He was less serene when a reasonable appeal in terms of light, if not of tactics, was turned down, and in between stabbing with martyred defiance at Davidson he glared savagely at the square leg umpire. Titmus drove occasionally through the covers, but in the main both he and Trueman, keeping the ball down skilfully, used the gap between second slip and gully. It was scarcely exhilarating, but it meant that England went in to lunch at 265 for 6, a situation with prospects.

Titmus now looked more intently for runs, but after three handsome strokes off the back foot he cut at Hawke and was taken at the wicket. He and Trueman had added a handy 51, the same as in the third Test here, and continuing evidence of their pleasure in each other's company. Benaud returned, and

Trueman, with sudden spite, lashed him to long-off where Burge, falling forward, uncovered his bald patch but failed to hang on. Unconvinced, Trueman tried again and this time Harvey at mid-on held a skier, his fourth catch of the innings. Smith and Allen pottered for twenty minutes, managing seven runs, with Harvey thrice saving certain boundaries with left-handed stops at cover. Simpson bowled Smith, who hit across something suspiciously close to a full toss, and then Allen hoisted 300 with a pull for four. Allen, joined by Statham, bucked up appreciably. He cut Simpson, drove Benaud almost cynically, and even went some way to restoring local approval. He quickly forfeited it by drying up almost completely. Statham, after a conciliatory overture, grew more out of touch the longer he was in: it was a mercy when Allen snicked Davidson to Benaud at second slip. The innings had lasted altogether nine and a half hours: it seemed like days. No one, theoretically, could complain too harshly of a total of 321 after Cowdrey and Sheppard had gone for 39. But the desiccated manner of its composition, the periods when nothing appeared to be happening at all, and the absence of anything approaching either grace or urgency created an ultimately stunning impression of desultoriness.

Australia began their innings in dismal light which Trueman emphasized by striking Simpson an introductory blow on the shoulder with a full toss. He beat him three times in this opening over with out-swingers Simpson knew precious little about. Against Statham, however, Simpson prospered. He repeatedly found the gap between cover and third man, and though Statham almost bowled him once he looked briskly confident. Lawry showed signs of sticking but Trueman got one to move late off the seam and Smith took a fine catch low and at full stretch. Trueman nearly knocked Booth's head off with his first ball and the second grazed the off stump. He survived, however, and with Simpson ran a series of ample singles that no English batsman would have contemplated. Trueman, sacrificing two slips, dropped to medium and Dexter, for no obvious reason, bowled at similar pace to an even more blatantly defensive field. Titmus broke the congealing ennui by bowling Booth as soon as he came on. Booth, having jumped down the pitch the ball before, hit all across one that drifted in from outside the leg stump. O'Neill, moving across his wicket, thrust his pads dumbly at the first ball and seemed in face of a concerted appeal distinctly lucky to get away with it. Dexter brought Trueman back for one over and O'Neill hooked a bouncer high but safely. Dexter returned when Allen might have been more to the point, and O'Neill drove him impatiently through the covers. After one over Allen did in fact come on, bowling into the wind with a cordon of five on the leg side halfway to the boundary. Titmus, using such breeze as there was, had two short legs, one in front, one behind, and both as close as good manners and Trueman's language would permit. Simpson now ran out of ideas and O'Neill, utterly cramped, pushed arthritically off the back foot. Titmus dropped one short in his sixth over, O'Neill swung at it, and Barrington at square leg nearly brought off a miraculous one-handed catch. The next ball turned appreciably and Simpson, pushing forward, was snapped up by Trueman round the corner. Once more the hypnosis by off-spin was complete. Burge, peering myopically out, understandably appealed against the onset of twilight. His plea was allowed, which was as well for him, if disappointing for his tormentors. For at last some kind of tension was building up, with the plot developing a discernible theme.

Titmus, bowling from the Randwick end, from which he had taken 7 for 79 a month earlier, gave away only 10 runs in 8 overs, which had included the wickets of Booth and Simpson. Allen bowled 3 overs for 5. Despite its tortoise-like motivation, the affair had acquired possibilities. Dexter had set himself a target of at least 300, which he had achieved, hoping that his spinners could bowl Australia out twice on a slow, turning wicket in three days. How realistic this was we should see.

ENGLAND – First Innings

D. S. Sheppard, c. and b. Hawke	19
M. C. Cowdrey, c. Harvey, b. Davidson	2
K. F. Barrington, c. Harvey, b. Benaud	101
E. R. Dexter, c. Simpson, b. O'Neill	47
T. W. Graveney, c. Harvey, b. McKenzie	14
R. Illingworth, c. Grout, b. Davidson	27
F. J. Titmus, c. Grout, b. Hawke	34
F. S. Trueman, c. Harvey, b. Benaud	30
A. C. Smith, b. Simpson	6
D. A. Allen, c. Benaud, b. Davidson	14
J. B. Statham, not out	17
Extras (b. 4, l.b. 6)	10
Total	321

FALL OF WICKETS. 1—5, 2—39, 3—129, 4—177, 5—189, 6—224, 7—276, 8—286, 9—293, 10—321.

AUSTRALIA – First Innings

W. M. Lawry, c. Smith, b. Trueman	11
R. B. Simpson, c. Trueman, b. Titmus	32
B. C. Booth, b. Titmus	11
N. C. O'Neill, not out	18
P. J. Burge, not out	0
Extras (b. 1, l.b. 1)	2
Total (3 wkts.)	74

FALL OF WICKETS. 1—28, 2—50, 3—71

Third Day: On Sunday night the Duke of Norfolk, in his suite overlooking the Rushcutters Bay Oval that was Victor Trumper's home ground, gave a cocktail party. It was the last weekend we should be in Sydney; by the next Sunday a depleted M.C.C. would be in New Zealand, the Press dispersed, the series decided. The lights came out over the harbour, the yachts, lapping at their moorings, dissolved into the dark. Ted Dexter, who later that night gave an accomplished TV performance in Meet the Press, expressed satisfaction in the situation of the game and some confidence in its outcome.

Monday was again cloudy and rather humid. Statham bowled the first over to Burge and off the first ball Barrington from cover threw the stumps down at the bowler's end, giving Burge two overthrows. O'Neill hit Titmus off the back foot to the cover boundary. He looked ominously secure. Dexter gave Statham three overs, then brought on Allen. His opening over, a maiden, had Burge worried, though the ball had yet to turn. Burge went to cut the second ball and it went through an inch past the off stump. O'Neill cut Titmus square for four and then, moving out, drove him hard enough to beat long on, where Parfitt, fielding for Cowdrey whose eye had flared up again, was slow starting.

O'Neill, satisfied now about the degree of expected turn, twice steered Allen past slip. Burge, who had been three quarters of an hour over five, was encouraged to do the same, taking seven runs. Down the other end he pushed out at Titmus and the ball spun off bat and then pad, Graveney at forward short leg falling on it just too late. O'Neill drove Allen to the sightscreen, cutting him again past slip. In an hour Australia had scored 45, O'Neill making 31 of them. Drinks were taken and Titmus shaved Burge's off stump as Burge lay back to cut. O'Neill reached 50, as good a one as any in the series, then was picked up on the half-volley by Trueman at leg slip off Titmus. Though wickets had not come, each bowler in turn was entitled to visions of one. The contest was absorbing, an inch either way making the difference. Dexter might perhaps have switched his bowlers, or tried Illingworth earlier, but he preferred to stick to Titmus and Allen. O'Neill crashed Titmus past mid-off, a stroke all melody and power. Illingworth, when after ninety minutes he did replace Allen, began with three full tosses, Burge swinging one over mid-wicket's head. Allen changed ends and again Trueman nearly snapped up O'Neill. Burge drove Illingworth to the sightscreen and Australia were 150. Graveney at short mid-on thought he had caught O'Neill in Allen's next over but O'Neill stayed put. Allen, flighting the ball cleverly, kept O'Neill from getting at him, and always there was the chance of a catch round the corner. Illingworth posed fewer problems of either spin or flight, but though Burge struck him hard and often he only once more got past the covers.

Australia, 163 for 3 at lunch, had come through, not without scratches, but convincingly enough. O'Neill and Burge had scored 89 off 33 overs, never wholly invulnerable, but moving freely up and down the pitch instead of stabbing from the back foot. The bowlers, without that final bit of luck that takes wickets, had given nothing away.

The luck was still missing afterwards, for Allen, throwing one up to O'Neill in the first over, drew him yards down the pitch. It almost bowled him but although Smith gathered it he did so awkwardly and O'Neill scraped back. Burge hit Titmus straight, then swept him, both times for four. Allen bowled three maidens in a row to O'Neill, each beautifully varied, and finally he got his reward. O'Neill jumped out and drove him scorchingly hard and low to the right of Graveney at short mid-on. Graveney, moving one way, twisted the other and caught the ball at full stretch with his right hand resting on the grass. There was a moment of stunned disbelief. Allen had taken 1 for 3 in 5 overs.

Harvey, affectionately greeted, swept Titmus off his leg stump; Burge swept Allen off his middle. Dexter made a fine stop at deep mid-off, throwing the wicket down from thirty yards.

Statham took the new ball at 200 and Burge, relishing its gloss, drove it to the long off boundary and cut it to the cover pickets. Trueman, at the Hill end, from which Allen had bowled nine overs for five runs, bowled his first over of the day at a quarter to three and Dexter at third slip put down a brutish left-handed catch from Burge. Two balls later Trueman again found the edge and the ball pitched a yard in front of Illingworth at second slip. In the next over Burge flicked at Statham and Smith, reaching across with no movement of the feet, dropped him. He was having a bad afternoon.

Harvey, never in touch properly, batted in subdued shadowy fashion, edging here and there, but rarely timing it. The clouds closed in, drizzle thickening to rain, so that the new ball seemed a liability rather than otherwise. Twenty minutes were lost, and then, on the stroke of tea, Harvey hooked Statham, got a top edge, and Parfitt, running in from long leg, caught him. Again it rained, and when, at five o'clock, they came out again Allen and Titmus found the ball altogether too wet to control. Davidson, after a meditative opening, swept and cut Allen, while Burge, freed from swing and spin, cruised towards his 100. Dexter, charitably deciding to suffer the inconveniences himself, went round the wicket but Davidson, waving the sight-screen back and forth, kept him waiting. Shrugging his shoulders Dexter dug the first ball in, Davidson hooked, and Allen at square leg caught him in front of his face.

Benaud came out in quite atrocious light, drove Statham and hooked Dexter, but was interrupted by the umpires. They conferred, decided it was too dark, and twenty minutes early called it off. Over an hour altogether was lost, and the narrative, in consequence, was gutted of purpose. It was a pity, for the quality of performance—O'Neill's batting, Allen's bowling—was the highest for some time.

ENGLAND – First Innings

Batsman	Runs
D. S. Sheppard, c. and b. Hawke	19
M. C. Cowdrey, c. Harvey, b. Davidson	2
K. F. Barrington, c. Harvey, b. Benaud	101
E. R. Dexter, c. Simpson, b. O'Neill	47
T. W. Graveney, c. Harvey, b. McKenzie	14
R. Illingworth, c. Grout, b. Davidson	27
F. J. Titmus, c. Grout, b. Hawke	34
F. S. Trueman, c. Harvey, b. Benaud	30
A. C. Smith, b. Simpson	6
D. A. Allen, c. Benaud, b. Davidson	14
J. B. Statham, not out	17
Extras (b. 4, l.b. 6)	10
Total	321

FALL OF WICKETS. 1—5, 2—39, 3—129, 4—177, 5—189, 6—224, 7—276, 8—286, 9—293, 10—321.

AUSTRALIA – First Innings

W. M. Lawry, c. Smith, b. Trueman..........	11
R. B. Simpson, c. Trueman, b. Titmus........	32
B. C. Booth, b. Titmus......................	11
N. C. O'Neill, c. Graveney, b. Allen..........	73
P. J. Burge, not out........................	98
R. N. Harvey, c. sub., b. Statham............	22
A. K. Davidson, c. Allen, b. Dexter............	15
R. Benaud, not out........................	13
Extras (b. 5, l.b. 5)........................	10
Total (6 wkts.)	285

FALL OF WICKETS. 1—28, 2—50, 3—71, 4—180, 5—231, 6—271.

Fourth Day: It was greyer, more blustery and a great deal colder. Dexter wound up his spinners and very much in clockwork fashion they bowled. Burge collected the two for his 100, Benaud once lifted Allen over mid-on, but in half an hour they managed nothing else. Both Titmus, into the breeze now, and Allen were mechanically accurate. Burge, having contained himself for nearly six hours, now swept at Titmus with his left leg down the pitch and was l.b.w. An over later McKenzie swung at a half-volley and Titmus, diving to his left, took a fine return catch. Australia, two wickets in hand, were 18 behind.

Hawke cut Allen to the pavilion but all the same Australia had managed only 28 in the hour. Statham replaced Allen, Trueman resting with a strained thigh in the pavilion. Benaud glanced Statham to send Australia ahead and then turned him to the square leg boundary. Dexter brought Allen back and Benaud hit him beautifully through the covers. Twice he struck Titmus past mid-off, the ball banging back off the fence. England were getting into trouble. Dexter seemed to be operating by remote control and when Allen suddenly spun one very sharply to Benaud there was cause for anxiety. Benaud now came down the pitch to Allen, the ball turned off a length and Graveney took a gentle catch at leg slip. He took another one off Titmus a few minutes later, Hawke hitting a half-volley to short mid-on. So Australia, after 110 minutes before lunch, were kept to a lead of 28. Titmus had taken 5 for 103, Allen 2 for 87. There were ten hours left for play.

Davidson began from the Hill end, the wind blowing across towards the slips. Benaud allowed him two slips only, setting a long leg and third man. Sheppard took a single off the first ball, and then Illingworth, who had come in with him, twice drove Davidson straight for two. McKenzie bowled one over, mostly wide of the off stump, Benaud then replacing him with Hawke. Illingworth played him nicely past cover and turned him with the swing past square leg. Sheppard hit a half-volley to the long-on boundary and most of Australia's lead had gone. At 23 Benaud got down to the real business himself and at once beat Sheppard with a leg-break of perfect length. Sheppard then played Davidson off his hip and McKenzie, at backward short leg, put down a simple catch. Davidson, cutting the ball off the seam, confined himself now almost exclusively to the leg stump, with two men close, and one by the umpire. Simpson crouched at slip alone. Benaud twice beat Illingworth with leg-breaks turning laboriously off a length. Neither were easy to get away and England, after a bright start, managed only 33 in an hour.

Drinks were taken and Illingworth, set, it seemed, on dealing with Benaud, pulled him to mid-wicket but then drove him straight to Hawke at extra cover. It had, nonetheless, been the best opening partnership since Brisbane – 40 as against 17, the highest in the 2nd, 3rd or 4th Tests. Barrington came next, not Dexter, which looked to be an admission of some kind, or plain thoughtlessness. Davidson, with five men on the leg side, continued to peg away around the leg stump at medium pace, the ball pitching over after over within an area of about six inches. It was invariably fielded by one of the short legs, or if not by them, by square leg too close for the single. Benaud, with four men on the off halfway to the boundary, pitched on the off stump, but Barrington, having warmed the fingers of each in turn, beat mid-off and cover in quick succession.

He now swept against the spin, Lawry at square leg making a hash of a catch that dropped just behind him. Sheppard was beaten in the flight by Benaud but, unlike at Adelaide, got back in time. Again Benaud beat him. Barrington cut Benaud past slip, earning himself an over from Davidson on the leg stump. Simpson bowled the last over before tea, beating and nearly bowling Barrington with his googly. Davidson, who had been on the whole afternoon, bowled 14 overs for 29. England at tea were 74, which is to say 46 runs on. Sheppard, in two hours, had scored 29.

McKenzie bowled with Simpson afterwards, and Sheppard hit him twice through the covers. He drove Simpson past mid-off to reach 50, and with Barrington at last responsive to the art of the short single – like a long-frigid bride awakened to the pleasures of the senses – England spurted.

Harvey bowled three overs of plausible off-breaks, then Davidson was back. Barrington hit Benaud twice high over mid-on, but was less in touch than Sheppard, who began now to see less of the bowling. Sheppard suddenly ran out to Davidson and hit him over mid-wicket. England plainly could begin to think in terms of an eventual declaration. Sheppard, cutting at Benaud, was caught by Harvey at cover. Dexter, hurrying out, played four balls unhappily from Benaud, then moved down the wicket to Davidson and hit him over mid-off. Benaud, bowling slower, threw the ball up to Dexter, who again came down the wicket, missed in the semi-dark and was stumped. It was an honourable sacrifice, though in terms of victory and imagery the one least desirable. Barrington reached 50, then was dropped by Grout on the leg side off Davidson.

It was colder and darker than at any time in the match, and any light appeal during the previous half-hour must have been upheld. Cowdrey showed signs of intended animation but after twenty minutes against Davidson and Benaud candles would have had to be called for. Seven minutes before stumps he did appeal.

So, for the third day running, the light triumphed. England, 165 for 3, were 137 ahead. Whatever Dexter might have hoped, there seemed just not time enough. Of the 55 overs bowled by Australia, Davidson, spinning and cutting, and Benaud, bowling slower and more accurately to a deeper onside field, had shared 41.

ENGLAND

	First Innings		Second Innings	
D. S. Sheppard,	c. and b. Hawke	19	c. Harvey, b. Benaud	68
M. C. Cowdrey,	c. Harvey, b. Davidson	2	not out	12
K. F. Barrington,	c. Harvey, b. Benaud	101	not out	57
E. R. Dexter,	c. Simpson, b. O'Neill	47	st. Grout, b. Benaud	6
T. W. Graveney,	c. Harvey, b. McKenzie	14		
R. Illingworth,	c. Grout, b. Davidson	27	c. Hawke, b. Benaud	18
F. J. Titmus,	c. Grout, b. Hawke	34		
F. S. Trueman,	c. Harvey, b. Benaud	30		
A. C. Smith,	b. Simpson	6		
D. A. Allen,	c. Benaud, b. Davidson	14		
J. B. Statham,	not out	17		
Extras	(b. 4, l.b. 6)	10	Extras (b. 1, l.b. 3)	4
Total		321	Total (3 wkts.)	165

FALL OF WICKETS. *First Innings:* 1—5, 2—39, 3—129, 4—177, 5—189, 6—224, 7—276, 8—286, 9—293, 10—321. *Second Innings:* 1—40, 2—137, 3—145.

AUSTRALIA – First Innings

W. M. Lawry,	c. Smith, b. Trueman	11
R. B. Simpson,	c. Trueman, b. Titmus	32
B. C. Booth,	b. Titmus	11
N. C. O'Neill,	c. Graveney, b. Allen	73
P. J. Burge,	l.b.w., b. Titmus	103
R. N. Harvey,	c. sub., b. Statham	22
A. K. Davidson,	c. Allen, b. Dexter	15
R. Benaud,	c. Graveney, b. Allen	57
G. D. McKenzie,	c. and b. Titmus	0
N. Hawke,	c. Graveney, b. Titmus	14
A. W. Grout,	not out	0
Extras	(b. 6, l.b. 5)	11
Total		349

FALL OF WICKETS. 1—28, 2—50, 3—71, 4—180, 5—231, 6—271, 7—299, 8—303, 9—347, 10—349.

Fifth Day: The clouds remained, it was again grey and cool, as if the weather was to provide suitable mood music to the end. Overnight Dexter and Benaud had made their usual wearisome proclamations, like tired oracles mechanically uttering cynical prophecies to an indifferent and sceptical public. England, Dexter said, would aim at a hundred before lunch, then set Australia to score at a run a minute for four hours.

The first hour brought 39 runs, 22 to Barrington, 17 to Cowdrey. Benaud bowled most of this time, switching to the Randwick end halfway through, with Hawke and Davidson alternating at the other. He set his field deep, and not a martial note was sounded by either side. Cowdrey pottered, Barrington, like a somnambulist who had already dreamed his second hundred of the match, pushed. They scored by singles, never more than gently persuasive. After seventy minutes Cowdrey lofted Hawke with the swing to the mid-wicket boundary, then drove him sweetly through the covers. The ball could be hit after all; Cowdrey looked almost injured at the revelation. Barrington remained distrustful, or at least disinclined to put it to the test.

Forty minutes before lunch, with England 229, Benaud gave Davidson the new ball. It was the last time we should see him with it. Cowdrey hooked him, then played one that dipped in late down to long leg. He cut McKenzie to reach 50, hit Davidson high back over his head and then steered him to Benaud at second slip. The change in tempo, with Barrington in permanent hibernation, had been too abrupt. Graveney, making haste, was caught and bowled by Davidson. McKenzie, getting one to lift in the next over, had Barrington caught by Grout. He had put the onus of losing their wickets on to others, and now, in his perspex cage, had lost his own six runs short of his second hundred. He reached the boundary only twice.

Trueman heaved his first two balls from McKenzie high to the fence. He faced up to the third, but Benaud decided to drop two men out and was hooted for doing so. Trueman swished again and was caught by Harvey at deep mid-off.

Titmus played half a dozen pugnacious strokes and then Smith, caught at slip, courteously provided Davidson with a wicket with his last ball in Test cricket. England, despite their slothful opening, had scored 103 in the morning. Dexter, having achieved his stated objective, fulfilled his obligation by declaring. Australia, with four hours left, needed 241 runs to win. The *dénouement* was clumsily contrived, but at least some propitiatory gesture had been made. Trueman, bowling cutters at medium pace, began from the Randwick end. He beat Simpson twice, then brought the fifth back to remove the leg stump. Two overs later he limped off the field. Dexter bowled somewhat wildly in his place, but soon there were spinners on at each end. After forty-five minutes Australia, taking it quietly, were 25, Harvey 17. Titmus now pitched one short at Harvey, Harvey slashed, and Cowdrey, at short slip, put it down. Lawry, stationary on 7 for twenty minutes, edged Titmus fine of Cowdrey for three. Harvey at the other end jumped out to Allen and snicked him past the leg stump. He cut Allen square for four, turned him off his pads, and in the same over was beaten in the air and bowled. Australia, after sixty-five minutes, were 39 for 2. Titmus, with Dexter and Barrington squatting off O'Neill's hip, bowled three good overs before O'Neill cut him past slip and then lay back to force him through the covers. At 50 Dexter replaced Allen with Barrington, presumably as some sort of votive offering, and then switched Allen to the Randwick end. Smith jollied Australia along further by letting through several byes and Barrington encouraged O'Neill with a long-hop and a full toss, both of which he thumped for four. Allen bowled a maiden to Lawry, who was 18 after 115 minutes, and handclapping began on the Hill. Allen pitched two short outside the off stump and O'Neill, cutting, missed the first and was caught at the wicket off the second. Allen's second ball to Booth turned, kept low and hit the middle stump. Booth stabbed as if electrocuted. Burge edged the last ball of the over and it flew to the left of Cowdrey, who had begun to move the other way. Dexter, able now to dismiss notions of defeat, luxuriantly crowded Lawry. Allen bowled to two short legs, two slips, two silly mid-offs. Australia, 75 for 4 at tea, had two hours to sweat out. A mirror had been held to the corpse and it had shown sudden signs of life.

Titmus and Allen bowled for twenty minutes and Lawry, leaning on the ball, dropped it in front of him like a trained retriever. Dexter gave Graveney four overs and once he found the edge, the ball flying low off Burge's bat between slip and gully. Lawry and Burge helped themselves to twenty-four runs meanwhile. With eighty minutes left Illingworth bowled for the first time. Allen, having bowled six overs for five runs, came off. The ball turned with ponderous solemnity and short of picking it off Lawry's bat nothing could be done about it. Dexter had a brief turn, Barrington came back, then Titmus. Burge dropped on the ball, smothering it as if in a sack. The sun, for the only time in five days, made a brief appearance. Drinks were taken and it became painfully evident that the drama was over. Both Burge and Lawry, long after all images of potential disaster had gone up in smoke, produced strokes of massive portentousness. The dwindling group on the Hill jeered, catcalled and shouted for Davidson. But they were denied their final glimpse. Lawry and Burge, like entombed miners tapping listlessly for help, saw the day through. No one was listening any longer.

It was a sorry end, an anti-play after all. Benaud had turned his back on an honest challenge. But the mistakes had been made earlier and he could afford to shrug. Had either of Burge's two edges wide of Cowdrey gone to hand it could have flared up. But England, on a lifeless pitch, had left themselves too little time. The weather had not helped. They had come out of the match on top, but the Ashes would be left behind. Drawing the series was more than anyone could have hoped before Brisbane, but the final encounter, which might have justified everything, never really materialized. Both teams got about their just deserts.

ENGLAND

First Innings		Second Innings	
D. S. Sheppard, c. and b. Hawke	19	c. Harvey, b. Benaud	68
M. C. Cowdrey, c. Harvey, b. Davidson	2	c. Benaud, b. Davidson	53
K. F. Barrington, c. Harvey, b. Benaud	101	c. Grout, b. McKenzie	94
E. R. Dexter, c. Simpson, b. O'Neill	47	st. Grout, b. Benaud	6
T. W. Graveney, c. Harvey, b. McKenzie	14	c. and b. Davidson	3
R. Illingworth, c. Grout, b. Davidson	27	c. Hawke, b. Benaud,	18
F. J. Titmus, c. Grout, b. Hawke	34	not out	12
F. S. Trueman, c. Harvey, b. Benaud	30	c. Harvey, b. McKenzie	8
A. C. Smith, b. Simpson	6	c. Simpson, b. Davidson	1
D. A. Allen, c. Benaud, b. Davidson	14		
J. B. Statham, not out	17		
Extras (b. 4, l.b. 6)	10	Extras (b. 1, l.b. 4)	5
Total	321	Total (8 wkts. dec.)	268

FALL OF WICKETS. *First Innings:* 1—5, 2—39, 3—129, 4—177, 5—189, 6—244, 7—276, 8—286, 9—293, 10—321. *Second Innings:* 1—40, 2—137, 3—145, 4—239, 5—247, 6—249, 7—257, 8—268.

AUSTRALIA

First Innings		Second Innings	
W. M. Lawry, c. Smith, b. Trueman	11	not out	45
R. B. Simpson, c. Trueman, b. Titmus	32	b. Trueman	0
B. C. Booth, b. Titmus	11	b. Allen	0
N. C. O'Neill, c. Graveney, b. Allen	73	c. Smith, b. Allen	17
P. J. Burge, l.b.w., b. Titmus	103	not out	52
R. N. Harvey, c. sub., b. Statham	22	b. Allen	28
A. K. Davidson, c. Allen, b. Dexter	15		
R. Benaud, c. Graveney, b. Allen	57		
G. D. McKenzie, c. and b. Titmus	0		
N. Hawke, c. Gravney, b. Titmus	14		
A. W. Grout, not out	0		
Extras (b. 6, l.b. 5)	11	Extras (b. 4, l.b. 6)	10
Total	349	Total (4 wkts.)	152

FALL OF WICKETS. *First Innings:* 1—28, 2—50, 3—71, 4—180, 5—231, 6—271, 7—299, 8—303, 9—347, 10—349. *Second Innings:* 1—0, 2—39, 3—70, 4—70.

Bowling Analysis

AUSTRALIA

	First Innings				Second Innings			
	O.	M.	R.	W.	O.	M.	R.	W.
Davidson ...	25.6	4	43	3	28	1	80	3
McKenzie ..	27	4	57	1	8	0	39	2
Hawke	20	1	51	2	9	0	38	0
Benaud	34	9	71	2	30	8	71	3
Simpson	18	4	51	1	4	0	22	0
O'Neill	10	0	38	1				
Harvey					3	0	13	0

ENGLAND

	First Innings				Second Innings			
	O.	M.	R.	W.	O.	M.	R.	W.
Trueman ...	11	0	33	1	3	0	6	1
Statham	18	1	76	1	4	1	8	0
Dexter......	7	1	24	1	4	1	11	0
Titmus	47.2	9	103	5	20	7	37	0
Allen	43	15	87	2	19	11	26	3
Illingworth..	5	1	15	0	10	5	8	0
Barrington ..					8	3	22	0
Graveney ...					4	0	24	0

UMPIRES: C. Edgar and I. Rowan
Total Attendance: 125,215
Total Receipts: £A28,483 11s.

10 Postscript

It had been my intention to write these final pages in Oahu, most accessible of the Hawaiian islands, to which I had flown in a Qantas Boeing immediately after the final Test. But the pleasures of Waikiki Beach, of surf-riding, catamarans and outrigger canoes, proved too seductive; in the evenings I preferred to gulp Daiquiries and Mai-Tais, brought by soft-footed Polynesian girls with hibiscus in their hair, and watch the sun go down behind the coconut palms. Also, Hawaiian music is no kind of accompaniment to stern analyses of the intricacies of Anglo-Australian Test cricket. I tried again in San Francisco, but somehow the procession of Old Fashioneds, the distractions of Chinatown and Fisherman's Wharf, or perhaps simply the proximity of Alcatraz, deterred me from effort. I made no attempt at all in New York, still snow-smeared and frozen, as was the whole of the Middle West, nor in Puerto Rico, where I flew for a week to escape the last of the winter. Instead, I lazed on the coral beaches of Dorado, picnicked in the rain-forests of El Yunque, and scrambled over the forts from which the Conquistadores had looked out over the Atlantic at invading Dutch and British fleets. Drake had sailed from San Juan on his last voyage and only annihilating attacks of dysentery among his troops prevented the Earl of Cumberland, who captured Puerto Rico in 1598, from maintaining the island as a British possession. Had it not been for this, Puerto Rico might now be part of the cricket-playing Caribbean, with Test matches in place of baseball games being staged in the arenas of San Juan. Instead, I watched cock-fights, which in their later stages made a partnership between Lawry and Mackay seem in comparison to be indecently eventful. However, they were passionately attended, for whole days at a time, and much money changed hands. So much so, it seemed to me quite clear that the single remedy to restore crowds to cricket would be the re-introduction of betting. After all, when cricket began, it was as much for its possibilites as an object of wager, as for its charms as a summer diversion or its displaying of personal skills that the nobility promoted it. Most cricketers are gamblers, and who would bother to go racing if betting was prohibited? Properly controlled, it would not affect the quality of the play at all; a maiden over would be a legitimate forecast, though if bowled to X or Y, one would be lucky to get evens. At the very least, it would be less harmful than artificial tinkering with the existing laws.

I find myself, therefore, recalling this series under the Sussex Downs, less green than I have ever seen them, and attempting to unearth some antidote to the universal feelings of disappointment these Tests have aroused. Or at least to discover what went wrong, and why. For, plainly, something did, though nothing as fatal as might be supposed from the barrage of abuse that rang in the ears of the withdrawing players, both from the English and Australian press. I have in front of me as I write Harvey's series of squalid articles, largely devoted to hysterical anecdote, detrimental to Dexter, and also a file of press-cuttings, mostly by Sports editors who scarcely saw a ball bowled, or who would not recognize a cut from a hook if they saw one. They leave one with a feeling more of pity than of contempt. Are their motives so mercenary, their interest so tenuous, that they cannot even try to understand what the game is about and how it is played? Test cricket needs constructive criticism, much more than it gets, but if it is not based on genuine feeling and an honest desire to get to grips with the complexities, it can only be harmful and a waste of time.

However, it was not only the uninformed and irresponsible critics who were left, finally, with a sense of anti-climax. I think everyone who saw the last day at either Adelaide or Sydney felt that too great a disparity existed between what went on in the minds of the players, and what passed through the minds of an audience who had paid to be entertained. It seemed, justifiably I think, that at moments there was no relation at all between the two. The batsmen were pursuing private activities that were only tangentially relevant to an overall strategy, let alone to the public. The reason was, quite simply, that there are dull, selfish, and bigoted cricketers just as there are dull, selfish and bigoted human beings. Captains of Test teams consider themselves to have two responsibilities, one is to lead their countries to victory, and, secondly, failing that, to avoid defeat. No one could possibly quarrel with this. At no stage does the obligation to entertain, as separate from either of these tasks, come into it. Nor should it. Once Test cricket ceased to be wholly competitive, in the purest sense, it would lose all intensity, and decay. Even in village cricket, popularly conceived to be the backbone of the game, people care passionately about the result. It would be very boring otherwise. The point is that in every form of cricket a bowling or batting performance acquires significance in exact relation to its context. Virtuosity as an end in itself means nothing; if it did, spectators would swarm to the nets to watch great technicians amusing themselves.

Somehow the true perspective, largely through understandable pique, has been lost. Australian crowds, thrilled by the West Indian series of a couple of years back, thirsted for Tests with the same exhilarating attack and counter-attack. In that instance Frank Worrell, supported by several of the greatest stroke-players in the game, forced Benaud into retaliatory tactics. He was obliged to reply in kind. As it was, the West Indians, narrowly losing the series after two crucial and questionable umpiring decisions, had every reason to consider themselves hard done by. They played with magnificent spirit, and they added to superb natural ability a growing realization of their own possibilities. The Australians, stung out of potential complacency, had the resources to match them in terms of sounder technique and greater experience, if not of sheer brilliance. The result was a contest in a thousand. The West Indians astonished even themselves, the Australians finally scraped home, the individual Tests were not only dramatically close but packed with thrilling performances and moments of high drama. Everyone went away happy.

What happened this time? Three Tests were drawn (one interestingly, two drably, though rain and bad light were substantial causes) and two ended one-sidedly, in margins of seven and eight wickets. There were, on the England side, three stroke-players capable of enhancing any Test, on the Australian side two. The two Australians, O'Neill and Harvey, achieved one convincing innings each, and those late in the series. Of the English three, Graveney missed two Tests, Cowdrey only twice moved beyond diffidence, Dexter played five commanding innings in ten. Each side had one fast bowler able to throw the whole proceedings into confusion, once he had struck, and supporting bowlers able to bowl accurately, and over long periods, to defensive fields. When England batted there was always the threat that if any wicket was thrown away unnecessarily Davidson or Benaud would step in and polish off the rest. The risk, in relation to the skills available, outweighed the advantages. The Australians, for their part, were consistently handicapped by the failures of Harvey and O'Neill, having continually to climb to security on the backs of Lawry, Simpson, Booth and Mackay. It was the length of their batting, with Benaud and Davidson repeatedly being required to graft their way out of trouble, that ultimately enabled them to achieve respectability. Catching less haphazard than England's would have overturned them comfortably. After Brisbane, England never once got off to a faintly encouraging start, with the result that the middle batsmen, aware of their comparatively long tail, bore an oppressive burden. Time after time Titmus and Trueman salvaged seeming wrecks, but against bowlers such as Davidson, McKenzie and Benaud, it could only be uphill work. The pitches were uniformly slow, unhelpful equally to batsmen and bowlers. Before the war, when larger and quicker scores were habitually achieved, wickets were uncovered – allowing far greater variety of conditions – captains were less adept at pacing the game to their own advantage, and geniuses of the order of Bradman and Hammond were able to make nonsense of defensive impositions. Geniuses, however, cannot be whistled up for the asking.

Dexter, in an unfortunately phrased farewell statement, expressed the view that had the Ashes not been at stake, but each match played for £1,000, then there would have been no drawn games. I trust he did not fully understand the implications of what he said; if he did, then he has forfeited every right to go on being England's captain. Even so, and despite the Duke of Norfolk's contention that he had not come out to watch drawn matches, there is no dishonour in a draw. Who could forget Watson's and Bailey's heroic, last-ditch effort against Australia at Lord's in 1953, a demonstration of character and determination that enabled England to win back the Ashes at the Oval after three losing series? There have been many such instances, not least when Australia saved the Adelaide Test against West Indies, Kline and Mackay hanging on for the last hour. I find nothing uninteresting about a drawn match, *per se*; what is important is the manner and the tactics that conduce to it.

In this present series there are three draws to investigate. At Brisbane, any one of three results was possible up to the very last hour. No one, in a five-day match, could ask fairer than that. The tempo all along may have been slowish, but the average total was around 300 runs a day, which, with the bowlers nearly always rather the stronger, is not sluggish.

At Adelaide, the responsibility was again with Benaud. Several hours were lost through rain and bad light, and Davidson was absent for most of the match. To the onlooker, there for kicks, the last day might well have seemed a steady descent into the futile. Benaud, convinced he could not win, settled on making losing as unlikely as possible. As a result, he gave himself inadequate time to do either. Had Titmus taken an easy catch on the last morning, England, despite everything, could have got home. Barrington scored a fine hundred on the last afternoon and the match petered out. But the rain and the dropped catch cannot be put against Benaud: restore the time lost and the match would have ended one way or the other. What irked most people was simply Benaud's realism. They would have preferred at least some gesture towards a decision, remote though it might have proved. Benaud is not one for gestures of that kind: his reading of the possibilities may be questioned, but once accepting them his tactics were perfectly logical. No one took pleasure from the desultory playing out of the game, but that was the way the cards fell. You cannot rig the hands. There is cause for complaint only when the batting captain, with a decipherable prospect of success, refuses to take the legitimate risk of losing. Where the Australians, both here at Adelaide and on the last afternoon at Sydney, displeased, was in their reluctance to enact a charade. But as Benaud later drily remarked, 'Matches are played over five days, not over one-and-a-half'.

At Sydney this proposition was underlined. Dexter, in consultation with his advisers, conceived that England's best chance of winning (not, I must emphasize, of drawing) was to score as many runs over 300 as they could manage, then hope, on what was a slow, turning wicket, to bowl Australia out twice in the time remaining. Obviously the quicker they scored, the longer would be the time at their disposal. The necessary premise to England's scoring 300 was that Davidson should be allowed to do as little damage with the new ball as possible. The precedents for this were not promising. Accordingly, with Cowdrey moved up to No. 2 in Pullar's place, it was decided that no strokes were to be attempted in front of the wicket for half-an-hour, after which most of the shine would have gone and Cowdrey could open out. I think it was, inevitably, a mistaken policy, but it had sensible motives. After 29 minutes Cowdrey, somewhat unluckily, was caught off his glove, and Sheppard followed him not long after. The Australians, having tasted blood, made certain that Dexter, despite his evident intentions, should find it hazardous to make good the time lost. Benaud set defensive fields, himself bowling with great accuracy, and Dexter, try as he might, failed to get through. The outfield, rain-softened and lush, was extraordinarily slow. Barrington assumed the strike, and the plan increasingly misfired. Benaud could afford to wait for mistakes: Dexter could not afford to make one, for with him gone any chance of achieving a large enough total to make Australia struggle on so laboriously turning a pitch would evaporate immediately. That both he and Barrington were forced, so early in the game, into an almost fatalistic approach, was a direct consequence of the loss of two cheap wickets, of tidy Australian bowling and magnificent fielding, and a pitch on which the ball came slowly on to the bat. Substitute Bradman for Barrington and all this would have been of no account. But players must be accepted for what they are. Barrington is a churlish runner between the wickets, he had the responsibility – which he bore nobly – of holding the innings together, and the ultimate policy, with its target of 300, remained valid. Dexter came out after tea intent on hurrying things up and got out in the first over. It was, of course, maddening; but England's slowness was scarcely wilful. It is impossible not to sympathize with barracked players when they offer their bats to their hecklers and invite them to do better. Things are not often that easy, though they may appear so from the stands. Bad balls seem to go unpunished, but fields are, after all, set against them, and when you have been concentrating for hours, with no margins allowed for error, the half-volley or one short of a length cannot be disposed of by magic. The ball runs for you, or it does not; and once the bowlers acquire the initiative, it requires more effort than is sometimes discernible to wrest it away. In this instance England might well have done better to go for the bowling from the start; but this is to assume that the batsmen were better players than they were. In fact, Sheppard usually had to hang on for his life, and only Dexter, Graveney at his infrequent best, and Cowdrey when out of his chrysalis, ever had the capacity to dictate matters. Criticism, to be realistic, must deal with the potentialities of those actually involved; it is crying for the moon to expect players to change their spots overnight.

No one was happy that England, hampered by a long stretch of appalling light, finally took a day and a half to reach 320. Australia, pinned down by Titmus, fared no better. By the second evening Dexter's strategy, allowing for everything, had still a 50-50 chance of success. On a pitch that gave the spinners progressive scope, England must have won the match. But the ball continued to turn painfully slowly. O'Neill, Burge and Benaud batted with skill and authority, and, predictably, time began to run out. England, in their second innings, hurried along as best they could, but Dexter lost his wicket in near darkness, and when, finally, prospects of defeat had been decently minimized – though altogether less so than Benaud had insisted on at Adelaide – there were only four hours left for play. On this last morning England, though they scored exactly a hundred before lunch, might well have striven harder for a longer and more imaginatively achieved lead. There were just grounds for dissatisfaction, for which Barrington, inching his way towards a second century in the match, must take most of the blame. This was a case where Dexter could, and should, have given precise instructions, something he rarely felt disposed to do.

His declaration, when it came, left Australia to score 60 an hour for four hours. Although this was more than had been managed at any stage of the match, it was not asking anything out of the ordinary. Unfortunately, Simpson was bowled by Trueman in the first over and then Harvey and O'Neill, each of whom began to show signs of accepting the challenge, got out. When Allen bowled Booth for nought with a shooter Benaud promptly shut up shop. For about twenty minutes Dexter's tactics even looked as if they might pay off – silencing his critics for good – but cleverly as Allen bowled the pitch was against him. Lawry and Burge, attempting nothing, played out the evening with few qualms.

Again, the *dénouement* had been sadly limp; but the pitch and the run of the game had conditioned what happened. It is one thing to mourn the absence of drama; it is quite another, understanding why and how things turned out as they did, to abuse the captains for not being able to reverse natural and logical processes. Had the two sides been less evenly matched, the results, as New Zealand proved, would have been decisive. Then one side would have had to have given way. But which? All through this series, the bowlers held slightly the whip hand, and when this is the case, the batsmen are bound to appear wary and obdurate. It sometimes turns out like this and there is no easy way out. Results cannot be contrived artificially; that is not what Test matches are about. The flaw in the pattern of this series was not in the tactics employed; it stemmed simply from the fact that there were no batsmen, on such pitches and against the bowling they were required to face, of the calibre to create images. By and large, these were two fairly pedestrian sides, the run of the mill players heavily outnumbering those of Test class.

Faster wickets, where mere occupation of the crease was no guarantee of immunity, would have altered the whole rhythm. Spin bowlers have a right to expect to come into their own on the last day of a five-day match. Yet this did not once happen. Benaud and Titmus were no more conclusive at the end of a match than at the beginning; if anything, the ball turned more slowly as the game proceeded. Again, there was nothing approaching a green wicket; the fast bowlers had to do it all themselves. On Hutton's tour, when England, winning three Test matches, only twice nosed beyond 300, it was quite otherwise. The scoring was even slower, but the matches were consistently exciting.

Covering the wickets, too, has tended to remove those elements of surprise and unpredictability that are natural to the game. Bradman, before the war, commented that you would not expect Lindrum to perform on a torn table-cloth. Nor would you, but then cricket is not billiards. That batsmen no longer need to pit their skills against bowlers on sticky wickets not only takes much of the variety from the game, robbing it of intrinsic waywardness, but it puts a premium on mere competence. Before wickets were covered the time lost after rain was more than compensated for by trickier conditions, with a consequent acceleration of narrative. The days of covering are, one hopes, numbered. Luck may play a greater part than at present, but weather hazards are infinitely preferable to stifled, placid pitches, devoid of spirit and humour.

These Tests were unique in one sense: never before (and one must hope never again) have both captains held press conferences in their dressing-rooms after each day's play. Benaud began this practice in England in 1961, for the benefit of touring correspondents. Dexter, for publicity reasons, was encouraged to emulate him. As an exercise in public relations it badly rebounded. Not only did the subsequent day's play bear scant relation to the predictions, prophecies and stated intentions of the two captains, but the repetitious nature of their often platitudinous comments created an inevitably stale and wearying effect.

It is of little interest what captains say they are going to do or what explanations they give for what they have done already. Critics and an informed public must judge by results, not on intentions. Moreover, this relentless intrusion into the dressing-room, whether captains affect to mind or not, leads to the expressing of opinions usually much better left unexpressed. The same applies to cricketers writing in the press about series in which they are, or have just been, playing. Harvey's articles have earned him some money, but they have done him harm quite incommensurate with his fee. Benaud, a professional journalist, who wrote a weekly column throughout the series, is a wiser bird altogether. Personal vindictiveness always recoils on the writer. Harvey may well dislike Dexter; he is at liberty to believe that Dexter does not play the kind of cricket he cares for, but the bald, unsubstantiated terms in which he voiced his disapproval cheapened him, not Dexter.

Australian papers as a whole give far fuller coverage to cricket than do English ones. The main papers in each city, the *Melbourne Age*, the *Sydney Morning Herald*, the *Adelaide Advertiser*, the *Brisbane Courier-Mail* and the *West Australian* in Perth, carry as a rule both a detailed account of the play by their cricket correspondent, and comments by former Test cricketers. Thus O'Reilly and Hassett grace the Press Box during Tests and what they have to say next day has a technical value especial to them. Having no obligation to describe, they are free to make points as they occur to them. They wouldn't, I imagine, set much store by dressing-room interviews. Jack Fingleton, by profession a Parliamentary correspondent in Canberra, chooses to write for non-Australian papers, who are the losers thereby. Keith Miller, when he can be prised from the race-course, alternately chastises and cheers in prose that has no use for half-measures. Barnes writes a column calculated to provoke; Lindwall does commentaries on television and radio; Archer broadcasts. Whatever the merits of individual styles, there is no absence of informed comment. Australian journalism may lack the kind of tradition that in England provided scope for Darwin, Cardus and Robertson-Glasgow; but what it loses in wit, grace and imagery, is offset by directness and authority. They take the finer points seriously. In addition, the wealth of illustration accompanying every report underlines the scantiness of English papers in this respect. The system whereby Lord's, the Oval, and other Test grounds sell sole photographic rights to one agency may simplify administration, but by removing the incentive of competition has lowered the standard quite disproportionately.

The consequence of this extensive Australian coverage of cricket – which is by no means limited to professional cricket writers – is that every quote or remark, every incident no matter how trivial, is likely to be inflated out of all proportion. Since a disparaging or disaffected comment is always better news than a reasonable one, all sense of perspective is quickly lost. A casual observer, flicking through the papers, might be forgiven for thinking all Test cricketers sado-masochists, riddled with resentment, intent on boring at all costs, and potential failures to a man. Cricket, like the upper classes and standards in general, is in permanent decline. No one would have it otherwise.

Whatever the merits of the Tests as entertainment – and for the reasons I have suggested the teams seemed finally never to get to grips – the fact remains that Dexter achieved in terms of results more than anyone expected before Brisbane. M.C.C. were soundly defeated by a Combined XI at Perth and trounced by New South Wales in Sydney. The odds were that England would be lucky to draw a couple of Tests and could expect to lose three. In the event, they proved extremely difficult to beat. We live in an era of anti-novels and anti-plays and in this sense the Tests were of their period. Their particular brand of non-committal inconclusiveness might have been invented by Harold Pinter, Samuel Beckett or N. F. Simpson. The scene-setting caution with which the contestants sized one another up overlapped into, and ultimately devoured, the time that belonged to action. Nevertheless, in thirty years only one English side, Hutton's in 1954/55, left for New Zealand with a better record and victorious. England, after all, drew the series, and of the two teams they came on the very last day the closer to winning. That is not an entirely negligible achievement. Dexter has since received almost unqualified abuse, but few captains have ever set a better personal example on the field and he joins Chapman, Jardine and Hutton as the only Test captains since the 1914–18 war to have held their own in Australia. He had his faults, certainly, but in the main these lay in his handling of his own players and they did not demonstrably affect the results of the Tests. He spent little time with his team off the field, but he was not alone in this. Jardine, Hammond, Hutton were equally remote characters, and similar complaints, one recalls, were constantly levelled at May. Bradman, during his playing days, was not usually regarded as a particularly sociable figure, nor one disposed to be free with friendly advice to his juniors. It would seem that the price of cricketing pre-eminence, added to captaincy's strains and responsibilities, is a kind of withdrawn aloofness that is not entirely separable from the single-mindedness essential to the great player. Keith Millers and Denis Comptons are not thrown up every day, and neither of these was ever saddled with the burdens, social, administrative and strategic, of captaining a side, let alone on tour. Irresponsibility was part of their charm, though Miller, especially, might have been a rewarding captain.

Social responsiveness, affability, evenness of mood are not noticeably part of Dexter's personality, though he is consistent to the extent that he would as unconcernedly cut the Duke of Norfolk or the Chairman of the Selectors as he would look through a plain hostess at a cocktail party. Where he failed in his relations with his team was that he left them overmuch to their own devices, often without guidance or consideration, when both would have been appreciated. Yet he is not without charm or warmth and if it lacked tact to greet the flannelled Bradman at Canberra with the remark 'Straight out of Madame Tussauds' it suggests a not displeasing irony too. He was generously accessible to the Press, and was never other than strictly to the point in his statements to them.

Much has been made of his tactical callowness *vis-à-vis* Benaud, and occasionally his field placings bore the look of a chess board that has been inadvertently knocked over by a waiter and the pieces reassembled at random. Often he seemed *distrait* during long partnerships, as if some opaque screen had come down between his private fantasies and what was actually going on. Unlike Benaud, who gives the appearance of identifying himself with every single one of his players all of the time, Dexter seems to abstract himself, as if the flow of events was no real concern of his. Yet I do not really think that

Benaud, for all his persuasiveness and skill in man-management, ever got the better of him strategically. For most of the series Benaud seemed obsessed by Dexter's presence, and if his own sparse haul of wickets included Dexter's more often than anyone else's, this was of only personal significance.

In the end Dexter had too much to do, the consequence of which was that he lost his own attacking flair. In the first two Tests he raised, by his personal aggressiveness, the whole level of the English batting, and by the time he had himself gone off the boil the standard had been set. England subsequently fought all the way down the line, with Barrington in almost permanent residence, but in the initial stages, when Benaud wore an aura of invincibility, and Davidson threatened to lay waste, it was Dexter, almost contemptuously, who reduced them to human scale. He repeatedly lost his way in the suburbs of a long innings, occasionally through impatience, occasionally through exhaustion, but generally, one felt, it was because at some stage in the sixties or seventies he ceased to play instinctively and became aware of the need to go on. He was then easy prey to the spinners, prodding forward without clear idea of the googly or the leg-break. But disappointment was relative: he played magnificent strokes in nearly every innings and the sight of him pacing his crease, or bent over his bat, all restless energy, was always one to lift the spirits. He will never, perhaps, be a great player of leg-spin, though he took a fair toll of Benaud and Simpson, but few batsmen have ever driven fast bowling harder or reduced stock bowlers more ruthlessly to insignificance. He was one of the few English fielders to match the Australians in mobility and crispness, and his bowling, while only spasmodically purposeful, earned both respect and wickets.

It was one of Dexter's problems that only three of his side could be said to have come off in the accepted sense – Trueman, Titmus, and Barrington. Trueman, hair blackly flopping over a face that never lost an industrial pallor, endeared himself almost alone to Australian crowds. He never put down a catch, he threw, either left-handed or right, from the boundary to the top of the stumps, and his curving, bandy-legged run, toe-caps glinting as the broad, untidy hips swivelled, was always the signal for dead quiet. He bowled beautifully with the new ball, controlling the swing and adjusting the angles of approach, and he varied a full, swerving length with others, fractionally short on the leg stump, that reared up at the ribs. He was often genuinely fast, but even off his shorter run, at moments when he moved round the field with an old sweat's assumed resentfulness, he was never other than accurate and probing.

Taken as a pair, there was little to choose between Trueman and Statham on the one hand, Davidson and McKenzie on the other. In each case, the new ball thrust came from Trueman and Davidson, with Trueman rather the more enduring of the two. On the same side, with their contrasting methods, they would have made a glorious combination. Trueman had a slight edge in pace, Davidson exploited the more bewildering swing. Between McKenzie and Statham, one developing, one running down, there was the difference between youthful strength and honest endeavour. In his prime Statham never swung the ball perceptibly, but he had pace and the ability to make one or two an over nip back devastatingly off the seam. These days he retains his control, his almost robot accuracy, but only rarely did he get any life out of the pitch or move the ball off it. He was often no more than fast medium and he bowled on long hot afternoons rather from memory than with anticipation. McKenzie, still lacking art and frequently wild in direction, takes little out of himself, has magnificent shoulders and an open action, and always made the ball get up off a length. On anything approaching a lively wicket, like Lord's, he must be an uncomfortable proposition. Whenever Benaud needed him to bowl long spells he kept his pace to the end.

The real revelation of the series was, I suppose, Titmus. He played first in a Test match as long ago as 1955, but Laker held sway until 1959, after which Allen, with his more pronounced spin, kept him out. Nevertheless Titmus kept bowling cheerfully away on a Lord's pitch kinder to seamers, taking his hundred wickets and making just over or under a thousand runs. He seemed a thoroughly good county cricketer.

It was not until the Second Test at Melbourne that he began to appear more than this. The Australians never played him convincingly, sweeping across the line or getting pushed crabbily back on their stumps. He varied his pace enough to deter too frequent or early moves down the wicket, and his curving trajectory, with the ball starting outside the leg stump and floating across, disconcerted everyone. He bowled few bad balls and was able to get away, for the most part, without deep fielders. In comparison with the great off-spinners his range is narrow; Booth occasionally showed up his limitations, for on Australian pitches he declined to give the ball much air, he was not able to get it to move the other way off the pitch, as Illingworth with his rounder action occasionally does, and his turn, compared with Allen's, is negligible. But he gave himself precise tasks, and he fulfilled them admirably. His batting, especially with Trueman at the other end, progressed from the plucky to the eloquent, and apart from his one sad lapse on the last morning at Adelaide, he fielded with safety and alertness.

In figures alone, only Hammond among English batsmen has ever exceeded Barrington's performances in Australia. This is to put Barrington way out of his natural class; but runs count, and whether at five or three Barrington delivered the goods. He prefers the higher position and when Dexter sent him in first wicket down he came up with scores of 63, 132 not out, 101 and 93. No one could ask more than that. Indeed his first-class scores on the tour make remarkable reading: 24, 0, 44, 104, 219*, 19, 183*, 78, 23, 52, 35, 0*, 35, 23, 63, 132*, 33, 67, 101 and 93. These he followed up with a century in the First Test in New Zealand. He is a magnificent cutter, an effective sweeper. He plays forward with bat almost exaggeratedly straight, though when driving the quicker bowlers outside the off stump he hits disturbingly far from the body, with the weight on the back foot. Yet he gets down on the ball, and if fast, short-pitched bowling induces an initial, marionettish jerkiness he soon settles to more convincing methods. He usually began an innings with a flourish of strokes, dropping to a steady jog-trot, enlivened by sudden onslaughts against the spinners. Had he the knack of taking the quick single for a forward push he would avoid the *longueurs* that often engulf him. He bowled less usefully than in the West Indies, not getting as much bounce nor being as economical, but his picking up and throwing from the boundary suffered nothing in comparison with the Australians.

Cowdrey, unobtrusive as vice-captain to the point of invisibility, had a fair but scarcely impressive series. He began nightmarishly when opening the innings, batted agreeably at Melbourne, but though he made two further Test fifties never looked quite to have his heart in it. His technique was the soundest on either side, the power was suggested but never fully exploited. He batted like a car being run-in. There were occasions when it was necessary, and seemed well within his capability, for him to take the attack to pieces. But he remained content to let the bowlers come to him, secure in the belief that for him timing and not aggression is the only weapon. He batted smoothly always, but he was never able, as a batsman of his gifts at number four should be able, to assume the initiative and disrupt calculations. Towards the end of the last tour of West Indies he roused himself against Hall and Watson in a fashion he never managed this time. He makes batting seem so absurdly easy that only about once a year does he appear to extend himself beyond mere display. He lacks the destructive element, a quality, one imagines, that cannot be acquired on demand. He took some beautiful catches at slip but was more fallible than usual.

Not since the break-up of the Hutton-Washbrook partnership over ten years ago, has England – except significantly when Cowdrey was pressed into opening – managed to get off to fluent starts in Tests that mattered. No one expected miracles from Pullar and Sheppard, but after Brisbane, when they passed fifty in the first innings, and a hundred in the second, one assumed they had weathered the worst. In the next three Tests they scraped into double figures only once, and four times failed to get beyond five. Pullar was scarcely ever in long enough to play badly, for his ideas about where Davidson was pitching in relation to the stumps were so hazy that he was consistently out, both to him and McKenzie, having either made no stroke or provided the merest sketch of one. He improved his fielding but his evident distaste for the whole business increased as the weeks went by. Sheppard passed thirty, a reasonable figure for an opening batsman against Davidson, five times in ten, a sequence that included a century and two fifties. That cannot be written off as failure. Had he not owed so many runs before he started, no one need have complained. He often seemed totally at sea against Davidson's swing, a fact not helped by his left shoulder pointing wide of mid-on, but he discernibly put his mind to the problem and sometimes played Benaud better than anyone.

Graveney, out of touch throughout the opening weeks, found himself dropped from the Brisbane Test – wrongly, I think – but towards the end batted with more incisiveness than I can remember. It was cruelly unfortunate that he should have been unfit at Sydney in January, when his character, temperament and technique would have been put to their most crucial test. He could, there, once and for all have proved whether he had the guts as well as the grace. As it was, he had no further opportunity of acquitting himself in an exacting context, and the ultimate question mark still hovers accusingly around him.

There remain the wicket-keepers, and those marginal figures who flitted in and out of the Tests without defining their positions either way. Only Larter of the seventeen players did not play at all in the Tests in Australia.

Murray, the first choice wicket-keeper, and technically much the superior of the two, began untidily and with Smith starting with a string of useful scores was obliged to make way. At Brisbane and Melbourne, Smith, a likeable and altogether pleasant cricketer, revealed suspected weaknesses to the spinners, and though he was fairly safe standing back he reached for the ball with little movement of the feet, making not only for awkwardness but for total abstention from the half-chance. Murray returned at Sydney, and immediately took the brilliant, shoulder-jarring catch which put him virtually out of the running for the rest of the tour. Smith kept well at Adelaide but had a wretched time with the spinners at Sydney.

Allen could count himself unlucky, in that he ought to have played in the Third Test, on a wicket that gave Titmus 7 for 79. Whenever the two subsequently bowled together, not least on the last afternoon of all, it was Allen who looked the more searching. Alec Bedser eventually prevailed on him, after a long, fruitless period, to add a couple of paces to his previously non-existent run-up, which, as Laker had long before insisted, was necessary for any significant changes in pace. But Allen, with quiet West country stubbornness, is resistant to experiment and he suffered in consequence.

Illingworth at Adelaide should have had 2 for 1 on the first morning; but the dropping of Harvey off him by Cowdrey and Sheppard in consecutive balls put a brutal end to any sudden flights of fancy. He had little to offer after that, though when required to open the innings, both at Sydney and in New Zealand, he made a respectable job of it.

Coldwell was strikingly useful in the Melbourne victory, but quite ineffectual after that. The pitches were too slow for him, or he for them; he trundled away accurately on an unhelpful wicket at Sydney, then was discarded.

Knight scraped into the Brisbane Test, largely by reason of his batting, which blossomed headily on the first time round. He played several fine innings in lesser matches, when the ball was pitched up to him, but once his weakness against the short, lifting ball had been exposed, he was reduced out of recognition. As a bowler he lacked the action, the physique, the pace and the guile. Larter picked up wickets here and there, but he alone never came into Test reckoning. Parfitt, after a valuable innings at Brisbane, lost his way completely, despite every effort.

The fielding, quite apart from the incredible number of dropped catches, was often untidy, sometimes downright inept, and only in the briefest flashes at all polished.

Only in the field were the Australians an eye-taking side. As a team they were short of personality, their batting had, perforce, to devolve round the least gifted stroke-players, and Benaud, as his own bowling shed lustre, grew defiantly constricted. He bore the manner of a small householder who, robbed of his watch-dog, had decided to barricade himself in. The Ashes lay in the grate and no Santa Claus was being allowed down the chimney. Anyone taking a detached but unblinking look at Benaud through this series would have found few instances of captaincy more imaginative or inspired than competence solicits. There were those who felt that some of Bradman's conservatism had rubbed off on Benaud; others smiled cynically at any rosy ideas about Benaud ever having taken risks, other than those (as at Manchester, 1961) forced on him. The truth is that in Test matches few captains ever take gambles of the kind the public relish; they play to win or to draw in that order, and the balance is rarely so delicate that attempting to win involves an ultimate forfeit. Benaud has been an immensely successful captain and Dexter the only opponent not to have to give him best.

On the field Benaud is a source of endless fascination. He adjusts his players as if by reference to some built-in electronic computer, assessing angles and distances. He appears calm, solicitous, involved; nothing happens that has not been foreseen, or that could alter the thoughtful deliberate walk from gully to gully, or back to his bowling mark. There has never been such a calculating cricketer and even at Melbourne, when England sailed steadily towards their target, it was only in the last half-hour that Benaud seemed at all disconcerted. Australians play relentlessly and Benaud, exuberant enough at moments of success, gives the impression, when things go wrong, of being able to afford to relax, for he knows, and we know, he has the ace up his sleeve.

How much his decline in effectiveness as a bowler was due to England's improved methods of playing him, and how much represented an actual falling-off, is hard to determine. He bowled beautifully in the first innings at Brisbane, but thereafter was expensive and on occasions extremely untidy. He alternated between long accurate spells and sudden descents into chaos. He seemed reluctant to throw the ball up, setting restrictive fields in consequence; the habit these days is for leg-spinners to drug batsmen into error rather than seduce them, which makes, on pitches where turn is minimal, for less exciting cricket. Benaud nearly always batted pleasantly; if, against fast bowling, some small gap between bat and pad is generally apparent, he remains nonetheless a crisp, front-footed player, never reluctant to hook nor charitable to the half-volley.

Harvey must thank his lucky stars for England's catching; he would otherwise have taken his leave of Test cricket in the gloomiest fashion. His one long innings should never have begun, and his only other score of consequence, a streaky effort in the Third Test, was again by kind permission of Sheppard. Still, he fielded superbly at cover, and in the last Test his catching of Graveney at leg slip – one of four catches by him – was electrifying.

No matter how plodding England's batting at any given moment, the Australians held the attention by their speed of movement, the deadly accuracy and swiftness of their throwing. Not one of them fielded other than well, while Harvey and O'Neill, with McKenzie and Shepherd scarcely inferior, were a constant delight. Davidson, weary with bowling, was not the claw of old, but Simpson and Benaud both took fine catches at slip. Grout, when he returned after his injury, was impressively clean and quick, though Bedser, used to thudding into

Evans's gloves, looked stonily at the sight of Grout standing back to Mackay.

In batting, only Booth of the earlier Australian players did full justice to themselves. There is something a bit stringy and colourless about Booth's presence, but he moves early into line, uses his feet and keeps his head. His Brisbane hundred was full of good things and in the mood he spanked the ball past mid-off. Infected by Lawry he would dry up at times, though at Adelaide he displayed an appetite for offspin, hitting Titmus, with Dexter's connivance, high into the untenanted areas wide of mid-on.

O'Neill played two magnificent innings, too few for a player of his all-round skill. Trueman unnerved him early on and he took some time to decide on the correct tactics against Titmus. He always promised well and he has a magnetism and power second only to Dexter.

Simpson and Lawry, as an opening pair, got going together little more than Sheppard and Pullar. Simpson began the season with a series of commanding innings all round Australia, but in the Tests he was curiously subdued. He set himself limited objectives, kept on the move with quickly-run singles, and glowed steadily, like a low-voltage bulb, without ever shining. Trueman beat him outside the off stump with monotonous regularity. Lawry was more adhesive than Pullar, but his snail-like proddings were calculated to empty any ground.

Burge lost his place for two Tests through substituting the sweep for the straight hit, but he is a dogged, burly player who, while late in maturing, has a tough resilience. Shepherd, his left-handed replacement, plays less straight than is desirable, but on good wickets has the strength and eye to score prolifically.

Of Mackay we must have seen the last: no batsman has ever made the most of such meagre talents, but now the timing and skill in placing had ebbed. What was left was the crude machinery, the fly-wheel missing. His bowling appeared commonplace, though neither Guest nor Hawke, called in subsequently to take some of the strain off Davidson, were spectacular improvements.

After an absence of eight years one cannot but notice, as one travels Australia, great changes: not only in the soaring skylines, the increase in sophistication and cosmopolitanism, but in less decipherable qualities of allegiance and attitude. Asia, as well as Europe, has grown nearer, and although the 100,000 migrants who arrive annually are still half of them British, that still leaves 50,000 Italians, Greeks, Hungarians and Jugoslavs to write their signatures across the blank years ahead.

George Molnar, a former Hungarian, some of whose cartoons embellish this book, has recently written: 'The new migrants introduced to Australia espresso bars, gallantry to ladies, flats with balconies, soccer, wine drinking, building in concrete, handshakes and smiles. They also introduced conversation as a way to pass time. . . . [Before they arrived] agriculture predominated. The country had still to be conquered. The general attitude was: "If it moves shoot it. If it stands still chop it down."

'The Australian is in the making. Maybe he will be a mixture of British values, of Continental enjoyment of life, of American techniques, with a touch of Eastern mysticism. Or perhaps he'll just be a tolerant, cheerful chap, with limited ambitions and a like for easy living. In any case he is rich, young and handsome . . . Lucky devil.'

The possibilities could not be more succinctly put. Either way, whether one prefers the old Australia of elegant, pillared, but internally frowsty country pubs and empty streets with wrought-iron bandstands, or the modern one of motels, highways, and space-contracting air travel, the essential characteristics show through. You can like them, or dislike them, but no one in future will be able to ignore them.

'You mean he is bringing out Hobbs?'

'My confidence is returning, Benaud prods better.'

'Cricket dull? It's jolly good fun.'

'No more bowling – too strenuous. Why not take up Test cricket?'

Scorebook

TEST MATCH AVERAGES IN AUSTRALIA

AUSTRALIA – BATTING

	Innings	Times not out	Runs	Highest score	Average
P. Burge	6	2	245	103	61.25
B. C. Booth	10	2	404	112	50.50
B. Shepherd	3	1	94	71*	47.00
R. B. Simpson	10	1	401	91	44.56
R. N. Harvey	10	0	395	154	39.50
K. D. Mackay	5	1	148	86*	37.00
W. M. Lawry	10	1	310	98	34.44
N. C. O'Neill	9	0	310	100	34.44
R. Benaud	7	0	227	57	32.43
A. K. Davidson	7	0	158	46	22.57
B. N. Jarman	4	2	23	11*	11.50
G. D. McKenzie	7	0	52	16	7.43
A. W. T. Grout	3	3	17	16*	—

Also batted: N. Hawke 14, C. Guest 11.

* Not out

AUSTRALIA – BOWLING

	Overs	Maidens	Runs	Wickets	Average
A. K. Davidson	175.6	30	480	24	20.00
G. D. McKenzie	205.3	25	619	20	30.95
R. Benaud	233	58	688	17	40.47
N. Hawke	29	1	89	2	44.50
R. B. Simpson	93	18	369	8	46.13
K. D. Mackay	86.5	19	227	4	56.75
N. C. O'Neill	33	8	118	2	59.00

Also bowled: B. C. Booth 2-0-4-0; R. N. Harvey 3-0-13-0; C. Guest 18-0-59-0.

Catches: R. Benaud 9, R. B. Simpson 9, R. N. Harvey 6, A. K. Davidson 4, W. M. Lawry 4, G. D. McKenzie 3, B. C. Booth 2, P. Burge 2, N. Hawke 2, N. C. O'Neill 2, B. Shepherd 1.

Wicket-keeping: A. W. T. Grout 7 catches, 2 stumpings; B. N. Jarman 7 catches, no stumpings.

TEST MATCH AVERAGES IN AUSTRALIA

ENGLAND – BATTING

	Innings	Times not out	Runs	Highest score	Average
K. F. Barrington	10	2	582	132*	72.75
E. R. Dexter	10	0	481	99	48.10
M. C. Cowdrey	10	1	394	113	43.78
F. J. Titmus	8	3	182	59*	36.40
D. S. Sheppard	10	0	330	113	33.00
T. W. Graveney	5	1	116	41	29.00
P. H. Parfitt	4	0	112	80	28.00
G. A. Pullar	8	0	170	56	21.25
F. S. Trueman	7	0	142	38	20.29
R. Illingworth	3	0	57	27	19.00
A. C. Smith	5	1	47	21	11.75
J. B. Statham	6	2	29	17*	9.75

Also batted: D. A. Allen 14; L. J. Coldwell 2*, 1 and 0; B. R. Knight 4* and 0; J. T. Murray 3* and 0.

ENGLAND – BOWLING

	Overs	Maidens	Runs	Wickets	Average
D. A. Allen	62	26	113	5	22.60
F. S. Trueman	159.3	8	521	20	26.05
F. J. Titmus	236.3	54	616	21	29.33
E. R. Dexter	95.2	6	373	11	33.91
B. R. Knight	31.5	3	128	3	42.67
J. B. Statham	165.2	15	580	13	44.62
L. J. Coldwell	57	5	159	3	53.00
R. Illingworth	40	9	131	1	131.00
K. F. Barrington	40	6	154	1	154.00

Also bowled: T. W. Graveney 7-1-34-0.

Catches: F. S. Trueman 7, K. F. Barrington 6, T. W. Graveney 6, M. C. Cowdrey 5, J. B. Statham 3, F. J. Titmus 3, E. R. Dexter 2, D. S. Sheppard 2, D. A. Allen 1, B. R. Knight 1.

Wicket-keeping: A. C. Smith 13 catches, no stumpings; J. T. Murray 1 catch, no stumpings.

FIRST-CLASS AVERAGES IN AUSTRALIA

Played 15, *Won* 4, *Lost* 3, *Drawn* 8

BATTING

	Innings	Times not out	Runs	Highest score	Average
K. F. Barrington	22	5	1,451	219*	85.35
T. W. Graveney	18	4	737	185	52.64
M. C. Cowdrey	24	3	1,028	307	48.95
E. R. Dexter	24	1	1,023	102	44.48
B. R. Knight	14	4	431	108	43.10
F. J. Titmus	17	5	503	137*	41.92
D. S. Sheppard	23	0	913	113	39.69
G. A. Pullar	19	1	564	132	31.33
R. Illingworth	12	3	248	65*	27.56
A. C. Smith	13	3	257	55	25.70
D. A. Allen	9	3	119	32*	19.83
P. H. Parfitt	17	1	305	80	19.06
F. S. Trueman	11	0	179	38	16.27
J. T. Murray	7	3	60	24*	15.00
J. B. Statham	11	2	96	30	10.67
J. D. F. Larter	2	1	4	4*	4.00
L. J. Coldwell	7	3	12	4	3.00

BOWLING

	Overs	Maidens	Runs	Wickets	Average
D. A. Allen	290.2	89	690	29	23.79
J. D. F. Larter	189.4	18	700	29	24.14
F. S. Trueman	230.3	18	773	30	25.77
J. B. Statham	290.5	33	1,043	33	31.61
F. J. Titmus	394.4	79	1,134	34	33.35
E. R. Dexter	185.2	17	711	18	39.50
B. R. Knight	128.4	15	506	11	46.00
L. J. Coldwell	202.5	27	706	15	47.07
R. Illingworth	186.5	34	611	12	50.92
K. F. Barrington	122.2	17	523	10	52.30

Also bowled: T. W. Graveney 9-2-36-2; G. Pullar 9-0-38-0.

Catches: T. W. Graveney 13, K. F. Barrington 12, E. R. Dexter 11, M. C. Cowdrey 9, D. S. Sheppard 8, F. J. Titmus 8, F. S. Trueman 8, P. H. Parfitt 7, J. B. Statham 6, D. A. Allen 5, L. J. Coldwell 5, R. Illingworth 5, B. R. Knight 1, J. D. F. Larter 1.

Wicket-keeping: A. C. Smith 27 catches, 1 stumping; J. T. Murray 9 catches, 1 stumping.

WESTERN AUSTRALIA

Perth, October 19, 20, 22. M.C.C. won by 10 wkts.

M.C.C.

First Innings		Second Innings	
G. A. Pullar, c. Punch, b. Hoare........	23	not out..................	27
M. C. Cowdrey, l.b.w., b. Bevan........	15	not out..................	20
E. R. Dexter, b. Hoare...............	76		
T. W. Graveney, c. Buggins, b. McKenzie	14		
K. F. Barrington, c. Bevan, b. Hoare.....	24		
P. H. Parfitt, c. McKenzie, b. Hoare.....	2		
R. Illingworth, st. Buggins, b. Lock......	0		
F. J. Titmus, st. Buggins, b. Lock........	88		
A. C. Smith, c. Hoare, b. Lock..........	42		
J. B. Statham, b. Lock................	3		
J. D. F. Larter, not out................	4		
Extras (b. 4, l.b. 2, n.b. 6)............	12	Extras (b.2)..........	2
Total..........................	303	Total (for no wkts.)..	49

FALL OF WICKETS. 1—32, 2—57, 3—91, 4—148, 5—154, 6—161, 7—161, 8—280, 9—292, 10—303.

WESTERN AUSTRALIA

K. Gartrell, c. Smith, b. Larter	23	c. Larter, b. Illingworth..	72
K. Punch, c. Smith, b. Larter...........	1	c. Smith, b. Statham.....	0
M. Vernon, c. Dexter, b. Statham.......	4	b. Illingworth...........	68
B. Shepherd, c. Illingworth, b. Titmus...	41	c. Graveney, b. Statham..	40
J. Parker, b. Statham................	0	c. Dexter, b. Statham.....	30
P. Wishart, c. Smith, b. Statham........	1	b. Statham..............	0
D. Hoare, c. Illingworth, b. Titmus......	8	b. Titmus...............	8
B. Buggins, c. Illingworth, b. Titmus.....	2	b. Illingworth...........	33
G. D. McKenzie, c. Smith, b. Larter....	0	l.b.w., b. Titmus.........	0
G. A. R. Lock, not out...............	0	not out.................	9
H. Bevan, b. Larter..................	0	c. sub., b. Larter.........	2
Extras (b. 3).......................	3	Extras (b. 3, l.b. 8, n.b. 2)	12
Total..........................	77	Total..............	274

FALL OF WICKETS. *First Innings:* 1—12, 2—21, 3—27, 4—27, 5—31, 6—66, 7—70, 8—77, 9—77, 10—77. *Second Innings:* 1—1, 2—138, 3—148, 4—215, 5—217, 6—222, 7—263, 8—263, 9—263, 10—274.

WESTERN AUSTRALIA

	O.	M.	R.	W.	O.	M.	R.	W.
Hoare	19	1	92	4				
McKenzie ..	22	2	69	1	4	0	15	0
Bevan	13	1	61	1	3	0	23	0
Punch	2	1	1	0				
Lock	20.3	5	68	4				
Shepherd					1	0	3	0
Gartell					0.2	0	6	0

M.C.C.

	O.	M.	R.	W.	O.	M.	R.	W.
Statham	8	3	21	3	18	4	49	4
Larter	9.1	1	25	4	14	1	52	1
Dexter......	4	0	17	0	8	3	17	0
Titmus	11	3	31	1	11	3	27	2
Barrington					10	1	47	0
Illingworth					19	4	70	3

COMBINED XI

Perth, October 26, 27, 29, 30. Combined XI won by 10 wkts.

M.C.C.

First Innings		Second Innings	
M. C. Cowdrey, c. Vernon, b. Hoare	0	c. Buggins, b. Hoare	0
D. S. Sheppard, c. Simpson, b. Lock	43	c. Simpson, b. McKenzie	92
E. R. Dexter, c. Bevan, b. Hoare	2	b. O'Neill	60
T. W. Graveney, c. Buggins, b. McKenzie	1	b. O'Neill	2
K. F. Barrington, c. Buggins, b. McKenzie	0	c. Vernon, b. Hoare	44
B. R. Knight, not out	65	c. Simpson, b. Hoare	2
R. Illingworth, c. Simpson, b. Lock	19	not out	27
D. A. Allen, c. Buggins, b. Hoare	4	c. Simpson, b. Hoare	1
J. T. Murray, b. McKenzie	13	c. Buggins, b. Hoare	11
F. S. Trueman, c. Vernon, b. McKenzie	2	c. Lawry, b. McKenzie	17
L. J. Coldwell, c. Hoare, b. Lock	4	c. Lawry, b. McKenzie	2
Extras (b. 2, l.b. 2)	4	Extras (b. 8, l.b. 1, w. 1, n.b. 2)	12
Total	157	Total	270

FALL OF WICKETS. *First Innings:* 1—3, 2—7, 3—14, 4—14, 5—85, 6—113, 7—118, 8—144, 9—146, 10—157. *Second Innings:* 1—7, 2—104, 3—106, 4—209, 5—211, 6—211, 7—212, 8—232, 9—265, 10—270.

COMBINED XI

First Innings		Second Innings	
W. Lawry, c. Graveney, b. Trueman	52	retired hurt	15
R. B. Simpson, c. Graveney, b. Allen	109	not out	66
M. Vernon, l.b.w., b. Allen	1	not out	26
N. C. O'Neill, c. Graveney, b. Allen	15		
B. Shepherd, c. Barrington, b. Allen	0		
J. Parker, c. Murray, b. Allen	55		
D. Hoare, c. Sheppard, b. Trueman	5		
B. Buggins, c. Sheppard, b. Coldwell	4		
G. A. R. Lock, c. Dexter, b. Trueman	24		
G. D. McKenzie, not out	48		
H. Bevan, b. Illingworth	2		
Extras (l.b. 2)	2	Extras (b. 4, l.b. 4)	8
Total	317	Total (no wkts.)	115

FALL OF WICKETS. 1—116, 2—119, 3—171, 4—171, 5—190, 6—208, 7—217, 8—248, 9—312, 10—317.

COMBINED XI

	O.	M.	R.	W.	O.	M.	R.	W.
Hoare	14	2	42	3	22	3	60	5
McKenzie	13	4	38	4	25.4	6	66	3
Bevan	3	0	19	0	7	0	31	0
Simpson	3	0	18	0	6	0	34	0
Lock	12.2	2	36	3	13	3	37	0
O'Neill					6	0	30	2

M.C.C.

	O.	M.	R.	W.	O.	M.	R.	W.
Trueman	21	2	65	3	5	0	23	0
Coldwell	20	4	67	1	6	1	29	0
Knight	2	0	12	0	3	0	20	0
Illingworth	18.1	2	73	1				
Allen	33	10	76	5				
Dexter	3	0	14	0				
Barrington	2	0	8	0	4	0	35	0

O

SOUTH AUSTRALIA

Adelaide, November 2, 3, 5, 6. Drawn.

SOUTH AUSTRALIA

First Innings		Second Innings	
L. Favell, c. Parfitt, b. Statham	7	b. Statham	36
J. Causby, run out	16	b. Statham	7
J. Lill, l.b.w., b. Titmus	87	l.b.w., b. Illingworth	19
G. Sobers, b. Knight	42	run out	99
N. Dansie, c. Smith, b. Knight	0	c. Parfitt, b. Titmus	8
I. McLachlan, c. Smith, b. Larter	53	c. Graveney, b. Illingworth	27
I. Chappell, hit wkt, b. Statham	36	l.b.w., b. Statham	34
N. Hawke, c. Titmus, b. Larter	46	not out	37
B. Jarman, not out	37	not out	7
P. Squires, b. Statham	0		
G. Brooks, b. Statham	3		
Extras (b. 4, l.b. 3, n.b. 1)	8	Extras (l.b. 8, n.b. 1)	9
Total	335	Total (7 wkts. dec.)	283

FALL OF WICKETS. *First Innings:* 1—12, 2—41, 3—154, 4—154, 5—154, 6—220, 7—264, 8—324, 9—331, 10—335. *Second Innings:* 1—25, 2—58, 3—64, 4—128, 5—137, 6—229, 7—249.

M.C.C.

First Innings		Second Innings	
M. C. Cowdrey, b. Brooks	0	not out	32
G. A. Pullar, b. Sobers	21	c. Hawke, b. Brooks	56
K. F. Barrington, c. Jarman, b. Hawke	104		
T. W. Graveney, b. Brooks	99		
P. H. Parfitt, c. McLachlan, b. Hawke	15		
F. J. Titmus, not out	137		
B. R. Knight, c. Jarman, b. Hawke	55	not out	3
A. C. Smith, c. Causby, b. Hawke	55		
R. Illingworth, c. and b. Hawke	1		
J. B. Statham, b. Hawke	8		
Extras (b. 6, l.b. 6, w. 1)	13	Extras (b. 1, l.b. 3)	4
Total (9 wkts. dec.)	508	Total (1 wkt.)	95

J. D. F. Larter did not go in.

FALL OF WICKETS. *First Innings:* 1—1, 2—56, 3—224, 4—232, 5—257, 6—365, 7—486, 8—493, 9—508. *Second Innings:* 1—91.

M.C.C.

	O.	M.	R.	W.	O.	M.	R.	W.
Statham	21.3	7	58	4	19	1	83	3
Larter	17	1	76	2	15	1	56	0
Knight	16	4	43	2	3	3	0	0
Titmus	22	3	80	1	18	1	55	1
Illingworth	12	0	43	0	28	2	80	2
Barrington	4	0	27	0				

SOUTH AUSTRALIA

	O.	M.	R.	W.	O.	M.	R.	W.
Hawke	30.7	5	130	6	4	0	37	0
Brooks	24	3	79	2	6	0	48	1
Sobers	34	0	141	1	2	0	6	0
Squires	11	0	52	0				
Chappell	15	0	76	0				
Dansie	3	0	17	0				

AUSTRALIAN XI

Melbourne, November 9, 10, 12, 13. Drawn.

M.C.C.

First Innings		Second Innings	
D. S. Sheppard, c. Martin, b. Guest	31	c. Misson, b. Guest	1
G. A. Pullar, c. Harvey, b. Misson	16	b. Misson	3
E. R. Dexter, c. Veivers, b. Simpson	102	c. Harvey, b. Guest	4
M. C. Cowdrey, l.b.w., b. Misson	88	c. Cowper, b. Guest	3
K. F. Barrington, not out	219	c. Misson, b. Veivers	19
F. J. Titmus, c. Harvey, b. Simpson	37	not out	14
B. R. Knight, c. Guest, b. Simpson	108	not out	10
D. A. Allen, b. Misson	11		
J. T. Murray, not out	9		
Extras (b. 2, l.b. 8, w. 2)	12	Extras (b. 9, l.b. 2, w. 3)	14
Total (7 wkts. dec.)	633	Total (5 wkts. dec.)	68

F. S. Trueman and J. D. F. Larter did not go in.

FALL OF WICKETS. *First Innings:* 1—26, 2—110, 3—183, 4—272, 5—366, 6—575, 7—600. *Second Innings:* 1—10, 2—19, 3—19, 4—28, 5—58.

AUSTRALIAN XI

First Innings		Second Innings	
R. B. Simpson, b. Trueman	130	c. Murray, b. Larter	9
G. Thomas, c. Murray, b. Knight	27	c. Barrington, b. Larter	1
R. N. Harvey, c. and b. Titmus	51	c. Murray, b. Titmus	21
B. Shepherd, run out	114	not out	91
I. McLachlan, c. Murray, b. Dexter	55	run out	68
F. Misson, c. Allen, b. Titmus	19		
R. Cowper, c. Dexter, b. Larter	17	not out	0
T. Veivers, c. Cowdrey, b. Larter	9		
J. Martin, c. Titmus, b. Trueman	4		
B. Jarman, not out	0		
C. Guest, c. Murray, b. Larter	12		
Extras (b. 5, l.b. 5, n.b. 2, w. 1)	13	Extras (b. 6, l.b. 4, n.b. 1)	11
Total	451	Total (4 wkts.)	201

FALL OF WICKETS. *First Innings:* 1—72, 2—172, 3—239, 4—354, 5—377, 6—415, 7—431, 8—436, 9—437, 10—451. *Second Innings:* 1—9, 2—18, 3—61, 4—201.

AUSTRALIAN XI

	O.	M.	R.	W.	O.	M.	R.	W.
Misson	24	3	103	3	6	2	13	1
Guest	27	1	113	1	4	0	22	3
Martin	12	0	101	0				
Veivers	27	1	146	0	2	0	19	1
Simpson	33	3	153	3				
Cowper	1	0	1	0				
Harvey	0.3	0	4	0				

M.C.C.

	O.	M.	R.	W.	O.	M.	R.	W.
Larter	17.3	1	83	3	3	0	16	2
Trueman	21	2	90	2	3	0	16	0
Knight	16	1	70	1	9	0	45	0
Dexter	4	1	20	1	9	0	47	0
Allen	30	3	95	0				
Titmus	26	4	80	2	8	1	33	1
Pullar					8	0	33	0

NEW SOUTH WALES

Sydney, Nov. 16, 17, 19. New South Wales won by an innings and 80 runs.

M.C.C.

First Innings		Second Innings	
G. A. Pullar, c. Simpson, b. Martin	132	b. Benaud	18
D. S. Sheppard, c. Ford, b. Martin	18	c. Ford, b. Davidson	7
E. R. Dexter, b. Martin	42	c. Misson, b. Benaud	5
M. C. Cowdrey, c. Davidson, b. O'Neill	50	c. Simpson, b. Martin	8
T. W. Graveney, c. Thomas, b. O'Neill	0	b. Benaud	9
P. H. Parfitt, b. Benaud	17	c. Thomas, b. Benaud	22
R. Illingworth, c. Thomas, b. Benaud	19	b. Martin	1
A. C. Smith, c. Simpson, b. Benaud	0	c. Thomas, b. Benaud	4
D. A. Allen, not out	18	not out	12
F. S. Trueman, c. Benaud, b. Martin	12	c. O'Neill, b. Benaud	6
J. B. Statham, st. Ford, b. Simpson	30	b. Benaud	0
Extras (b. 7, l.b. 2, n.b. 1)	10	Extras (b. 9, l.b. 3)	12
Total	348	Total	104

FALL OF WICKETS. *First Innings:* 1—31, 2—92, 3—180, 4—180, 5—251, 6—279, 7—280, 8—291, 9—303, 10—348. *Second Innings:* 1—17, 2—29, 3—36, 4—44, 5—51, 6—58, 7—83, 8—83, 9—97, 10—104.

NEW SOUTH WALES

G. Thomas, b. Trueman	7
R. B. Simpson, c. Smith, b. Illingworth	110
N. C. O'Neill, c. Allen, b. Dexter	143
B. C. Booth, hit wkt, b. Dexter	41
R. N. Harvey, b. Statham	63
A. K. Davidson, b. Illingworth	55
R. Flockton, not out	62
R. Benaud, not out	40
Extras (b. 2, l.b. 8, n.b. 1)	11
Total (6 wkts. dec.)	532

J. Martin, F. Misson and D. Ford did not go in.

FALL OF WICKETS. 1—16, 2—250, 3—271, 4—366, 5—385, 6—449.

NEW SOUTH WALES

	O.	M.	R.	W.	O.	M.	R.	W.
Davidson	11	2	34	0	10	4	11	1
Misson	11	1	46	0	3	0	25	0
Benaud	25	9	61	3	18.1	10	18	7
Martin	24	1	122	4	12	3	38	2
Simpson	10.2	1	34	1				
O'Neill	7	1	36	2				
Flockton	1	0	5	0				

M.C.C.

	O.	M.	R.	W.	O.	M.	R	W.
Trueman	11	1	45	1				
Statham	22	0	94	1				
Allen	24	1	117	0				
Dexter	26	1	116	2				
Illingworth	32	3	144	2				
Pullar	1	0	5	0				

QUEENSLAND

Brisbane, November 23, 24, 26, 27. Drawn.

QUEENSLAND

First Innings		Second Innings	
D. Bull, c. Parfitt, b. Coldwell	8	l.b.w., b. Dexter	29
S. Trimble, c. Coldwell, b. Knight	95	b. Larter	8
T. Veivers, c. and b. Coldwell	36	b. Dexter	26
P. Burge, b. Larter	34	b. Graveney	13
G. Bizzell, b. Larter	59	b. Dexter	2
D. Hughson, l.b.w., b. Barrington	25	b. Dexter	0
K. D. Mackay, not out	105	not out	0
W. A. Grout, c. Titmus, b. Knight	56		
J. Mackay, not out	0	not out	5
W. Hall	—	c. Murray, b. Graveney	2
Extras (l.b. 4, n.b. 10, w. 1)	15	Extras (b. 6, l.b., 2, n.b. 1)	9
Total (7 wkts. dec.)	433	Total (7 wkts.)	94

C. Westaway did not go in.

FALL OF WICKETS. *First Innings:* 1—9, 2—67, 3—125, 4—233, 5—249, 6—334, 7—422. *Second Innings:* 1—12, 2—63, 3—63, 4—72, 5—73, 6—92, 7—94.

M.C.C.

P. H. Parfitt, b. Westaway	47
D. S. Sheppard, b. K. Mackay	94
E. R. Dexter, b. Veivers	80
K. F. Barrington, not out	183
T. W. Graveney, b. Westaway	52
F. J. Titmus, b. Westaway	52
B. R. Knight, c. Hughson, b. Westaway	81
A. C. Smith, not out	22
Extras (b. 9, l.b. 8)	17
Total (6 wkts. dec.)	581

D. A. Allen, L. J. Coldwell, and J. D. F. Larter did not go in.

FALL OF WICKETS. 1—101, 2—211, 3—233, 4—326, 5—332, 6—512.

M.C.C.

	O.	M.	R.	W.	O.	M.	R.	W.
Coldwell	31	4	106	2	3	0	8	0
Larter	20	1	63	2	7	2	12	1
Dexter	1	1	0	0	8	3	8	4
Titmus	29	6	93	0				
Knight	13.7	1	58	2	3	0	12	0
Allen	9	0	27	0	10	5	15	0
Barrington	8	1	71	1	12	3	28	0
Graveney					1	0	2	0

QUEENSLAND

	O.	M.	R.	W.
Hall	27	2	106	0
J. Mackay	24	4	88	0
Westaway	27	5	156	3
K. Mackay	28	5	56	1
Veivers	24	1	145	2
Trimble	1	0	13	0

VICTORIA

Melbourne, December 14, 15, 17, 18. M.C.C. won by 5 wkts.

VICTORIA

	First Innings		Second Innings	
W. M. Lawry, c. Statham, b. Allen		177	run out	26
I. Redpath, c. Illingworth, b. Statham		5	c. Illingworth, b. Coldwell	1
J. Potter, c. Cowdrey, b. Statham		44	c. Graveney, b. Allen	44
R. Cowper, run out		7	b. Coldwell	10
N. West, c. Cowdrey, b. Knight		70	c. Smith, b. Statham	31
W. O'Halloran, c. Coldwell, b. Knight		8	c. Statham, v. Allen	28
R. Jordan, b. Statham		2	c. Statham, b. Coldwell	3
C. Guest, b. Statham		4	c. Parfitt, b. Coldwell	9
I. Meckiff, b. Allen		3	c. Smith, b. Coldwell	7
A. Connolly, c. sub., b. Allen		4	not out	4
K. Kirby, not out		8	b. Coldwell	2
Extras (l.-b. 8)		8	Extras (b. 8, l.-b. 2)	10
Total		340	Total	175

FALL OF WICKETS. *First Innings:* 1—7, 2—102, 3—110, 4—268, 5—292, 6—305, 7—309, 8—326, 9—328, 10—340. *Second Innings:* 1—2, 2—44, 3—81, 4—87, 5—133, 6—149, 7—160, 8—167, 9—170, 10—175.

M.C.C.

	First Innings		Second Innings	
D. S. Sheppard, c. Jordan, b. Connolly		12	l.b.w., b. Guest	50
P. H. Parfitt, c. Meckiff, b. Connolly		13	c. Potter, b. Meckiff	7
M. C. Cowdrey, run out		46	c. Jordan, b. Guest	63
T. W. Graveney, c. and b. Kirby		40	not out	24
B. R. Knight, c. Jordan, b. Kirby		2	b. West	20
R. Illingworth, b. Meckiff		50	not out	9
G. Pullar, c. Cowper, b. Meckiff		91	c. Cowper, b. Guest	2
A. C. Smith, c. Jordan, b. Meckiff		41		
D. A. Allen, c. Potter, b. Kirby		2		
J. B. Statham, c. Redpath, b. Connolly		26		
L. J. Coldwell, not out		0		
Extras (b. 3, w. 5, l.-b. 5)		13	Extras (b. 4, l.-b. 1)	5
Total		336	Total (5 wkts.)	180

FALL OF WICKETS. *First Innings:* 1—23, 2—26, 3—107, 4—115, 5—116, 6—212, 7—291, 8—300, 9—336, 10—336. *Second Innings:* 1—3, 2—12, 3—116, 4—125, 5—163.

VICTORIA

	O.	M.	R.	W.	O.	M.	R.	W.
Statham	24	2	112	4	13	1	46	1
Coldwell	12	2	37	0	17·6	2	49	6
Illingworth	25	9	43	0	3	0	16	0
Allen	29·2	11	57	3	23	9	42	2
Knight	16	0	83	2	1	0	12	0

M.C.C.

	O.	M.	R.	W.	O.	M.	R.	W.
Meckiff	23	7	53	3	9	1	37	1
Guest	10	1	35	0	10	0	32	3
Connolly	18·2	2	71	3	5	0	25	0
Kirby	30	3	137	3	11	1	49	0
Potter	3	0	10	0				
O'Halloran	10	3	17	0	6	0	18	0
West					3·4	1	8	1
Lawry					1	0	6	0

SOUTH AUSTRALIA

Adelaide, December 22, 24, 26, 27. Drawn.

M.C.C.

	First Innings		Second Innings	
D. S. Sheppard, b. Sobers		81	b. Sobers	5
P. H. Parfitt, b. Brooks		2	c. Jarman, b. Brooks	7
E. R. Dexter, c. Chappell, b. Sobers		16	c. Chappell, b. Sangster	37
M. C. Cowdrey, c. Chappell, b. Dansie		307	c. McLachlan, b. Sobers	2
K. F. Barrington, run out		52	not out	52
T. W. Graveney, not out		122	b. Sincock	35
F. J. Titmus		—	c. Lill, b. Dansie	4
J. T. Murray		—	not out	24
Extras (b. 1, w. 2, l.b. 3)		6	Extras (l.b. 1)	1
Total (5 wkts. dec.)		586	Total (6 wkts. dec.)	167

D. A. Allen, L. J. Coldwell, and J. D. F. Larter did not go in.

FALL OF WICKETS. *First Innings:* 1—2, 2—39, 3—144, 4—242, 5—586. *Second Innings:* 1—8, 2—12, 3—23, 4—62, 5—108, 6—121.

SOUTH AUSTRALIA

	First Innings		Second Innings	
L. Favell, c. Dexter, b. Allen		120	c. Cowdrey, b. Coldwell	3
K. Cunningham, c. Sheppard, b. Coldwell		15	hit wkt., b. Larter	29
T. Lill, c. Dexter, b. Titmus		55	b. Coldwell	2
G. Sobers, c. Allen, b. Barrington		89	not out	75
I. McLachlan, b. Allen		62	b. Larter	2
N. Dansie, c. and b. Barrington		64	not out	0
J. Chappell, run out		2		
J. Sangster, c. Parfitt, b. Barrington		19		
B. Jarman, c. Barrington, b. Titmus		11		
D. Sincock, c. Graveney, b. Titmus		0		
G. Brooks, not out		2		
Extras (b. 2, l.b. 4, n.b. 5)		11	Extras (l.b. 1, w. 1)	2
Total		450	Total (4 wkts.)	113

FALL OF WICKETS. *First Innings:* 1—27, 2—165, 3—215, 4—343, 5—357, 6—375, 7—425, 8—442, 9—445, 10—450. *Second Innings:* 1—8, 2—16, 3—89, 4—97.

SOUTH AUSTRALIA

	O.	M.	R.	W.	O.	M.	R.	W.
Brooks	18	0	74	1	8	0	30	1
Sobers	25	2	124	2	9	1	44	2
Sincock	26	1	153	0	10	0	55	1
Sangster	10	0	75	0	3	0	23	1
Chappell	9	1	49	0				
Dansie	10.2	1	59	1	5	1	14	1
Cunningham	2	0	28	0				
McLachlan	3	0	14	0				
Favell	1	0	4	0				

M.C.C.

	O.	M.	R.	W.	O.	M.	R.	W.
Larter	22	1	113	0	5	0	23	2
Coldwell	19	3	69	1	8.7	0	65	2
Dexter	15	1	60	0	1	0	15	0
Allen	21	4	54	2	2	0	8	0
Titmus	21.1	1	88	3				
Barrington	18	2	55	3				

COMBINED XI

Launceston, Tasmania, January 4, 5, 7. M.C.C. won by 313 runs.

M.C.C.

First Innings		Second Innings	
P. H. Parfitt, c. Lawry, b. Aldridge	2	not out	38
D. S. Sheppard, c. Shepherd, b. Connor	82	c. Brakey, b. Booth	67
E. R. Dexter, c. Booth, b. Brakey	5	not out	8
K. F. Barrington, c. Aldridge, b. Patterson	73		
F. J. Titmus, c. Connor, b. Patterson	1		
B. R. Knight, b. Brakey	68		
R. Illingworth, not out	65		
J. T. Murray, c. and b. Connor	0		
D. A. Allen, not out	32		
Extras (b. 3)	3	Extras (l.b. 1, n.b. 2)	3
Total (7 wkts. dec.)	331	Total (1 wkt. dec.)	116

F. S. Trueman and J. D. F. Larter did not go in.

FALL OF WICKETS. *First Innings:* 1—2, 2—7, 3—154, 4—155, 5—178, 6—251, 7—256. *Second Innings:* 1—106.

COMBINED XI

First Innings		Second Innings	
W. M. Lawry, c. Parfitt, b. Trueman	12	c. Sheppard, b. Larter	4
G. Connor, b. Murray, b. Trueman	7	c. Dexter, b. Allen	0
B. C. Booth, c. Sheppard, b. Trueman	3	b. Allen	7
N. C. O'Neill, c. Dexter, b. Knight	22	b. Allen	4
B. Shepherd, b. Larter	0	l.b.w., b. Illingworth	3
B. Hyland, b. Larter	0	c. Titmus, b. Illingworth	2
L. Maddocks, hit wkt., b. Larter	0	c. Dexter, b. Illingworth	8
I. Crowden, c. Barrington, b. Trueman	21	c. Trueman, b. Allen	0
B. Patterson, c. Murray, b. Larter	0	not out	10
K. J. Aldridge, st. Murray, b. Barrington	8	c. Sheppard, b. Barrington	15
G. Brakey, not out	0	absent injured	0
Extras (b. 4)	4	Extras (b. 4)	4
Total	77	Total	57

FALL OF WICKETS. *First Innings:* 1—16, 2—19, 3—24, 4—28, 5—36, 6—44, 7—44, 8—44, 9—77, 10—77. *Second Innings:* 1—4, 2—6, 3—25, 4—34, 5—42, 6—45, 7—47, 8—47, 9—57, 10—57.

COMBINED XI

	O.	M.	R.	W.	O.	M.	R.	W.
Aldridge	15	2	63	1				
Brakey	13	3	67	2	4	0	14	0
O'Neill	4	0	29	0	4	0	24	0
Connor	19	3	73	2	6	0	42	0
Patterson	11	2	34	2	2	0	6	0
Crowden	5	0	62	0				
Booth					3	0	27	1
Shepherd					0.2	0	0	0

M.C.C.

	O.	M.	R.	W.	O.	M.	R.	W.
Trueman	10	5	13	4				
Larter	13	4	24	4	4	1	7	1
Knight	11	2	20	1	3	1	3	0
Barrington	2.4	1	16	1	2	0	8	1
Allen					10	5	19	4
Illingworth					9.4	5	11	3
Dexter					2	0	5	0

VICTORIA

Melbourne, February 1, 2, 4, 5. Drawn.

M.C.C.

	First Innings		Second Innings	
G. A. Pullar, c. Jordon, b. Meckiff		5		
P. H. Parfitt, c. Redpath, b. Meckiff		0	c. Cowper, b. Connolly	21
K. F. Barrington, c. Cowper, b. Guest		33	c. Jordon, b. Meckiff	66
E. R. Dexter, b. Connolly		35	b. West	70
T. W. Graveney, c. Lawry, b. Meckiff		185	not out	38
B. R. Knight, c. Meckiff, b. Connolly		5	b. Meckiff	8
F. J. Titmus, b. Meckiff		28	c. Cowper, b. Stackpole	7
A. C. Smith, c. Jordon, b. Stackpole		46	not out	0
D. A. Allen, c. Potter, b. Meckiff		25		
L. J. Coldwell, not out		3		
J. D. F. Larter, c. West, b. Stackpole		0		
Extras (l.b. 6, w. 1, n.b. 3)		10	Extras (l.b. 4, w. 4)	8
Total		375	Total (5 wkts. dec.)	218

FALL OF WICKETS. *First Innings:* 1—1, 2—6, 3—62, 4—78, 5—96, 6—202, 7—309, 8—355, 9—372, 10—375. *Second Innings:* 1—13, 2—39, 3—155, 4—199, 5—218.

VICTORIA

	First Innings		Second Innings	
W. M. Lawry, c. Smith, b. Larter		15	c. Illingworth, b. Allen	26
I. Redpath, c. Smith, b. Allen		26	b. Larter	8
K. Stackpole, c. Coldwell, b. Allen		33	run out	21
J. Potter, st. Smith, b. Allen		106	b. Allen	0
R. Cowper, c. and b. Allen		28	c. Smith, b. Allen	51
N. West, b. Larter		37	b. Larter	1
B. Jordon, b. Larter		0	c. and b. Barrington	15
C. Guest, b. Larter		23	c. Smith, b. Larter	10
I. Meckiff, l.b.w., b. Allen		5	c. Coldwell, b. Barrington	38
K. Kirby, not out		18	not out	10
A. Connolly, c. Parfitt, b. Barrington		5	not out	2
Extras (b. 5, l.b. 5, w. 1)		11	Extras (b. 2, l.b. 2, w. 1, n.b. 1)	6
Total		307	Total (9 wkts.)	188

FALL OF WICKETS. *First Innings:* 1—25, 2—69, 3—84, 4—162, 5—238, 6—238, 7—279, 8—279, 9—286, 10—307. *Second Innings:* 1—19, 2—42, 3—42, 4—73, 5—78, 6—105, 7—116, 8—148, 9—182.

VICTORIA

	O.	M.	R.	W.	O.	M.	R.	W.
Meckiff	29	6	93	5	19	3	47	2
Guest	11	1	53	1	7.4	1	27	0
Connolly	28	2	86	2	7	1	32	1
Kirby	7	0	55	0	13	1	67	0
Stackpole	8.3	0	50	2	4	0	20	1
West	5	1	28	0	3	1	17	1
M.C.C.								
Coldwell	16	3	77	0	12	3	40	0
Larter	29	2	105	4	14	2	45	3
Dexter	8	0	19	0	1	1	0	0
Allen	24	9	43	5	13	6	24	3
Titmus	14	3	38	0	4	1	13	0
Barrington	2.6	0	14	1	17	3	60	2
Graveney					1	1	0	0

MINOR MATCHES

Kalgoorie, W.A. Oct. 16, 17. Drawn. M.C.C. 247 for 4 wkts. dec. (Pullar 102) and 314 for 8 wkts. (Murray 102, Sheppard 59, J. Menegola 4 for 101); WESTERN AUSTRALIAN COUNTRY DISTRICTS XI 212 (I. Campbell 66, Trueman 4 for 22, Barrington 4 for 44).

Griffith, N.S.W. Nov. 14. M.C.C. won by 7 wkts. SOUTHERN N.S.W. COUNTRY XI 186 for 6 wkts. dec. (M. Rudd 82, Dexter 2 for 29); M.C.C. 187 for 3 wkts. (Pullar 77 not out, Dexter 76 not out).

Toowoomba, Queensland. Nov. 28. M.C.C. won by 7 wkts. SOUTH QUEENSLAND COUNTRY XI 202 for 4 wkts. dec. (I. Oxenford 66, W. Brown 56 retired); M.C.C. 204 for 3 wkts. (Parfitt 128 not out).

Townsville, Queensland. Dec. 7, 8. M.C.C. won by an innings and 120 runs. QUEENSLAND COUNTRY XI 165 (M. Campbell 40, Larter 3 for 39, Illingworth 3 for 46) and 138 (W. Brown 47, Allen 5 for 57, Statham 2 for 8); M.C.C. 423 for 9 wkts. dec. (Graveney 118, Parfitt 98, Sheppard 67, Illingworth 58).

Bendigo, Victoria. Dec. 10, 11. Drawn. VICTORIA COUNTRY XII 110 (Barrington 4 for 29, Larter 4 for 31) and 158 for 4 wkts. (F. Watts 63); M.C.C. XII 360 for 8 wkts. dec. (Cowdrey 111, Barrington 90, Graveney 59 not out).

Shepparton, Victoria. Dec. 12. M.C.C. won by 5 wkts. VICTORIA COUNTRY XII 191 for 6 wkts. dec. (G. Leyden 46, W. Jones 39 not out, Illingworth 4 for 65); M.C.C. XII 196 for 5 wkts. (Pullar 51, R. Marshall 3 for 39).

Port Lincoln, S.A. Dec. 21. M.C.C. won by 10 wkts. SOUTH AUSTRALIAN COUNTRY XI 55 (Trueman 4 for 9); M.C.C. 56 for 0 wkt.

Hobart, Tasmania. Jan. 8, 9. Drawn. TASMANIA 203 (R. Stokes 82, Barrington 4 for 35) and 181 for 6 wkts. (R. Stokes 76 not out, B. Hyland 44); M.C.C. 324 (Parfitt 121, Pullar 63, J. O'Brien 7 for 73).

Newcastle, N.S.W. Jan. 18, 19, 21. M.C.C. won by 145 runs. M.C.C. 319 (Knight 73, Pullar 53, R. Ring 4 for 105) and 190 for 4 wkts. dec. (Dexter 71 not out); N.S.W. COUNTRY XI 203 (D. Dives 71, Coldwell 3 for 32, Allen 3 for 35) and 161 (Allen 5 for 38, Pullar 3 for 26).

Canberra. Feb. 7. M.C.C. won by 3 runs. M.C.C. 253 for 7 wkts. dec. (Sheppard 72, G. Smith 3 for 61); PRIME MINISTER'S XI 250 (Benaud 68, Allen 5 for 68).

Dubbo, N.S.W. Feb. 8, 9. Drawn. N.S.W. COUNTRY XI 137 (Trueman 4 for 45) and 227 for 5 wkts. (L. Drake 101, Allen 3 for 51); M.C.C. 451 for 8 wkts. dec. (Graveney 106, Cowdrey 97, Sheppard 93, Knight 70).

Tamworth, N.S.W. Feb. 10, 11. M.C.C. won by 10 wkts. N.S.W. COUNTRY XI 109 (B. Weissel 51, Allen 4 for 29) and 222 (Illingworth 3 for 58, Titmus 3 for 72); M.C.C. 322 for 6 wkts. dec. (Dexter 87, Illingworth 62 not out, Knight 62) and 10 for 0 wkt.

NEW ZEALAND

Auckland, February 22, 23, 25, 26. England won by an innings and 215 runs

ENGLAND – First Innings

D. S. Sheppard, c. Dick, b. Cameron	12
R. Illingworth, c. Reid, b. Cameron	20
K. F. Barrington, c. Playle, b. Cameron	126
E. R. Dexter, c. Barton, b. Yuile	7
M. C. Cowdrey, c. Barton, b. Cameron	86
P. H. Parfitt, not out	131
B. R. Knight, b. Alabaster	125
F. J. Titmus, st. Dick, b. Sparling	26
J. T. Murray, not out	9
Extras (b. 18, l.b. 1, n.b. 1)	20
Total (7 wkts. dec.)	562

J. D. F. Larter and L. J. Coldwell did not go in.

FALL OF WICKETS 1—24, 2—45, 3—63, 4—229, 5—258, 6—498, 7—535.

NEW ZEALAND

First Innings		Second Innings	
G. T. Dowling, b. Coldwell	3	b. Illingworth	14
W. R. Playle, c. Dexter, b. Larter	0	c. Dexter, b. Coldwell	4
P. T. Barton, c. Sheppard, b. Larter	3	l.b.w., b. Titmus	16
J. R. Reid, b. Titmus	59	not out	21
B. Sinclair, c. Coldwell, b. Titmus	24	b. Larter	2
J. T. Sparling, c. Murray, b. Larter	3	c Barrington, b. Illingworth	0
E. C. Dick run out	29	c. Illingworth, b. Larter	0
B. W. Yuile, run out	64	l.b.w., b. Larter	1
R. C. Motz, c. Murray, b. Knight	60	c. & b. Illingworth	20
J. C. Alabaster, b. Knight	2	c. Titmus, b. Illingworth	0
F. J. Cameron, not out	0	b. Larter	1
Extras (b. 5, l.b. 3, n.b. 2, w. 1)	11	Extras (b. 2, l.b. 8)	10
Total	258	Total	89

FALL OF WICKETS. *First Innings:* 1—0, 2—7, 3—7, 4—62, 5—71, 6—109, 7—161, 8—256, 9—258, 10—258. *Second Innings:* 1—15, 2—42, 3—42, 4—42, 5—46, 6—46, 7—56, 8—83, 9—83, 10—89.

NEW ZEALAND

	O.	M.	R.	W.
Motz	42	12	98	0
Cameron	43	7	118	4
Alabaster	40	6	130	1
Yuile	21	4	77	1
Reid	28	8	67	0
Sparling	12	2	52	1

ENGLAND

	O.	M.	R.	W.	O.	M.	R.	W.
Coldwell	27	9	66	1	5	2	4	1
Larter	26	12	51	3	14·1	3	26	4
Knight	10·4	2	23	2	10	2	13	0
Titmus	25	9	44	2	6	5	2	1
Barrington	12	4	38	0				
Dexter	9	4	20	0				
Illingworth	1	0	5	0	18	7	34	4

NEW ZEALAND

Wellington, March 1, 2, 4. England won by an innings and 47 runs.

NEW ZEALAND

First Innings		Second Innings	
G. T. Dowling, c. Smith, b. Trueman	12	c. Knight, b. Trueman	2
W. R. Playle, c. Smith, b. Knight	23	c. and b. Illingworth	65
P. T. Barton, c. Cowdrey, b. Trueman	0	c. Barrington, b. Knight	3
J. R. Reid, c. Smith, b. Knight	0	c. Barrington, b. Titmus	9
B. Sinclair, b. Trueman	4	c. and b. Barrington	36
M. J. Shrimpton, l.b.w., b. Knight	28	c. Parfitt, b. Barrington	10
A. E. Dick, c. Sheppard, b. Trueman	7	not out	38
B. W. Yuile, c. Illingworth, b. Titmus	13	b. Titmus	0
R. W. Clair, not out	64	c. Larter, b. Titmus	5
B. D. Morrison, run out	10	c. Larter, b. Titmus	0
F. J. Cameron, l.b.w., b. Barrington	12	l.b.w., b. Barrington	0
Extras (b. 13, l.b. 5, n.b. 3)	21	Extras (b. 13, l.b. 4, n.b. 2)	19
Total	194	Total	187

FALL OF WICKETS. *First Innings:* 1—32, 2—32, 3—35, 4—40, 5—61, 6—74, 7—96, 8—129, 9—150, 10—194. *Second Innings:* 1—15, 2—18, 3—41, 4—122, 5—126, 6—158, 7—159, 8—172, 9—179, 10—187.

ENGLAND – First Innings

D. S. Sheppard, b. Blair	0
R. Illingworth, c. Morrison, b. Blair	46
K. F. Barrington, c. Dick, b. Reid	76
E. R. Dexter, b. Morrison	31
P. H. Parfitt, c. Dick, b. Morrison	0
B. R. Knight, c. Dick, b. Cameron	31
F. J. Titmus, run out	33
M. C. Cowdrey, not out	128
F. S. Trueman, b. Cameron	3
A. C. Smith, not out	69
Extras (b. 3, l.b. 7, n.b. 1)	11
Total (8 wkts. dec.)	428

J. D. F. Larter did not go in.

FALL OF WICKETS. *First Innings:* 1—0, 2—77, 3—125, 4—125, 5—173, 6—197, 7—258, 8—265.

ENGLAND

	O.	M.	M.	W.	O.	M.	R.	W.
Trueman	20	5	46	4	18	7	27	1
Larter	14	2	52	0	7	1	18	0
Knight	21	8	32	3	4	1	7	1
Titmus	18	3	40	1	32	16	50	4
Barrington	2·3	1	1	1	11	3	32	3
Dexter	1	0	2	0				
Illingworth					26	13	34	1

NEW ZEALAND

	O.	M.	R.	W.
Blair	33	11	82	2
Morrison	31	5	129	2
Cameron	43	16	98	2
Reid	32	8	72	1
Yuile	10	1	36	0

OTAGO INVITATION XI

Dunedin, March 8, 9, 11. M.C.C. won by an innings and 10 runs.

OTAGO

	First Innings		Second Innings	
B. Congdon	b. Coldwell	0	c. Knight, b. Trueman	17
R. Holloway	b. Trueman	1	l.b.w., b. Trueman	4
R. Hendrey	c. Illingworth, b. Trueman	2	c. Titmus, b. Barrington	32
B. H. Pairaudeau	b. Coldwell	46	c. Trueman, b. Coldwell	6
B. Sutcliffe	b. Trueman	4	c. Sheppard, b. Trueman	22
L. R. Pearson	c. Smith, b. Coldwell	16	c. Smith, b. Trueman	0
J. T. Ward	c. Parfitt, b. Trueman	14	c. Smith, b. Trueman	19
J. C. Alabaster	l.b.w., b. Titmus	8	l.b.w. b. Barrington	1
F. J. Cameron	b. Trueman	7	b. Trueman	18
G. R. Anderson	b. Titmus	14	not out	28
J. Hill	not out	0	l.b.w., b. Barrington	6
Extras	(l.b. 1, n.b. 3)	4	Extras (b. 11, n.b. 6)	17
Total		116	Total	170

FALL OF WICKETS. *First Innings:* 1—1, 2—3, 3—4, 4—18, 5—43, 6—72, 7—91, 8—95, 9—111, 10—116. *Second Innings:* 1—16, 2—31, 3—39, 4—79, 5—79, 6—98, 7—100, 8—125, 9—153, 10—170.

M.C.C. – First Innings

D. S. Sheppard, c. Hill, b. Alabaster	76
R. Illingworth, c. Ward, b. Cameron	13
P. H. Parfitt, c. Sutcliffe, b. Hill	54
K. F. Barrington, l.b.w., b. Cameron	18
M. C. Cowdrey, c. Holloway, b. Hill	60
B. R. Knight, c. Alabaster, b. Hill	36
F. J. Titmus, not out	29
F. S. Trueman, b. Hill	1
J. T. Murray, run out	0
A. C. Smith, b. Cameron	2
L. J. Coldwell, not out	2
Extras (b. 2, l.b. 1, n.b. 2)	5
Total (9 wkts. dec.)	296

FALL OF WICKETS. 1—42, 2—140, 3—148, 4—169, 5—263, 8—264, 9—269.

M.C.C.

	O.	M.	R.	W.	O.	M.	R.	W.
Trueman	15·2	5	19	5	18	1	64	6
Coldwell	19	7	33	3	10	3	12	1
Knight	6	1	22	0	5	1	11	0
Titmus	7	1	38	2				
Illingworth					5	0	25	0
Barrington					9·5	2	41	3

OTAGO INVITATION XI

	O.	M.	R.	W.
Cameron	38	8	74	3
Anderson	15	2	74	0
Hill	25	8	61	4
Alabaster	18	3	63	1
Sutcliffe	2	0	19	0

NEW ZEALAND

Christchurch, March 15, 16, 18, 19. England won by 7 wickets.

NEW ZEALAND

First Innings		Second Innings	
G. T. Dowling, c. Dexter, b. Titmus....	40	c. Smith, b. Larter.......	2
W. R. Playle, c. Barrington, b. Trueman	0	c. Smith, b. Trueman....	3
B. W. Sinclair, hit wkt., b. Trueman	44	l.b.w., b. Larter.........	0
J. R. Reid, c. Parfitt, b. Knight	74	b. Titmus	100
P. T. Barton, c. Smith, b. Knight	11	l.b.w., b. Knight	12
M. J. F. Shrimpton, c. Knight, b. Trueman..............................	31	b. Titmus	8
A. E. Dick, b. Trueman..............	16	c. Parfitt, b. Titmus	1
R. C. Motz, c. Parfitt, b. Trueman......	7	b. Larter...............	3
R. W. Blair, c. Parfitt, b. Trueman	0	b. Titmus	0
J. C. Alabaster, not out	20	c. Parfitt, b. Trueman ...	1
F. J. Cameron, c. Smith, b. Trueman....	1	not out	0
Extras (b. 1, l.b. 9, w. 3, n.b. 9)	22	Extras (l.b. 7, n.b. 2) ..	9
Total..........................	266	Total...............	159

FALL OF WICKETS. *First Innings:* 1—3, 2—83, 3—98, 4—127, 5—195, 6—234, 7—235, 8—235, 9—252, 10—266. *Second Innings:* 1—16, 2—17, 3—66, 4—91, 5—129, 6—133, 7—151, 8—154, 9—159, 10—159.

ENGLAND

First Innings		Second Innings	
D. S. Sheppard, b. Cameron...........	42	b. Alabaster	31
R. Illingworth, c. Dick, b. Cameron	2		
K. F. Barrington, l.b.w., b. Motz.......	47	c. Reid, b. Blair.........	45
E. R. Dexter, b. Alabaster.............	46		
M. C. Cowdrey, c. Motz, b. Blair	43	not out	35
P. H. Parfitt, l.b.w., b. Reid	4	c. Shrimpton, b. Alabaster	31
B. R. Knight, b. Blair	32	not out	20
F. J. Titmus, c. Dick, b. Motz	4		
F. S. Trueman, c. Reid, b. Alabaster ...	11		
A. C. Smith, not out	2		
J. D. F. Larter, b. Motz	2		
Extras (b. 4, l.b. 6, w. 5, n.b. 3)......	18	Extras (b. 9, n.b. 2) ...	11
Total..........................	253	Total (3 wkts.)........	173

FALL OF WICKETS. *First Innings:* 1—11, 2—87, 3—103, 4—186, 5—188, 6—210, 7—225, 8—243, 9—250, 10—253. *Second Innings:* 1—70, 2—96, 3—149.

ENGLAND

	O.	M.	R.	W.	O.	M.	R.	W.
Trueman	30·2	9	75	7	19·4	8	16	2
Larter........	21	5	59	0	23	9	32	3
Knight	23	5	39	2	10	3	38	1
Titmus	30	13	45	1	21	8	46	4
Dexter........	9	3	8	0	10	2	18	0
Barrington	5	0	18	0				

NEW ZEALAND

	O.	M.	R.	W.	O.	M.	R.	W.
Motz	19·5	3	68	3	20	6	33	0
Cameron......	24	6	47	2	12	3	38	0
Blair	24	11	42	2	12	3	34	1
Alabaster	20	6	47	2	15·3	3	57	2
Reid	8	1	31	1				

'Yes . . . they need 257?' 'Millions or runs, Artie?'

'Got everything? . . . Bat, pads, gloves, ashcan?'

THE PAVILION LIBRARY

New Titles

Australia 63
Alan Ross

Pavilioned in Splendour
A. A. Thomson

Backlist

Cricket Cauldron
Alex Bannister

Masters of Cricket
Jack Fingleton

Cricket All His Life
E. V. Lucas

The Cricket Captains of England
Alan Gibson

Farewell to Cricket
Don Bradman

Jack Hobbs
Ronald Mason

In Celebration of Cricket
Kenneth Gregory

The Best Loved Game
Geoffrey Moorhouse

Bowler's Turn
Ian Peebles

Lord's 1787-1945
Sir Pelham Warner

Lord's 1946-1970
Diana Rait Kerr and Ian Peebles

Through the Caribbean
Alan Ross

Double Century Vol I
Marcus Williams (ed.)

Double Century Vol II
Marcus Williams (ed.)

In Search of Cricket
J. M. Kilburn

Sort of a Cricket Person
E. W. Swanton

End of an Innings
Denis Compton

Ranji
Alan Ross

Batter's Castle
Ian Peebles

The Ashes Crown the Year
Jack Fingleton

Life Worth Living
C. B. Fry

Cricket Crisis
Jack Fingleton

P. G. H. Fender
Richard Streeton

Hirst and Rhodes
A. A. Thomson